Professional Library Organization and Knowledge Organization Systems

Professional Library Organization and Knowledge Organization Systems

Manvendra Bhattacharya

RANDOM PUBLICATIONS
NEW DELHI - 110 002 (INDIA)

Professional Library Organization and Knowledge Organization Systems

ISBN 978-93-5111-311-9

Published in 2014 in India by
RANDOM PUBLICATIONS
4376-A/4B, Gali Murari Lal, Ansari Road
New Delhi-110 002
Phone: +9111-43580356, 23289044
E-mail: randomexports@gmail.com; sales@randompublications.com; info@randompublications.com

Reprinted 2019

Type Setting by: Friends Media, Delhi-110089
Digitally Printed at: Replika Press Pvt. Ltd.

Preface

A library classification is a system of coding, assorting and organizing documents, library materials or any information (books, serials, audiovisual materials, computer files, maps, manuscripts, realia) according to their subject and allocating a call number to that information resource. Bibliographic classification systems group entities together that are relevant the same subject, typically arranged in a hierarchical tree structure (like classification systems used in biology). A different kind of classification system, called a faceted classification system, is also widely used which allows the assignment of multiple classifications to an object, enabling the classifications to be ordered in multiple ways. Library management is a sub-discipline of institutional management that focuses on specific issues faced by libraries and library management professionals. Library management encompasses normal management tasks as well as intellectual freedom, anti-censorship, and fund-raising tasks. Issues faced in library management frequently overlap those faced in management of non-profit organizations. The term knowledge organization (KO) (or "organization of knowledge", "organization of information" or "information organization") designates a field of study related to Library and Information Science (LIS).

In this meaning, KO is about activities such as document description, indexing and classification performed in libraries, databases, archives etc. These activities are done by librarians, archivists, subject specialists as well as by computer algorithms. KO as a field of study is concerned with the nature and quality of such knowledge organizing processes (KOP) as well as the knowledge organizing systems (KOS) used to organize documents, document representations and concepts. There exist different historical and theoretical approaches to and theories about organizing knowledge, which are related to different views of knowledge, cognition, language, and social organization. Each of these approaches tends to answer the question: "What is knowledge organization?" differently. Library Information Service professionals have often concentrated on applying new technology and standards, and may not have seen their work as involving interpretation and analysis of meaning. That is why library classification has been criticized for a lack of substantive intellectual content. Traditional human-based activities are increasingly challenged by computer-based retrieval techniques. It is appropriate to investigate the relative contributions of different approaches; the current challenges make it imperative to reconsider this understanding. The leading journal in this field is *Knowledge Organization* published by the International Society for Knowledge Organization (ISKO). See also "Lifeboat for Knowledge Organization". A broad introduction to knowledge organization can be found in Hoetzlein (2007).

This book titled, "Professional Library Organization and Knowledge Organization Systems", provides readers with an introductory overview of library organization. An introduction to library organization is given with focus on role of major processes involved. Attempts are made towards understanding the significance of knowledge organization systems in library organization. The role of data and data retrieval are discussed in detail. A case study of select library organization systems is provided herein. Efforts have been made to focus on select additional factors in library organization and use. In addition, this book also is helpful in understanding common library practices on collection and protection. Efforts are made towards analyzing the role of select library professionals in library organization. A detailed bibliography, *glossary* and elaborate index make this publication user-friendly.

—Editor

Contents

1

Library Organization: An Introductory Overview

> "An idea can only become a reality once it is broken down into organized, actionable elements."
>
> —*Scott Belsky*

INTRODUCTION TO LIBRARY ORGANIZATION

Definition

A library is an institution that keeps a collection of books and other publications for reading, study and reference.

Tasks

Important tasks that a library has to perform for its proper operation and to impart efficient services to its clientele are as under:

(i) Selection
(ii) Acquisition
(iii) Processing
(iv) Circulation
(v) Reference
(vi) Serials
(vii) Binding
(viii) Preservation of library materials
(ix) Readers services

Services

It is necessary to understand that in a traditional library setting there are two main service activities, i.e.:

(i) Readers services and
(ii) technical services.

The various jobs covered under these two services can be understood better by the following graphic presentation:

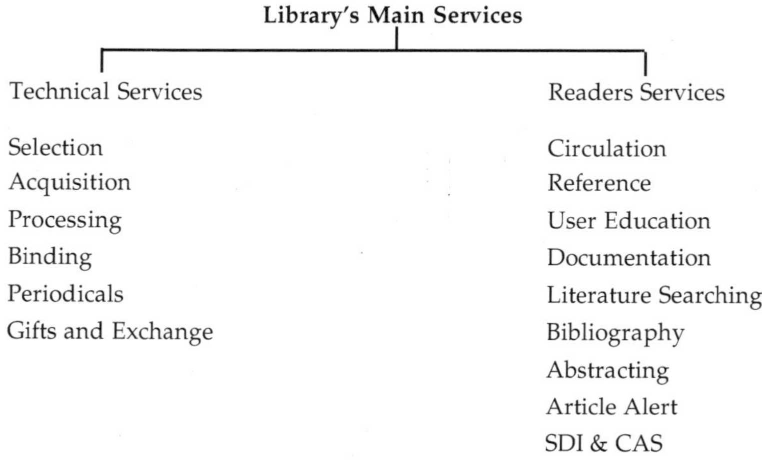

Administrative Services

The maintenance/upkeep of library is another job, which is undertaken by Administrative Unit/Section alongwith day-to-day administration of the library. Administration Unit/Section has to do overall supervision for the following jobs:

1. Posting and Transfer of staff to various sections/ departments.
2. Daily attendance of staff.
3. Maintaining leave record of staff.
4. Maintenance of discipline and issuing orders.
5. Daily cleaning of floors, furniture and other equipments.
6. Dusting of books.
7. Spray of insecticides.
8. Repairs of building, furniture and other equipments.
9. Maintenance and watering of flower plants.

Structure or Small and Medium Libraries

A number of departments, sections and units constitute a structure of a library depending upon its size and staff. In libraries which are of reasonably good size only a few sections are created by integrating the related tasks. In smaller libraries two or three persons handle all the jobs together. For example, Selection, Acquisition and Processing functions can be combined to form one section, Circulation and Reference into another, Periodicals and Binding can also be combined to form third section. The work of Documentation, Bibliography, Abstracting, Current Awareness Service, Selected Dissemination of Information and Article Alert Service etc. should be dealt with in one section as far as possible, otherwise this work can be combined with Reference Section.

The structure of medium sized libraries can be illustrated by the following chart

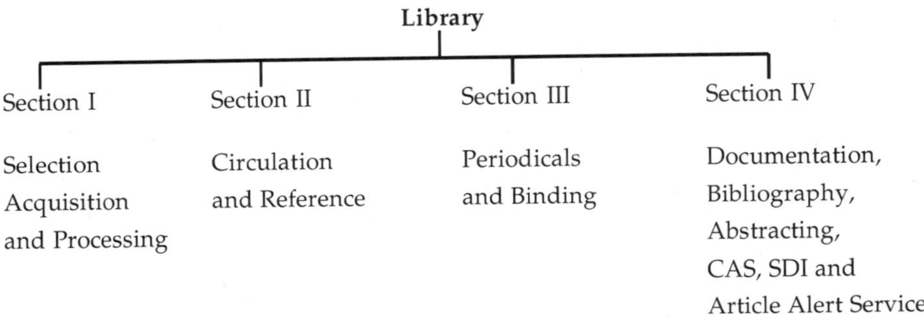

Large Libraries

Large libraries can be organized into Divisions, Departments and Sections. For example:

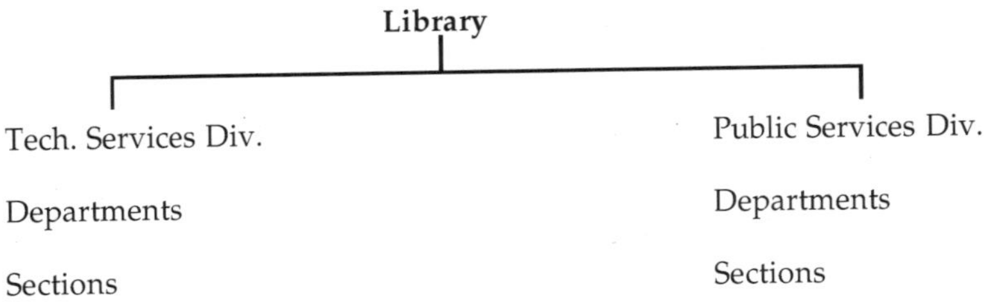

These sections can further be subdivided into units if so required. The number of Departments and Sections will depend upon the need and administrative convenience of the library.

The structure of large libraries can be illustrated in Chart I.

Staff

The staff employed in the libraries varies in designations and numbers in accordance with the size of the library. There are no standards for staff complement and the number of staff in a library depends on various factors such as:

- Workload

- Finances
- Approach of authorities
- Skill of the Librarian
- Circumstances at the time of sanction

The Staff Inspection Unit, Ministry of Finance, Government of India, have laid down standards of work for the jobs in the library, but these are very strict and conservative. By applying those norms one can only determine/project the number of library staff complement but do not specify the number of technical and non-technical persons. Librarians may feel that such norms are not suitable which have been laid down without much vision and thought.

Designations of Library Staff

The general hierarchy of the staff in a library is as follows:

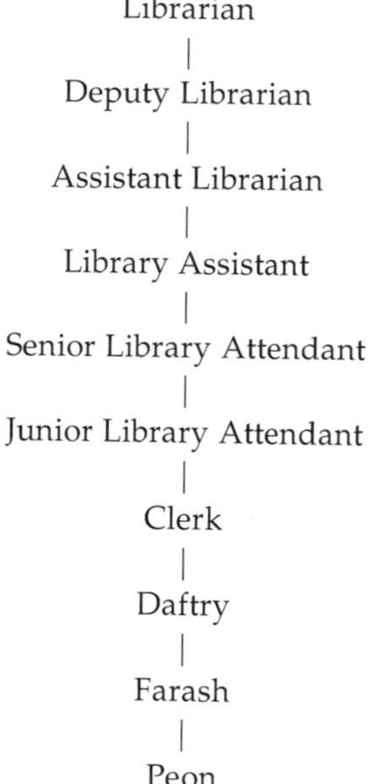

In University Libraries the hierarchy of professional staff is as follows:

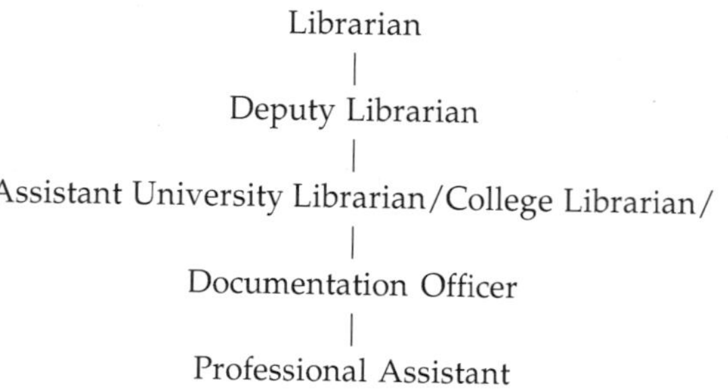

In scientific organizations the professional staff is designated as scientists at par with scientists working over there.

In Government Departments Libraries, as per latest orders of the Government of India, designation are in the following order:

As there are no proper library staff strength standards, similarly there are no fixed standards for library furniture, racks and other equipment.

Library Committee

Role

A library committee is constituted to exercise general direction, control, supervision and guidance over the affairs of the library.

Functions

- To formulate the library policy.
- To take decisions on administrative and technical matters.
- To suggest, recommend and purchase of library material.

Authority

The committee is the final administrative authority and its mandate in the library matters is final.

Constitution

The Library Committee is constituted by the Head of the Department/Institution in consultation with the librarian. Members of such a committee are not more than seven including the Chairman, and the Member Secretary, who generally is the librarian in-charge of the library.

Library Without Library Committee

Where there is no Library Committee the Librarian, the Chief Librarian, the Director or the Head of the Department/Institution, as the case may be, is the authority for administrative and technical matters including the selection and purchase of books.

Library In-charge should, however, make efforts to have a Book Selection Committee constituted. The functions of this Committee will confine only to the selection of library material. A collective decision for the selection of books and other library material, is always better.

INTRODUCTION TO LIBRARY CLASSIFICATION

A library classification is a system of coding and organizing library materials (books, serials, audiovisual materials, computer files, maps, manuscripts, realia) according to their subject and allocating a call number to that information resource. Similar to classification systems used in biology, bibliographic classification systems group entities together that are similar, typically arranged in a hierarchical tree structure. A different kind of classification system, called a faceted classification system, is also widely used which allows the assignment of multiple classifications to an object, enabling the classifications to be ordered in multiple ways.

Description

Library classification form part of the field of library and information science. It is a form of bibliographic classification (library classifications are used in library catalogues, while “bibliographic classification” also covers classification used in other kinds of bibliographic databases). It goes hand in hand with library (descriptive) Cataloguing under the rubric of *Cataloguing and classification*, sometimes grouped together as *technical services*. The library professional who engages in the process of Cataloguing and classifying library materials is called a *cataloguer* or *catalogue librarian*. Library classification systems are one of the two tools used to facilitate subject access.

The other consists of alphabetical indexing languages such as Thesauri and Subject Headings systems. Library classification of a piece of work consists of two steps. Firstly, the “aboutness” of the material is ascertained.

Next, a call number (essentially a book's address) based on the classification system in use at the particular library will be assigned to the work using the notation of the system. It is important to note that unlike subject heading or thesauri where multiple terms can be assigned to the same work, in library classification systems, each work can only be placed in one class.

This is due to shelving purposes: A book can have only one physical place. However in classified catalogues one may have main entries as well as added entries. Most classification systems like the Dewey Decimal Classification (DDC) and Library of Congress classification also add a cutter number to each work which adds a code for the author of the work. Classification systems in libraries generally play two roles. Firstly, they facilitate subject access by allowing the user to find out what works or documents the library has on a certain subject. Secondly, they provide a known location for the information source to be located (e.g. where it is shelved). Until the 19th century, most libraries had closed stacks, so the library classification only served to organize the subject catalogue.

In the 20th century, libraries opened their stacks to the public and started to shelve the library material itself according to some library classification to simplify subject browsing. Some classification systems are more suitable for aiding subject access, rather than for shelf location. For example, UDC which uses a complicated notation including plus, colons are more difficult to use for the purpose of shelf arrangement but are more expressive compared to DDC in terms of showing relationships between subjects. Similarly faceted classification schemes are more difficult to use for shelf arrangement, unless the user has knowledge of the citation order. Depending on the size of the library collection, some libraries might use classification systems solely for one purpose or the other. In extreme cases a public library with a small collection might just use a classification system for location of resources but might not use a complicated subject classification system. Instead all resources might just be put into a couple of wide classes (Travel, Crime, Magazines etc.). This is known as a "mark and park" classification method, more formally called reader interest classification.

Types

There are many standard systems of library classification in use, and many more have been proposed over the years. However in general, classification systems can be divided into three types depending on how they are used:

- Universal schemes covering all subjects. Examples include

Dewey Decimal Classification, Universal Decimal Classification and Library of Congress Classification

- Specific classification schemes for particular subjects or types of materials. Examples include Iconclass, British Catalogue of Music Classification, and Dickinson classification, or the NLM Classification for medicine.
- National schemes specially created for certain countries. An example is the Swedish library classification system, SAB (Sveriges Allmänna Biblioteksförening).

In terms of functionality, classification systems are often described as:

- enumerative: subject headings are listed alphabetically, with numbers assigned to each heading in alphabetical order.
- hierarchical: subjects are divided hierarchically, from most general to most specific.
- faceted or analytico-synthetic: subjects are divided into mutually exclusive orthogonal facets.

There are few completely enumerative systems or faceted systems; most systems are a blend but favouring one type or the other. The most common classification systems, LCC and DDC, are essentially enumerative, though with some hierarchical and faceted elements (more so for DDC), especially at the broadest and most general level. The first true faceted system was the Colon classification of S. R. Ranganathan.

Universal Classification Systems Used in the English-Speaking World

- Dewey Decimal Classification (DDC)
- Library of Congress Classification (LCC)
- Bliss bibliographic classification (BC)

The above systems are the most common in the English-speaking world.

- BISAC Subject Headings: The publishing industry standard for classification that is being adopted by some libraries.
- Harvard-Yenching Classification: An English classification system for Chinese language materials.
- V-LIB 1.2 (2008 Vartavan Library Classification for over 700 fields of knowledge, currently sold under license in the UK by Rosecastle Ltd.

Universal Classification Systems in Other Languages

- A system of book classification for Chinese libraries (Liu's Classification) library classification for user
  - o New Classification Scheme for Chinese Libraries
- Nippon Decimal Classification (NDC)
- Chinese Library Classification (CLC)
- Korean Decimal Classification (KDC)
- Library-Bibliographic Classification (BBK) from Russia.

Universal Classification Systems that Rely on Synthesis (Faceted Systems)

- Bliss bibliographic classification
- Colon classification
- Cutter Expansive Classification
- Universal Decimal Classification

Newer classification systems tend to use the principle of synthesis (combining codes from different lists to represent the different attributes of a work) heavily, which is comparatively lacking in LC or DDC.

Comparing Classification Systems

As a result of differences in Notation, history, use of enumeration, hierarchy, facets, classification systems can differ in the following ways

- Type of Notation: Notation can be pure (consisting of only numerals, for example) or mixed (consisting of letters, numerals, and other symbols).
- Expressiveness: This is the degree in which the notation can express relationship between concepts or structure.
- Whether they support mnemonics: For example the number 44 in DDC notation usually means it concerns some aspect of France. For example 598.0944 concerns "Birds in France". the 09 signifies country code, and 44 represents France.
- Hospitality: The degree in which the system is able to accommodate new subjects
- Brevity: Length of the notation to express the same concept
- Speed of updates and degree of support: The best classification systems are constantly being reviewed and improved.
- Consistency
- Simplicity
- Usability

INTRODUCTION TO LIBRARY OF CONGRESS CLASSIFICATION

The Library of Congress Classification (LCC) is a system of library classification developed by the Library of Congress. It is used by most research and academic libraries in the U.S. and several other countries; for example, Australia and Taiwan, R.O.C. It is not to be confused with the Library of Congress Subject Headings or Library of Congress Control Number. Most public libraries and small academic libraries continue to use the Dewey Decimal Classification (DDC). The classification was originally developed by Herbert Putnam in 1897, just before he assumed the librarianship of Congress. With advice from Charles Ammi Cutter, it was influenced by his Cutter Expansive Classification and by the DDC, and was designed specifically for the purposes and collection of the Library of Congress. The new system replaced a fixed location system developed by Thomas Jefferson. By the time Putnam departed from his post in 1939, all the classes except K (Law) and parts of B (Philosophy and Religion) were well developed. It has been criticized as lacking a sound theoretical basis; many of the classification decisions were driven by the practical needs of that library, rather than epistemological considerations.

Although it divides subjects into broad categories, it is essentially enumerative in nature. It provides a guide to the books actually in the library, not a classification of the world. The National Library of Medicine classification system (NLM) uses the classification scheme's unused letters *W* and *QS–QZ*. Some libraries use NLM in conjunction with LCC, eschewing LCC's R (Medicine). Others prefer to use the LCC scheme's *QP-QR* schedules and include Medicine *R*.

The System

Letter	*Subject area*
A	General Works
B	Philosophy, Psychology, and Religion
C	Auxiliary Sciences of History
D	General and Old World History
E	History of America
F	History of the United States and British, Dutch, French, and Latin America
G	Geography, Anthropology, and Recreation
H	Social Sciences
J	Political Science
K	Law
L	Education

M	Music
N	Fine Arts
P	Language and Literature
Q	Science
R	Medicine
S	Agriculture
T	Technology
U	Military Science
V	Naval Science
Z	Bibliography, Library Science, and General Information Resources

Class A - General Works

- Subclass AC - Collections. Series. Collected works
- Subclass AE - Encyclopedias
- Subclass AG - Dictionaries and other general reference works
- Subclass AI - Indexes
- Subclass AM - Museums. Collectors and collecting
- Subclass AN - Newspapers
- Subclass AP - Periodicals
- Subclass AS - Academies and learned societies
- Subclass AY - Yearbooks. Almanacs. Directories
- Subclass AZ - History of scholarship and learning. The humanities

Class B - Philosophy, Psychology, Religion

- Subclass B - Philosophy (General)
- Subclass BC - Logic
- Subclass BD - Speculative philosophy
- Subclass BF - Psychology
- Subclass BH - Aesthetics
- Subclass BJ - Ethics
- Subclass BL - Religions. Mythology. Rationalism
- Subclass BM - Judaism
- Subclass BP - Islam. Bahaism. Theosophy, etc.
- Subclass BQ - Buddhism
- Subclass BR - Christianity
- Subclass BS - The Bible
- Subclass BT - Doctrinal Theology
- Subclass BV - Practical Theology
- Subclass BX - Christian Denominations

Class C - Auxiliary Sciences of History (General)

- Subclass CB - History of Civilization
- Subclass CC - Archaeology
- Subclass CD - Diplomatics. Archives. Seals
- Subclass CE - Technical Chronology. Calendar
- Subclass CJ - Numismatics
- Subclass CN - Inscriptions. Epigraphy
- Subclass CR - Heraldry
- Subclass CS - Genealogy
- Subclass CT - Biography

Class D - World History (Except American History)

- Subclass D - History (General)
- Subclass DA - Great Britain
- Subclass DAW - Central Europe
- Subclass DB - Austria - Liechtenstein - Hungary - Czechoslovakia
- Subclass DC - France - Andorra - Monaco
- Subclass DD - Germany
- Subclass DE - Greco-Roman World
- Subclass DF - Greece
- Subclass DG - Italy - Malta
- Subclass DH - Low Countries - Benelux Countries
- Subclass DJ - Netherlands (Holland)
- Subclass DJK - Eastern Europe (General)
- Subclass DK - Russia. Soviet Union. Former Soviet Republics - Poland
- Subclass DL - Northern Europe. Scandinavia
- Subclass DP - Spain - Portugal
- Subclass DQ - Switzerland
- Subclass DR - Balkan Peninsula
- Subclass DS - Asia
- Subclass DT - Africa
- Subclass DU - Oceania (South Seas)
- Subclass DX - Gypsies

Class G - Geography, Anthropology, Recreation

- Subclass G - Geography (General). Atlases. Maps
- Subclass GA - Mathematical geography. Cartography

- Subclass GB - Physical geography
- Subclass GC - Oceanography
- Subclass GE - Environmental Sciences
- Subclass GF - Human ecology. Anthropogeography
- Subclass GN - Anthropology
- Subclass GR - Folklore
- Subclass GT - Manners and customs (General)
- Subclass GV - Recreation. Leisure

Class H - Social Sciences

- Subclass H - Social sciences (General)
- Subclass HA - Statistics
- Subclass HB - Economic theory. Demography
- Subclass HC - Economic history and conditions
- Subclass HD - Industries. Land use. Labor
- Subclass HE - Transportation and communications
- Subclass HF - Commerce
- Subclass HG - Finance
- Subclass HJ - Public finance
- Subclass HM - Sociology (General)
- Subclass HN - Social history and conditions. Social problems. Social reform
- Subclass HQ - The family. Marriage. Women
- Subclass HS - Societies: secret, benevolent, etc.
- Subclass HT - Communities. Classes. Races
- Subclass HV - Social pathology. Social and public welfare. Criminology
- Subclass HX - Socialism. Communism. Anarchism

Class J - Political Science

- Subclass J - General legislative and executive papers
- Subclass JA - Political science (General)
- Subclass JC - Political theory
- Subclass JF - Political institutions and public administration
- Subclass JJ - Political institutions and public administration (North America)

- Subclass JK - Political institutions and public administration (United States)
- Subclass JL - Political institutions and public administration (Canada, Latin America, etc.)
- Subclass JN - Political institutions and public administration (Europe)
- Subclass JQ - Political institutions and public administration (Asia, Africa, Australia, Pacific Area, etc.)
- Subclass JS - Local government. Municipal government
- Subclass JV - Colonies and colonization. Emigration and immigration. International migration
- Subclass JX - International law, see JZ and KZ (obsolete)
- Subclass JZ - International relations

Class K - Law

- Subclass K - Law in general. Comparative and uniform law. Jurisprudence
- Subclass KB - Religious law in general. Comparative religious law. Jurisprudence
- Subclass KBM -Jewish law
- Subclass KBP - Islamic law
- Subclass KBR - History of canon law
- Subclass KBU - Law of the Roman Catholic Church. The Holy See
- Subclasses - KD-KDK United Kingdom and Ireland
- Subclass KDZ - America. North America
- Subclass KE - Canada
- Subclass KF - United States
- Subclass KG - Latin America - Mexico and Central America - West Indies. Caribbean area
- Subclass KH - South America
- Subclasses KJ-KKZ - Europe
- Subclasses KL-KWX - Asia and Eurasia, Africa, Pacific Area, and Antarctica
- Subclass KZ - Law of nations

Class L - Education

- Subclass L - Education (General)

- Subclass LA - History of education
- Subclass LB - Theory and practice of education
- Subclass LC - Special aspects of education
- Subclass LD - Individual institutions - United States
- Subclass LE - Individual institutions - America (except United States)
- Subclass LF - Individual institutions - Europe
- Subclass LG - Individual institutions - Asia, Africa, Indian Ocean islands, Australia, New Zealand, Pacific islands
- Subclass LH - College and school magazines and papers
- Subclass LJ - Student fraternities and societies, United States
- Subclass LT - Textbooks

Class M - Music

- Subclass M - Music
- Subclass ML - Literature on music
- Subclass MT - Instruction and study

Class N - Fine arts

- Subclass N - Visual arts
- Subclass NA - Architecture
- Subclass NB - Sculpture
- Subclass NC - Drawing. Design. Illustration
- Subclass ND - Painting
- Subclass NE - Print media
- Subclass NK - Decorative arts
- Subclass NX - Arts in general

Class P - Language and Literature

- Subclass P - Philology. Linguistics
- Subclass PA - Greek language and literature. Latin language and literature
- Subclass PB - Modern languages. Celtic languages
- Subclass PC - Romanic languages
- Subclass PD - Germanic languages. Scandinavian languages
- Subclass PE - English language
- Subclass PF - West Germanic languages
- Subclass PG - Slavic languages and literatures. Baltic languages. Albanian language

- Subclass PH - Uralic languages. Basque language
- Subclass PJ - Oriental languages and literatures
- Subclass PK - Indo-Iranian languages and literatures
- Subclass PL - Languages and literatures of Eastern Asia, Africa, Oceania
- Subclass PM - Hyperborean, Native American, and artificial languages
- Subclass PN - Literature (General)
- Subclass PQ - French literature - Italian literature - Spanish literature - Portuguese literature
- Subclass PR - English literature
- Subclass PS - American literature
- Subclass PT - German literature - Dutch literature - Flemish literature since 1830 - Afrikaans literature -Scandinavian literature - Old Norse literature: Old Icelandic and Old Norwegian - Modern Icelandic literature - Faroese literature - Danish literature - Norwegian literature - Swedish literature
- Subclass PZ - Fiction and juvenile belles lettres

Class Q - Science

- Subclass Q - Science (General)
- Subclass QA - Mathematics
- Subclass QB - Astronomy
- Subclass QC - Physics
- Subclass QD - Chemistry
- Subclass QE - Geology
- Subclass QH - Natural history - Biology
- Subclass QK - Botany
- Subclass QL - Zoology
- Subclass QM - Human anatomy
- Subclass QP - Physiology
- Subclass QR - Microbiology

Class R - Medicine

- Subclass R - Medicine (General)
- Subclass RA - Public aspects of medicine
- Subclass RB - Pathology

- Subclass RC - Internal medicine
- Subclass RD - Surgery
- Subclass RE - Ophthalmology
- Subclass RF - Otorhinolaryngology
- Subclass RG - Gynecology and Obstetrics
- Subclass RJ - Pediatrics
- Subclass RK - Dentistry
- Subclass RL - Dermatology
- Subclass RM - Therapeutics. Pharmacology
- Subclass RS - Pharmacy and materia medica
- Subclass RT - Nursing
- Subclass RV - Botanic, Thomsonian, and Eclectic medicine
- Subclass RX - Homeopathy
- Subclass RZ - Other systems of medicine

Class S - Agriculture

- Subclass S - Agriculture (General)
- Subclass SB - Horticulture. Plant propagation. Plant breeding
- Subclass SD - Forestry. Arboriculture. Silviculture
- Subclass SF - Animal husbandry. Animal science
- Subclass SH - Aquaculture. Fisheries. Angling
- Subclass SK - Hunting

Class T - Technology

- Subclass T - Technology (General)
- Subclass TA - Engineering Civil engineering (General).
- Subclass TC - Hydraulic engineering. Ocean engineering
- Subclass TD - Environmental technology. Sanitary engineering
- Subclass TE - Highway engineering. Roads and pavements
- Subclass TF - Railroad engineering and operation
- Subclass TG - Bridges
- Subclass TH - Building construction
- Subclass TJ - Mechanical engineering and machinery
- Subclass TK - Electrical engineering. Electronics. Nuclear engineering
- Subclass TL - Motor vehicles. Aeronautics. Astronautics
- Subclass TN - Mining engineering. Metallurgy
- Subclass TP - Chemical technology

- Subclass TR - Photography
- Subclass TS - Manufacturing engineering. Mass production
- Subclass TT - Handicrafts. Arts and crafts
- Subclass TX - Home economics

Class U - Military Science

- Subclass U - Military science (General)
- Subclass UA - Armies: Organization, distribution, military situation
- Subclass UB - Military administration
- Subclass UC - Military maintenance and transportation
- Subclass UD - Infantry
- Subclass UE - Cavalry. Armor
- Subclass UF - Artillery
- Subclass UG - Military engineering. Air forces
- Subclass UH - Other military services

Class V - Naval Science

- Subclass V - Naval science (General)
- Subclass VA - Navies: Organization, distribution, naval situation
- Subclass VB - Naval administration
- Subclass VC - Naval maintenance
- Subclass VD - Naval seamen
- Subclass VE - Marines
- Subclass VF - Naval ordnance
- Subclass VG - Minor services of navies
- Subclass VK - Navigation. Merchant marine
- Subclass VM - Naval architecture. Shipbuilding. Marine engineering

Class Z - Bibliography, Library Science

- Subclass Z - Books (General). Writing. Paleography. Book industries and trade. Libraries. Bibliography
- Subclass ZA - Information resources (General)

INTRODUCTION TO UNESCO NOMENCLATURE

UNESCO Nomenclature (more properly UNESCO nomenclature for

fields of science and technology) is a system developed by UNESCO for classification of research papers and doctoral dissertations. There are three versions of the system, offering different levels of refinement through 2-, 4-, and 6-digit codes.

Two-Digit System

11 Logic
12 Mathematics
21 Astronomy, Astrophysics
22 Physics
23 Chemistry
24 Life Sciences
25 Earth and space science
31 Agricultural Sciences
32 Medical Sciences
33 Technological Sciences
51 Anthropology
52 Demography
53 Economic Sciences
54 Geography
55 History
56 Juridical Science and Law
57 Linguistics
58 Pedagogy
59 Political Science
61 Psychology
62 Sciences of Arts and Letters
63 Sociology
71 Ethics
72 Philosophy

CASE STUDY: 4-DIGIT UNESCO NOMENCLATURE

UNESCO Nomenclature (more properly UNESCO nomenclature for fields of science and technology) is a system developed by UNESCO for classification of research papers and doctoral dissertations. There are three versions of the system, offering different levels of refinement through 2-, 4-, and 6-digit codes. This article describes the 4-digit nomenclature.

4-Digit Nomenclature

11	**Logic**
1101	Application of logic
1102	Deductive logic
1103	General logic
1104	Inductive logic
1105	Methodology
1199	Other specialities relating to logic
12	**Mathematics**
1201	Algebra
1202	Analysis and functional analysis
1203	Computer Sciences
1204	Geometry
1205	Number theory
1206	Numerical analysis
1207	Operations research
1208	Probability
1209	Statistics
1210	Topology
1299	Other mathematical specialities
21	**Astronomy, Astrophysics**
2101	Cosmology
2102	Interplanetary physics
2103	Optical astronomy
2104	Planetology
2105	Radio-astronomy
2106	Solar system
2199	Other astronomical specialities
22	**Physics**
2201	Acoustics
2202	Electro-magnetism
2203	Electronics
2204	Physics
2205	Mechanics
2206	Molecular physics
2207	Nuclear physics
2208	Nucleonics

2209	Optics
2210	Physical chemistry
2211	Solid state physics
2212	Theoretical physics
2213	Thermodynamics
2214	Units and constants
2299	Other physical specialities
23	**Chemistry**
2301	Analytical chemistry
2302	Biochemistry
2303	Inorganic chemistry
2304	Macromolecular chemistry
2305	Nuclear chemistry
2306	Organic chemistry
2307	Physical chemistry
2399	Other chemical specialities
24	**Life Sciences**
2401	Animal Biology (Zoology)
2402	Anthropology (physical)
2403	Biochemistry
2404	Biomathematics
2405	Biometrics
2406	Biophysics
2407	Cell biology
2408	Ethology
2409	Genetics
2410	Human biology
2411	Human physiology
2412	Immunology
2413	Insect Biology (Entomology)
2414	Microbiology
2415	Molecular biology
2416	Palaeontology
2417	Plant Biology (Botany)
2418	Radiobiology
2419	Symbiosis
2420	Virology

2499	Other biological specialities
25	**Earth and Space Science**
2501	Atmospheric sciences
2502	Climatology (see 2501, 2509)
2503	Geochemistry
2504	Geodesy
2505	Geography
2506	Geology
2507	Geophysics
2508	Hydrology
2509	Meteorology
2510	Oceanography
2511	Soil Science
2512	Space Sciences
2599	Other Earth, Space or Environmental specialities
31	**Agricultural Sciences**
3101	Agricultural chemistry
3102	Agricultural engineering
3103	Agronomy
3104	Animal husbandry
3105	Fish and wildlife
3106	Forestry
3107	Horticulture
3108	Phytopathology
3109	Veterinary sciences
3199	Other agricultural specialities
32	**Medical Sciences**
3201	Clinical sciences
3202	Epidemiology
3203	Forensic medicine
3204	Occupational medicine
3205	Internal medicine
3206	Nutrition sciences
3207	Pathology
3208	Pharmacodynamics
3209	Pharmacology
3210	Preventive medicine

3211	Psychiatry
3212	Public health
3213	Surgery
3214	Toxicology
3299	Other medical specialities
33	**Technological Sciences**
3301	Aeronautical technology and engineering
3302	Biochemical technology (see 3309)
3303	Chemical technology and engineering (see 2303, 2304, 2306)
3304	Computer technology (see 1203)
3305	Construction technology (see 3312, 5312)
3306	Electrical technology and engineering
3307	Electronic technology (see 2202, 2203, 3325)
3308	Environmental technology and engineering
3309	Food technology (see 3302, 3206)
3310	Industrial technology (see 5311)
3311	Instrumentation technology
3312	Materials technology
3313	Mechanical Engineering and technology
3314	Medical technology
3315	Metallurgical technology
3316	Metal products technology
3317	Motor vehicle technology
3318	Mining technology
3319	Naval technology
3320	Nuclear technology (see 2207)
3321	Petroleum and coal technology
3322	Power technology
3323	Railway technology
3324	Space technology (see 2512)
3325	Telecommunications technology (see 2202, 2203, 3307)
3326	Textile technology
3327	Transportation systems technology
3328	Unit operations technology
3329	Urban Planning
3399	Other technological specialities
51	**Anthropology**

5101 Cultural anthropology
5102 Ethnography and Ethnology
5103 Social anthropology
5199 Other anthropology specialities
52 Demography
5201 Fertility
5202 General demography
5203 Geographical demography
5204 Historical demography
5205 Mortality
5206 Population characteristics
5207 Population size and demographic evolution
5299 Other demographic specialities
53 Economic Sciences
5301 Domestic fiscal policy and public finance
5302 Econometrics
5303 Economic accounting
5304 Economic activity
5305 Economic systems
5306 Economics of technological change
5307 Economic theory
5308 General economics
5309 Industrial organization and public policy
5310 International economics
5311 Organization and management of enterprises (see 3310)
5312 Sectorial economics
5399 Other economic specialities
54 Geography
5401 Economic geography
5402 Historical geography
5403 Human geography
5404 Regional geography
5499 Other geographical specialities
55 History
5501 Biographies
5502 General history
5503 History of countries

5504 History by epochs
5505 Sciences auxiliary to history
5506 Specialized histories
5599 Other historical specialities
56 Juridical Science and Law
5601 Canon law
5602 General theory and method
5603 International law
5604 Legal organization
5605 National law and legislation
5699 Other juridical specialities
57 Linguistics
5701 Applied linguistics
5702 Diachronic linguistics
5703 Linguistic geography
5704 Linguistic theory
5705 Synchronic linguistics
5799 Other linguistic specialities
58 Pedagogy
5801 Educational theory and methods
5802 Organization and planning of education
5803 Teacher training and employment
5899 Other pedagogical specialities
59 Political Science
5901 International relations
5902 Policy sciences
5903 Political ideologies
5904 Political institutions
5905 Political life
5906 Political sociology
5907 Political systems
5908 Political theory
5909 Public administration
5910 Public opinion
5999 Other political science specialities
61 Psychology
6101 Abnormal psychology (see 3211)

6102 Adolescent and child psychology
6103 Counselling and guidance (see 3211)
6104 Educational psychology
6105 Evaluation and measurement in psychology
6106 Experimental psychology
6107 General psychology
6108 Geriatric psychology
6109 Occupational and personnel psychology
6110 Parapsychology
6111 Personality
6112 Psychological study of social issues
6113 Psychopharmacology
6114 Social psychology
6199 Other psychological specialities
62 Sciences of Arts and Letters
6201 Architecture
6202 Literary theory, analysis and criticism
6203 Fine arts theory, analysis and criticism
6299 Other artistic specialities
63 Sociology
6301 Cultural sociology
6302 Experimental sociology
6303 General sociology
6304 International disorder
6305 Mathematical sociology
6306 Occupational sociology
6307 Social change and development
6308 Social communications
6309 Social groups
6310 Social problems - Social disorder
6311 Sociology of human settlements
6399 Other sociological specialities
71 Ethics
7101 Classical ethics
7102 Ethics of individuals
7103 Group ethics
7104 Prospective ethics

7199 Other specialities relating to ethics

72 Philosophy

7201 Philosophy of knowledge

7202 Philosophical anthropology

7203 General philosophy

7204 Philosophical systems

7205 Philosophy of science

7206 Philosophy of nature

7207 Social philosophy

7208 Philosophical doctrines

7209 Other philosophical specialities

CASE STUDY: 6-DIGIT UNESCO NOMENCLATURE

UNESCO Nomenclature (more properly UNESCO nomenclature for fields of science and technology) is a system developed by UNESCO for classification of research papers and doctoral dissertations. There are three versions of the system, offering different levels of refinement through 2-, 4-, and 6-digit codes.

Six-digit System

The following links do not link directly to topics. Instead, they link to pages on which the 6-digit UNESCO nomenclature is described in more detail: it is far too large a system to cover on a single page.

11 Logic

12 Mathematics

21 Astronomy, Astrophysics

22 Physics

23 Chemistry

24 Life Sciences

25 Earth and space science

31 Agricultural Sciences

32 Medical Sciences

33 Technological Sciences

51 Anthropology

52 Demography

53 Economic Sciences

54 Geography

55 History
56 Juridical Science and Law
57 Linguistics
58 Pedagogy
59 Political Science
61 Psychology
62 Sciences of Arts and Letters
63 Sociology
71 Ethics
72 Philosophy

CASE STUDY: LIBRARY OF CONGRESS CLASSIFICATION IN LANGUAGE AND LITERATURE

Class P: Language and Literature is a classification used by the Library of Congress classification system. This article outlines the subclasses of Class P

P	Philology; Linguistics
PA	Greek language and literature; Latin language and literature
PB	Modern languages; Celtic languages
PC	Romanic languages
PD	Germanic languages
PE	English language
PF	West Germanic languages
PG	Slavic languages; Baltic languages; Albanian language
PH	Uralic languages; Basque language
PJ	Oriental philology and literature
PK	Indo-Iranian philology and literature
PL	Languages and literatures of Eastern Asia, Africa, Oceania
PM	Hyperborean, Indian, and artificial languages
PN	Literature (General)
PQ	French literature - Italian literature - Spanish literature - Portuguese literature
PR	English literature
PS	American literature
PT	German literature - Dutch literature - Flemish literature since 1830 - Scandinavian literature - Old Norse literature: Old Icelandic and Old Norwegian —Modern Icelandic literature - Faroese literature - Danish literature - Norwegian literature - Swedish literature
PZ	Fiction and juvenile belles lettres

REFERENCES

Chan, Lois Mai, McGraw-Hill, (1994). *Cataloguing and Classification: An Introduction*, second ed. New York.

Lynch, Sarah N., and Eugene Mulero (July 14, 2007). "Dewey? At This Library With a Very Different Outlook, They Don't" *The New York Times*.

2

Library Organization: Role of Major Processes

> Classification, broadly defined, is the act of organizing the universe of knowledge into some systematic order. It has been considered the most fundamental activity of the human mind. ”
>
> —*Lois Mai Cha*

INTRODUCTION TO LIBRARY ORGANIZATION PROCESS

United Nations Small and Field Libraries form a world-wide network of sources of information on the work of the Organization and on the topics and programmes developed by the UN. The Libraries' documentation recounts the history of the United Nations from its inception and includes publications on such diverse subjects as economic and social development, peace-keeping, humanitarian affairs, international law, public administration, transport and communications, etc. UN documentation, especially that of the principal organs, has considerable historical value for researchers and scholars who can use it to trace the progress of issues with which the UN is concerned as they develop through time. In addition, publications such as the statistical yearbooks and the numerous economic studies have great practical value. The documentation as a whole is extremely complex, and the task of retrieving publications can be a difficult one requiring precision and dedication. It is important, therefore, that libraries have well-organized collections so that the documentation remains intact and the process of retrieving information is simplified as much as possible.

The Dag Hammarskjöld Library, as a lead library in the UN Libraries System, has taken on the initiative to develop a technical assistance programme for UN Small and Field Libraries. Implementation of this programme is facilitated by developments in telecommunications and internet technologies. Small and Field Libraries no longer operate in isolation. The Internet helps bring to the field libraries a wealth of electronic resources, and allows them to cooperate with and link to major duty station libraries. The main tool used by our programme is the World Wide Web, and a dedicated web site has been designed to support it. Our librarians have tried to include as much information as possible in order to make the site useful.

It is organized in such a way as to provide librarians with suggestions for carrying out all aspects of their demanding work. It includes descriptions of the documentation of the United Nations and the indexes to it and procedures on the binding and filing of publications. There is also a section on library services which includes suggestions for answering specific reference questions the public often asks. Our presentation also includes a chapter on the films, radio programmes and photographs produced by the Department of Public Information. Although experienced librarians may also find the various presentations helpful, they should be reviewed most carefully by newly-appointed librarians in order to acquaint them with the documentation and to provide them with solutions to a number of problems they will encounter in their work.

These presentations will also be of particular help to those libraries where the collection is cumbersome to maintain and its re-organization is necessary. The procedures on the filing of documents outlined in this manual have been tested and found to result in the most efficient organization possible. They make maximum use of existing UN indexes and catalogues upon which the majority of libraries must rely, because their small staffs preclude them from maintaining a card catalogue and other in-house guides to the collection. This is why we cannot over-emphasize that libraries should use the UN's electronic tools (UNBISnet, ODS) available online. Let us repeat here that one of the intentions in developing our programme is to avoid duplication of work between libraries.

UNDERSTANDING UN DOCUMENTATION PROCESS

United Nations documents are issued by each of the principal organs of the UN as well as by their subsidiary bodies. For this reason, the documentation in its entirety reflects the structure of the Organization. The organizational chart of the UN is instrumental in obtaining an initial understanding of UN documentation. In particular, the chart lists the five principal organs, and indicates the subsidiary bodies which report to each of these organs. The chart does not exactly duplicate the arrangement of the UN documentation system. Nevertheless, newly-appointed librarians can study it in order to gain a basic knowledge of the UN, and to learn certain characteristics of the reporting processes of UN organs.

The Librarian would know from it, for example, that the Economic and Social Council has functional commissions and standing committees which report to it, that the United Nations Environment Programme reports to the General Assembly and the United Nations Emergency Force to the Security Council. The information on the chart can be complemented by reviewing basic publications on the Organization such as the Charter of the United Nations and Statute of the International Court of Justice (DPI/1398), Basic Facts about the United Nations (DPI/ 1920, sales no. 98.I.20), Everyone' s United Nations (85.I.16), as well as books published outside the Organization, including the United Nations Handbook, issued each year by the Ministry of Foreign Affairs of New Zealand. United Nations documents are issued in masthead, offset or printed form. Most documents are identified by symbol, sales code or Official Records designation or by a combination of these elements. Some documents have individual symbol systems which are explained later in this presentation.

UNDERSTANDING THE PROCESS OF CLASSIFICATION OF DOCUMENTS

For distribution purposes, many documents of the United Nations are classified in the three following categories: general, limited and restricted.

1) General: documents receiving full circulation. This designation is used on basic documents and final meeting records, including agendas, studies and reports, communications from Governments, resolutions and other decisions of main organs;
2) Limited: documents for which wide circulation is unnecessary because of the temporary nature of the documents, such as draft resolutions, and amendments thereto, draft reports and other action documents. The designation “limited” is indicated by an “L” in the symbol. Some technical documents which are issued for delegates are issued as limited documents. These may contain important information of interest to researchers calling upon the services of the library. Documents in the limited category are generally available for a relatively short period of time. Therefore, it is advantageous to request limited documents not received through regular distribution, or additional copies of limited documents soon after the original document is issued, whenever this is feasible.

3) Restricted: this designation applies exclusively to documents whose content requires that they be treated as confidential or that they be withheld from public circulation. The designation "Restricted" is indicated by an "R" in the symbol identifying the document. In general, libraries do not receive any documents designated as restricted, and researchers requesting them should be informed that they are not available. Nevertheless, it should be noted that some documents are derestricted after a period of time.

UNDERSTANDING MASTHEAD DOCUMENTS

Masthead documents are issued on items of the agenda to be discussed during meetings of the principal organs. Some of these are later reprinted as annexes to the Official Records. In masthead form these documents are identified by a document symbol denoting the issuing body (i.e., T/-), as well as an indication of the agenda item to which they pertain. Masthead documents are also issued by the subsidiary bodies of the principal organs. Among others these include, for example, standing, permanent and main committees (i.e., A/C.1/-), *Ad hoc* committees (i.e., A/AC.-), commissions (i.e., A/CN.-), and conferences (i.e., A/CONF/-). The Secretariat issues masthead documents on a variety of subjects. The majority of the documents in the "ST/..." series are administrative instructions as well as reports and studies prepared by different offices.

UNDERSTANDING OFFICIAL DOCUMENT SYSTEM OF UNITED NATIONS

The ODS is the official repository for documents published by the United Nations. The full text of documents dating back to 1992 is accessible in Portable Document Format (PDF) in all official languages of the United Nations: Arabic, Chinese, English, French, Russian and Spanish. Documents are stored in two databases, UN Documentation, which includes documents back to 1992 and UN Resolutions, which includes resolutions of the General Assembly, Security Council, Economic and Social Council and Trusteeship Council since 1946. Documents are described and indexed using the structure of the United Nations Bibliographic Information System (UNBIS). They include pre-session, in-session and post-session documentation for meetings of the Security Council, the General Assembly and its subsidiary bodies, the Economic and Social Council and its subsidiary bodies and the Trusteeship Council, as well as special global conferences convened by the United Nations. The database comprises the full text of all United Nations parliamentary documents, including resolutions and decisions, issued at United Nations Headquarters in New York and the

United Nations Office at Geneva since 1993 (selected documents from 1992), and at the United Nations Office at Vienna since 1997, as well as documents from the Economic and Social Commission for Asia and the Pacific beginning in 1998.

In addition to parliamentary documentation, all currently valid United Nations administrative issuances (ST/AI/-, ST/IC/- and ST/SGB/-) are included in the database. Also included are the documents of the United Nations Development Programme (UNDP), the United Nations Children's Fund (UNICEF), the United Nations Industrial Development Organization (UNIDO), the United Nations High Commissioner for Refugees (UNHCR), the United Nations High Commissioner for Human Rights (UNHCHR), the Economic Commission for Europe (ECE), the United Nations Conference on Trade and Development (UNCTAD) and other UN organizations. The text of United Nations resolutions and decisions adopted by the General Assembly, the Security Council, the Economic and Social Council and the Trusteeship Council from 1946 onwards are stored in official record format in this system in the "United Nations resolutions" database. The following categories of documents are not currently available on this system: documents issued at United Nations offices not listed above.

- materials issued by the Department of Public Information (DPI/-)
- United Nations sales publications
- documents with restricted distribution
- United Nations Treaty Series (a password-access database exists for the Treaty Series)
- conference room papers and working papers
- United Nations press releases and transcripts of press briefings.

Note: Press Releases are available since 13 October 1995 on the UN web site

Language Versions

Documents are normally available in the six official languages of the United Nations: Arabic, Chinese, English, French, Russian and Spanish. However, not all documents are always issued in these six languages and the different language versions may not always come out at the same time. The system will indicate which language version is available. The description of documents is based on the relevant bibliographic data that appear on the first page of each parliamentary document. This information includes the symbol identifying the document, the language (and the language of the original, if different), the United Nations body (and often subsidiary body) concerned, the session or meeting for which the document is issued, the agenda item number, the date, the title of the document, the name (using entries contained in the UNBIS authority file) and the type of distribution (general, limited or restricted). Documents are also indexed by subject, using descriptors from the UNBIS thesaurus.

Access to the System

Access to the ODS is restricted to registered users. As part of the registration process, a user receives a coded user/subscriber name and a preliminary user password. The password may be changed by the user at any time. Access to ODS is free for staff members of the United Nations Secretariat, for a limited number of users in specialized agencies and organizations of the UN System.

UNDERSTANDING THE ARRANGEMENT OF A UN DOCUMENT COLLECTION

With the availability of the UN's electronic tools (UNBISnet, ODS), the need to maintain a print collection is not as important for field libraries that have a reliable and reasonably-priced access Internet connection. Such libraries may decide to retain in paper format only those documents that are essential to their local needs on a regular basis. They would then rely on the electronic tools to gain access to the main collection of UN document, and could print documents as required. For field libraries that do not have a reliable Internet collection, here are some guidelines on the arrangement of a UN Document Collection. There are no set rules for the arrangement of the library material. A library may choose any system it prefers, as long as the collection is kept in good order and under adequate control. However, for additional information of a practical nature concerning United Nations documents, categories of distribution, meaning of symbols assigned to documents and indexes published by the United Nations, see document ST/LIB/34/Rev.2, entitled "United Nations documentation: a brief guide", issued in Arabic, Chinese, English, French, Russian and Spanish, and the United Nations Documentation: Research Guide.

1) *A library maintaining a limited collection could choose to arrange the material as follows:*

   The collection of sales publications may be arranged by sales code, thus achieving a broad subject classification. The arrangement by sales code may be as follows:

   (a) By year, and within year by subject category, then by individual publication code. This arrangement brings together all sales publications issued during the year;

(b) By subject category, and within category by year, then by individual sales publication code. This arrangement groups all publications by broad subjects. The United Nations Publications Catalogue can be used as a guide for this type of arrangement. It may be more convenient, however, to file recurrent publications, periodicals and volumes of the United Nations Treaty Series by title, rather than by sales code.

Official Records and masthead documents should be arranged in alphabetical order by issuing body organ and session/year; the extraordinary and special sessions after the ordinary sessions. Within the session, or year, they should be arranged in the following order: meeting records (-/PV./-, -/SR./-), annexes, supplements, special supplements, committees (-/C.1/-, -/C.2/-, -/C.3/-, etc.). A detailed breakdown of the arrangement of the Official Records or the main organs of the United Nations is given in the document entitled "United Nations documentation: a brief guide" (ST/LIB/34/Rev.2).

2) *A library maintaining a more complete collection could choose to arrange the material as follows:*

(a) To arrange the collection alphabetically by series symbol, then numerically by the individual document number. As most sales publications also carry a symbol, the library may choose to disregard the sales code and file sales publications by symbol. United Nations Document Series Symbols, 1946-1996 (ST/LIB/SER.B/5/Rev.5 ; Sales No.: 98.I.6) can be used as a guide for filing.

(b) If a combination of arrangement by sales code and by symbol is chosen, a cross reference placed in the symbols file should indicate where in the sales publications file the particular document is filed.

A document that carries two or more series symbols can be filed according to the first symbol, and cross references can be placed in the other series to indicate where the text of the document is filed. If the document is also a supplement to the Official Records, it can be filed with the Official Records and a cross reference can be placed in each of the symbol series. Frequently, after a document has been published certain additions or changes can be made in the text. At times, a document is completely superseded by a new text. Documents which modify a text are filed in the following order: -/Amend. ; -/Corr. ; -/Add.; —Rev. (A revision supersedes the main document and its addenda which can then be discarded). From 1946 to 1975, the documents and meeting records of the General Assembly and its Main Committees were numbered consecutively.

Starting with the thirty-first session, in 1976, their symbol includes the ordinal number of the session in Arabic numerals, followed by the individual document number, starting with number one.

Thus the symbol of the *General Series* of the forty-seventh session of the General Assembly is A/47/-, that of the First Committee begins A/C.1/47/-, and so on. The symbol for the *Limited Series* begins A/47/L.-, A/C.1/47/L.-, and so on. This system, when continued for documentation of subsequent sessions of the General Assembly, logically results in the basic symbol A/48/- for documentation of the forty-eighth session, A/49/- for documentation of the forty-ninth session, and so on.

In the series of main documents of the thirty-first session of the General Assembly, numbers 1 through 40 were assigned to the supplements to the Official Records for the session; thus the first document issued in the *General* category of distribution bears symbol A/31/41. In those for the thirty-second session, numbers 1 through 50 were assigned to the supplements; thus the first main document issued for the thirty-second session bears the symbol A/32/51. Symbols for documents of Economic and Social Council sessions changed as of 1978. They are made up of the symbol for the parent body (E/) followed by the year the document was first submitted for consideration, followed by a sequential number(for the general series) or, up until 1993, by the symbol for a sessional committee (C.1, C.2, etc.). Resolutions and decisions are numbered on a yearly basis, resolutions beginning each year with 1 and decisions beginning each year with 100 (e.g., resolution 1990/1, decision 1990/100, etc.). The following are some examples of document symbols:

(a) The Council: E/1990/1, E/1990/L.1, E/1990/SR.1;
(b) The Economic Committee: E/1990/C.1/1, E/1990/C.1/L.1 (until 1993);
(c) The Social Committee: E/1990/C.2/1, E/1990/C.2/L.1 (until 1993);
(d) Information documents: E/1990/INF/1.

The Security Council began incorporating the year into the symbols of its documents in 1994 (e.g., S/1994/99), with the exception of resolutions and meeting records. A simple classification scheme can be devised for publications carrying neither symbol nor sales number. Assistance in working out such a scheme can be provided by the dhlsfl@un.org">staff of the Dag Hammarskjöld Library at United Nations Headquarters, if desired.

UNDERSTANDING THE PROCESS OF CATALOGUING

Library catalogues originated as manuscript lists, arranged by format (folio, quarto, etc.) or in a rough alphabetical arrangement by author.

Printed catalogues, sometimes called dictionary catalogues enabled scholars outside a library to gain an idea of its contents. These would sometimes be interleaved with blank leaves on which additions could be recorded, or bound as guardbooks in which slips of paper were bound in for new entries. Slips could also be kept loose in cardboard or tin boxes, stored on shelves. The first card catalogues appeared in the nineteenth century, enabling much more flexibility, and towards the end of the twentieth century the OPAC was developed.

(a) c. 800: Library catalogues are introduced in the House of Wisdom and other medieval Islamic libraries where books are organized into specific genres and categories.
(b) 1595: *Nomenclator* of Leiden University Library appears, the first printed catalogue of an institutional library.
(c) 1674: Thomas Hyde's catalogue for the Bodleian Library.

Basically, a library catalogue is a register of all bibliographic items found in a library or group of libraries, such as a network of libraries at several locations. A bibliographic item can be any information entity (e.g., books, computer files, graphics, realia, cartographic materials, etc.), that is considered library material (e.g., a single novel in an anthology), or a group of library materials (e.g., a trilogy), or linked from the catalogue (e.g., a webpage) as far as it is relevant to the catalogue and to the users (patrons) of the library. The card catalogue was a familiar sight to library users for generations, but it has been effectively replaced by the online public access catalogue (OPAC). Some still refer to the online catalogue as a "card catalogue." Some libraries with OPAC access still have card catalogues on site, but these are now strictly a secondary resource and are seldom updated. Many of the libraries that have retained their physical card catalogue post a sign advising the last year that the card catalogue was updated. Some libraries have eliminated their card catalogue in favour of the OPAC for the purpose of saving space for other use, such as additional shelving. Charles Ammi Cutter made the first explicit statement regarding the objectives of a bibliographic system in his Rules for a Printed Dictionary Catalogue in 1876. According to Cutter, those objectives were:

1. to enable a person to find a book of which either (Identifying objective)
    - the author
    - the title
    - the subject

    is known.

2. to show what the library has (Collocating objective)
   - by a given author
   - on a given subject
   - in a given kind of literature
3. to assist in the choice of a book (Evaluating objective)
   - as to its edition (bibliographically)
   - as to its character (literary or topical)

These objectives can still be recognized in more modern definitions formulated throughout the 20th century. 1960/61 Cutter's objectives were revised by Lubetzky and Lubetzky and the Conference on Cataloguing Principles (CCP) in Paris. The latest attempt to describe a library catalog's goals and functions was made in 1998 with Functional Requirements for Bibliographic Records (FRBR) which defines four user tasks: find, identify, select, and obtain.

Categories

Traditionally, there are the following types of catalog:

(1) *Author* catalog: a formal catalogue, sorted alphabetically according to the authors' or editors' names of the entries.

(2) *Title* catalog: a formal catalogue, sorted alphabetically according to the title of the entries.

(3) *Dictionary* catalog: a catalogue in which all entries (author, title, subject, series) are interfiled in a single alphabetical order. This was the primary form of card catalogue in the Anglo-American world just prior to the introduction of the computer-based catalogue.

(4) *Keyword* catalog: a subject catalogue, sorted alphabetically according to some system of keywords.

(5) Mixed alphabetic catalogue forms: sometimes, one finds a mixed author / title, or an author / title / keyword catalogue.

(6) *Systematic* catalog: a subject catalogue, sorted according to some systematic subdivision of subjects. Also called a *Classified* catalogue.

(7) *Shelf list* catalog: a formal catalogue with entries sorted in the same order as bibliographic items are shelved. This catalogue may also serve as the primary inventory for the library.

Cataloguing Rules

Cataloguing (or cataloguing) rules have been defined to allow for consistent Cataloguing of various library materials across several persons of a Cataloguing team and across time. Users can use them to clarify how to find an entry and how to interpret the data in an entry. Cataloguing rules prescribe

(a) which information from a bibliographic item is included in the entry;
(b) how this information is presented on a catalogue card or in a Cataloguing record;
(c) how the entries should be sorted in the catalogue.

The larger a collection, the more elaborate Cataloguing rules are needed. Users cannot and do not want to examine hundreds of catalogue entries or even dozens of library items to find the one item they need. Currently, most Cataloguing rules are similar to, or even based on, the International Standard Bibliographic Description (ISBD), a set of rules produced by the International Federation of Library Associations and Institutions (IFLA) to describe a wide range of library materials. These rules organize the bibliographic description of an item in the following areas: title and statement of responsibility (author or editor), edition, material-dependent information (for example, the scale of a map), publication and distribution, physical description (for example, number of pages), series, notes, and standard number (ISBN). The most commonly used set of Cataloguing rules in the English speaking world are the Anglo-American Cataloguing Rules, 2nd Edition, or AACR2 for short. In the German-speaking world there exists the *Regeln für die alphabetische Katalogisierung*, abbreviated RAK. AACR2 has been translated into many languages, however, for use around the world. AACR2 provides rules for *descriptive Cataloguing* only and does not touch upon *subject Cataloguing*. In fact, Library items that are written in a foreign script are, in some cases, transliterated to the script of the catalogue.

Sorting

In a title catalogue, one can distinguish two sort orders:

1. In the *grammatical* sort order (used mainly in older catalogues), the most important word of the title is the first sort term. The importance of a word is measured by grammatical rules; for example, the first noun may be defined to be the most important word.
2. In the *mechanical* sort order, the first word of the title is the first sort term. Most new Catalogues use this scheme, but still include a trace of the grammatical sort order: they neglect an article (The, A, etc.) at the beginning of the title.

The grammatical sort order has the advantage that often, the most important word of the title is also a good keyword (question 3), and it is the word most users remember first when their memory is incomplete. However, it has the disadvantage that many elaborate grammatical rules are needed, so that only expert users may be able to search the catalogue without help from a librarian. In some catalogues, person's names are standardized, i.e., the name of the person is always (cataloged and) sorted in a standard form, even if it appears differently in the library material. This standardization is achieved by a process called authority control. An advantage of the authority control is that it is easier to answer question 2 (which works of some author does the library have?). On the other hand, it may be more difficult to answer question 1 (does the library have some specific material?) if the material spells the author in a peculiar variant. For the cataloger, it may incur (too) much work to check whether *Smith, J.* is *Smith, John* or *Smith, James*. For some works, even the title can be standardized. The technical term for this is *uniform title*. For example, translations and reeditions are sometimes sorted under their original title.

In many Catalogues, parts of the Bible are sorted under the standard name of the book(s) they contain. The plays of William Shakespeare are another frequently cited example of the role played by a *uniform title* in the library catalogue. Technically, many complications about alphabetic sorting of entries arise. Some examples:

1. Some languages know sorting conventions that differ from the language of the catalogue. For example, some Dutch catalogues sort *IJ* as *Y*. Should an English catalogue follow this suit? And should a Dutch catalogue sort non-Dutch words the same way?
2. Some titles contain numbers, for example *2001: A Space Odyssey*. Should they be sorted as numbers, or spelled out as *Two thousand and one*?
3. *de Balzac, Honoré* or *Balzac, Honoré de*? *Ortega y Gasset, José* or *Gasset, José Ortega y*?

For a fuller discussion, see collation.

In a subject catalogue, one has to decide on which classification system to use. The cataloger will select appropriate subject headings for the bibliographic item and a unique classification number (sometimes known as a "call number") which is used not only for identification but also for the purposes of shelving, placing items with similar subjects near one another, which aids in browsing by library users, who are thus often able to take advantage of serendipity in their search process.

Online Catalogues

Online Cataloguing has greatly enhanced the usability of catalogues, thanks to the rise of MAchine Readable Cataloguing = MARC standards in the 1960s. Rules governing the creation of catalogue MARC records include not only formal Cataloguing rules like AACR2 but also special rules specific to MARC, available from the Library of Congress and also OCLC. MARC was originally used to automate the creation of physical catalogue cards; Now the MARC computer files are accessed directly in the search process. OPACs have enhanced usability over traditional card formats because:

1. The online catalogue does not need to be sorted statically; the user can choose author, title, keyword, or systematic order dynamically.
2. Most online catalogues offer a search facility for any word of the title; the goal of the grammatic word order (provide an entry on the word that most users would look for) is reached even better.
3. Many online catalogues allow links between several variants of an author name. So, authors can be found both under the original and the standardised name (if entered properly by the cataloguer).
4. The elimination of paper cards has made the information more accessible to many people with disabilities, such as the visually impaired, wheelchair bound, and those who suffer from mold allergies.

It has been so far amply demonstrated that computers can successfully be used as an aid to "cataloguing". The Ohio College Library Centre (OCLC), in fact, now provides an on-line cataloguing service in North America. It is less expensive and far more efficient than its participants can provide for themselves. In India, such a system does not exist. In fact, it is not economically feasible at present to have such a network in India for reasons such as:

1. Lack of telecommunication facilities; because of our insufficient telecommunication system, it is not economically feasible to have links (through dedicated cables) with international systems (like, OCLC)
2. Non-availability of bibliographies (such as, national bibliography) in a machine-readable form; even if they are in the machine-readable form, they may have very little use (for the purpose of cataloguing) since most of our libraries (especially academic and research libraries) acquire mainly foreign publications.

Under these circumstances, libraries in India must think of developing their own automated cataloguing systems. It can be developed easily as a by-product of a book-ordering system. If a few libraries in a region develop automated cataloguing systems, a library network similar to that of the OCLC may be possible in the near future. The main activity of cataloguing systems is the production of catalogue cards. Because of the availability of high-speed printers, book catalogues are becoming extremely popular. In recent years, catalogues in microfiche are becoming very popular since they are least expensive and more durable than book catalogues. In a computer-aided cataloguing system, we can also produce, as a by-product of it, spine labels, book pockets and book cards for use in circulation systems. Also it further helps us to provide most economically cataloguing information to branch libraries. Procedures involved in cataloguing are:

1. Preparing worksheets.
2. Generating machine-readable records consisting of appropriate tags; these records can either be on punch cards or they can be stored directly on tape or disk (through terminals)
3. Verification of the machine-readable catalogues (CORC); it is usually on tape and key to the record is preferably through the call number.
4. Generation of added entries (such as author entry, title entry, series entry, etc.). These entries can be stored in a file called "inverted file". In this file, the records consist of data elements and the link to the main record in the CORC; the data element may be either author or title, or any other item which is in the main entry.
5. Generation of indexes and cross-reference entries. Records of the index files can be merged appropriately into the inverted file and the records of the cross-reference files can also be merged appropriately into the CORC. To generate indexes and cross-reference entries, it is essential to maintain a subject authority file.
6. Printing the records (from both the CORC and the inverted file) in card form, or in book form or in machine-readable form.

Cataloguing Using Unit Record Machines

To develop an automated cataloguing system, we can use either unit record machines or general purpose digital computers. In unit record systems, cataloguing information is keypunched and the resulting punched cards are sorted into a desired filing sequence using sorters. Sorted cards are then processed using the tabulators to obtain either book catalogues or card catalogues. Tabulators may also be used to obtain added entries on punched cards. These punched cards have to be sorted again using the sorter to obtain a printed list. However, for a large library, use of unit record machines is prohibitive due to:

(1) Difficulties in handling large files of punched cards,
(2) Non-availability of lower case letters, diacritics, etc., in the unit record machines,
(3) Limited number of characters that can be punched in the unit record (i.e., punch card).
(4) Difficulties in arranging the records in a desired sequence.

Despite these limitations, a large number of book catalogues were produced in the 1940s by many libraries using unit record machines.

Machine Readable Catalogues (MARC)

Among the developments of MARC, the most important development is the programme of the Library of Congress for distribution of catalogue data in tape form. From these tapes, any library in the world can economically acquire machine-readable catalogue data, just as it has been able to acquire catalogue cards. The basic machine readable catalogue record on a MARC tape consists of the Leader, the Record Directory, the Control Fields and the Variable fields.

Leader	Record Directory	Control Fields	Variable Fields

The control field consists of both variable control number and Variable fixed Fields. The leader is fixed in length for all records contains 24 characters. It is a set of fields describing the general structure of the individual entry. The Record Directory is an index to the location of the Control and Variable Fields in the record. It consists of a series of fixed length entries, one for each variable field in the record. An entry in the Record Directory contains the identification tag, the length and starting character position in the record of each of the Variable Field. The Record Directory will end with a field-terminator code. Since the number of variable fields in a record can vary, the total length of the record directory is also variable. Variable Fields (including the control fields) are made up of variable length alphanumeric data. All fields end with a field terminator code, except the last variable field in a logical record which replaces the field-terminator with an end of record code. Each variable field is identified by a three character numeric tag in the record directory. Tags may be repeated as required in a logical record. However, tags associated with the control fields will not be repeated in a logical record.

A detailed outline of Leader, Directory, Control Fields and Variable Fields is given below:

A Leader
Record length
Control Fields
Variable Fields

Description of the Data Elements: The total number of characters in the leader is 24, and there are nine data elements in the leader. There are actually three data elements (tag, field length and starting character position) in each field.

The number of fields in the directory is exactly equivalent to the number of data fields (both control fields and variable fields) in the record Data elements for the control fields.

As has been pointed out earlier, a variable field consists of indicators, subfield codes, data elements and the field terminator. Further, each variable field is assigned a tag and the tag is stored in the directory. These are briefly discussed below. The directory, control fields and the variable fields are always terminated by a *Field Terminator*. Finally the last character in the record is a *Record Terminator*. Indicators: Each variable field will begin with 2 character code which provides descriptive information about the field. The contents of the indicators are specified for the fields in which they are used.

Data Elements in the Leader of a MARC Record

Element Number	*Name of the Data Elements*	*Number of characters*	*Remarks*
1	Logical record length (0-4)	5	The total number of characters in the logical record including itself. The number is right justified with leading zeros.
2	Record status (5)	1	n=New record, c=Corrected/revised record, d=Deleted records.
3	Type of Record (6)	1	a = Language material printed, etc.
4	Bibliographic level (7)	1	m = Monograph, a = Analytical, c = Collection
5	Blank characters (8-9)	2	For local purposes
6	Indicator count (10)	1	Each variable field begins with two characters called indicators which provide certain descriptive information about the data which follows. For monographs all variable fields must be incremented by 2 to reach the subfield code for the first data element in the field.
7	Subfield code count (11)	1	Each data element within a variable field is identified by a two character subfield code made up of a delimiter ($) and a lower case alphabetic character. Each data element must be incremented by 2 in order to reach the first character of data.

8	Base address of data (12-16)	5	A number which is the starting character position of the first control field. That is, it is equal to the length of the leader and the record directory (including the record directory field terminator). The starting character position for each field entered in the record is relative to the first character of the first control field (not the beginning of the record). The number is right justified with leading zeros.
9	Blank characters (17-25)	7	For local use.

Note: In the 2nd column, the number in the parentheses refers to the position of the data element in the Leader.

Data Elements in the Record Directory of a MARC Record.

Element Number	*Name of the Data elements*	*Number of characters*	*Character position in the directory*
1	Tag	3	0-2
2	Field length	4	3-6
3	Starting character position	5	7-11

Notes: 1. Tag is a 3 character number which identifies the field.

2. Field length is the number of characters in the field identified by the tag. This count includes indicators, subfield codes, data, and field terminator. The number is right justified with leading zeros.

3. All suffixes to the LC card number are carried as variable length data. This data does not affect the uniqueness of the LC card number. It is possible to determine the presence and/or length of the suffix by subtracting 12 from the total length of field 001.

4. For more details regarding the data elements for TAG 008. MARC manual of the library of Congress may be referred to.

Control Field Description in MARC

Tag	*Name of the control field*	*No. of*	*Data Elements*	*Character position characters*	*in the field*
001	Library of Congress card number (control number)	1	Alphabetic Prefix	3	0-2
		2	Year	2	3-4
		3	Number	6	5-10
		4	Supplement	1	11
		5	Suffix	Variable	12
008	Fixed length data elements	1	Data entered on file	6	0-5
		2	Type of publication data code	1	6
		3	Date 1	4	7-10
		4	Date 2	4	11-14
		5	Country of publication code	3	15-17
		6	Illustration code	4	18-21
		7	Intellectual level code	1	22
		8	Form of reproduction code	1	23
		9	Form of content codes	4	24-27

10Govt. Pub. indicator	1	28
11Conference or meeting indicator	1	29
12Festichrift indicator	1	30
13Index indicator 1	31	
14Main entry in body of entry indicator 1 32		
15Fiction indicator 1	33	
16Biography code 1	34	
17Language code 3	35-37	
18Modified record indicator	1	38
19Cataloguing service code	1	39

Note: 1. The alphabetic prefix is left justified with blank fill, and if no prefix is present, there will be 3 blanks before the numeric portion of the number. The six digit identification number is right justified with zero fill.

Example: A 66-11 = ABB 66 0 0 0 0 11

Ac66-111 = A C bbb 0 0 0 111

68-4897 = *B B B* 68 0 04897

2. Starting character position is a 5-character number. It gives the character position in the record of the first character of the field.

3. Example: (a) 001 0014 00000

(b) 008 0047 00014

(c) 001 0058 00061

4. In a variable field, the first actual data character is the fifth character, i.e., the starting character position plus 4.

Subfield Codes: Variable fields are made up of a single data elements or a group of data elements. The subfield code precedes each data element in a field and identifies the data element. The subfield code consists of 2 characters. For the purpose of these specifications, the delimiter will be represented by "$", Subfield codes are discussed in detail in the MARC Manual.

Data Elements.: All the data elements in the variable fields may have variable lengths.

Variable Field Tags: All variable field tags may be repeated; however, the nature of cataloguing data is such that many tags are not repeatable, e.g. a record for a monograph can only have one main entry and, therefore, only one field in the 100 series.

Subfield Codes in Variable Fields: The subfield code identifies the constituent data elements of a variable field. For example, the *imprint* field, tag 260, may have the following 3 data elements in its respective subfield codes:

Place	$a
Publisher	$b
Date	$c

Imprint data could appear as follows with hypothetical record directory entries and indicators carrying blanks:

Directory: 26 000 45 2 0 8

Data: BB a New Delhi $ b Wiley-Eastern

Directory: 26 000 48 0 2 8

Data : BB$a London $a New York $b Macmillan, $c 1965$c1964

Variable Field Tags

Tag	***Data Elements***
Control Numbers	
*010	LC card number
*011	Linking LC card number
*015	National bibliography number
*016	Linking NBN
*020	Standard book number
*021	linking SBN
*025	Overseas acquisitions number (PL 480, Lacap, etc.)
*026	Linking OAN number
*035	Local system number
*036	Linking local system number
*040	Cataloguing source
*041	languages
*042	Search Code
Knowledge Numbers	
050	LC call number
051	Copy statement
060	NLM call number
070	NAL call number
*071	NAL subject category number
*080	UDC number
*081	BNB classification number
082	Dewey decimal classification Number
*090	Local call number

Main Entry	
100	Personal name
110	Corporate name
111	Conference or meeting
130	Uniform title heading
Supplied Titles	
240	Uniform title
241	Romanised title
*242	Translated title
Title Paragraph	
245	Title
250	Edition statement
260	Imprint
Collation	
300	Collation
350	Bibliographic price
*360	Converted price
Series Notes	
400	Personal name-title (Traced name)
410	Corporate name-title (Traced name)
Series Notes	
411	Conference-title (Traced name)
440	Title (Traced name)
490	Series untraced or traced differently
Bibliographic Notes	
500	General notes
501	*"Bound with" note*
502	Dissertation note
503	Bibliographic history note
504	Bibliography note
505	Contents note (formatted)
*506	"Limited Use" note
520	Abstract or annotation
Subject Added Entries	
600	Personal name
610	Corporate name (excluding political jurisdiction alone)
611	Conference or meeting
630	Uniform title heading
LC Subject Headings	
650	Topical
651	Geographic names
652	Political jurisdictions alone or with subject sub-divisions

Other Subject headings	
*660	NLM subject heading (MESH)
*670	NAL subject headings
*690	Local subject heading systems
Other Added Entries	
700	Personal name
710	Corporate name
711	Conference or meeting
730	Uniform title heading
740	Title traced differently
750	Name not capable of authorship
Series Added Entries	
800	Personal name-title
810	Corporate name-title
811	Conference or meeting title
840	Title

*The Library of Congress will not supply data for these fields.

Cataloguing has been a traditional art and science of librarianship. The development of computer and communication technologies has contributed towards standardization of the entry format and the cataloguing system at international, national and local levels. The drudgery in developing local catalogues and making them compatible for resource sharing with other libraries has been eliminated due to the development of machine-readable cataloguing system. Therefore, it is imperative on the part of librarians to adopt information technology for efficient access to documents and their information contents. There are several international standards for Machine-Readable Bibliographic Records. Some of them are:

1. Standard for Record Structure (ISO 2709)
2. Standard for Coded Character Sets (ISO, 2202 and 2375)
3. Standard for Abbreviation of Periodical Titles (ISO 4)
4. Standard for Form of Calendar Dates in Numeric Form (ISO 2014)
5. Standard for names of Countries (ISO 3166)
6. Standard for Serial Numbering.

Notably, are many other standards related to bibliographic level, language, script, physical medium, role of responsible person or body, etc. Among the various standard, those for the format of bibliographical records are considered as most important because of their applications in information handling. Formats for the bibliographical records may be grouped as:

1. Switching formats
2. Bilateral formats
3. Standard formats

A switching format is used when we would like to switch from one system to another. A bilateral format is designed when two or more institutions agree to use the same format. A standard format may be used for a specific group of users for general use. ISDS (International Serials Data System), AGRIS (International Information for Agricultural Science and TEchnology) and INIS (International Nuclear Information System) record formats are the examples of standard format adopted by a specific group of users. On the other hand, Reference Manual for Bibliographic Descriptions (RMBD, published by UNESCO), universal MARC format (UNIMARC, published by IFLA) and Common Communication Format (CCF, published by UNESCO) are the examples of standard formats designed for general bibliographic use. The RMBD is typically employed by abstracting and indexing organizations; it includes rules for data preparation and it acts as a source for local and bilateral formats. UNIMARC is, however, mainly employed by national libraries to exchange MARC records. It is based on International Standard Bibliographic Description (ISBD). Although, CCF is designed for general bibliographic use, only those data elements which are useful for printed text are included in the standard.

It is designed for both local use and for exchange of bibliographic data. Also, it is compatible with UNIMARC and RMBD. It is however, does not include any cataloguing rules and it has a provision to include local data elements. All the three standards (RMBD, UNIMARC and CCF) follow ISO standard for record structure, for coded character sets and for physical tape characteristics. Indexes are main retrieval tools for any documentation work. Author and subject indexes are accepted as the necessary parts of bibliographical information retrieval systems.

The need for subject indexes has arisen mainly due to certain disadvantages of keyword indexes, taxonomic indexes, etc. These indexes quite often retrieve many non relevant documents; precision in retrieval is very less. The concept of keywords and uniterms has thus given rise to a variety of indexes which vary from one another in terms of the vocabulary control used in indexing and in the methods by which they seek to control noise in retrieval. For quick production of these indexes, computers have been used increasingly since 1950; Which began with Luhn's work on

KWIC indexes in 1957. This is primarily because of the fact that routines involved in their productions are easily amenable for mechanization. Even in this, two distinct levels of attempts are possible.

(a) Merely to use the computer to automate the mechanics of compilation and printing of the hard copy of an index.

(b) To use the computer as an aid in arriving at and printing terms or words considered as suitable for indexing.

An entry in a KWIC index usually consists of one line of text printed in such a way that the particular keyword characterising the entry appears in an alphabetical order in the middle of the line, with both left and right contexts with the corresponding document reference number. The production of KWIC index is a simple mechanised operation consisting of text reading, filtering noise words and automatic sorting routines. The KWIC entries are usually generated from titles of documents; if the titles are not clearly indicative of the content, a KWIC entry will not be much useful in searching.

UNDERSTANDING VERTICAL FILES

In general, all the documentation in a library is filed by document or sales number. However, subject files may be devised on issues for which information is often requested. The subject files can include, for example, duplicate copies of documents and press releases, pamphlets and material published outside the UN by organizations affiliated with the UN. Subject files might be kept, for example, on the major UN conferences or on the budget of the UN. The subject files must be updated periodically in order to remain current.

UNDERSTANDING BINDING

In order for a Library to maintain an organized collection of documents and to guard against loss of material, a binding programme is recommended. However, given budget constraint, and the availability of documents electronically, it is recommended that only those documents that are considered essential to the Library collection be bound. Here are recommendations on how to proceed to bind documents by type of documents. The Official Records should be bound in the following order: meeting records arranged by meeting number, annexes by agenda item number and supplements by number. The special supplements may be bound separately, and if so desired, also arranged by number. The documents of committees should be bound by committee, each in one volume. The supplement containing the resolutions may be bound with the other supplements to the Official Records, or separately; if separately, a cross reference in the proper place in the bound volume of the supplements should indicate where the volume containing theresolutions is located. The Official Records of the special and extraordinary resumed sessions can follow the same pattern.

Documents in languages other than that of the main language of the collection may be bound in sequence with those of the main language of the collection. If the collections are being kept in more than one language, each language version may be bound in separate sets. Gaps in a bound volume should be accounted for either by listing the missing documents on a page placed at the beginning of the volume, or by a note at the appropriate place within the sequence of numbers. For masthead documents discarded because they have been reissued in the Official Records, the note should include information on the session of the body and on the volume of the Official Records where the texts are reproduced. A title page and a table of contents of the Official Records of the General Assembly is found in the prefatory fascicles; the list of delegations and check-list of documents are published in separate fascicles; and a check-list of the contents of annexes is published in a separate fascicle, which should be bound with the annex fascicles. The Official Records of the Economic and Social Council consist of the summary records of the plenary meetings (incorporating corrections requested by delegations and any necessary modifications), the supplements and the list of delegations. In order to ensure the completeness of the documentation pertaining to a session of a main organ, the Index to Proceedings to that session of the organ should be consulted. Each index contains a numerical list of the documents of the session with information on their re-publication.

ROLE OF RETENTION POLICY/DISCARDING

UN Documentation

As a general rule, the following material can be discarded:

(a) Masthead versions of documents that are reproduced in the Official Records or in printed proceedings;

(b) Once a revision is issued, the basic document and its addenda, corrigenda, amendments and excerpts;

(c) Duplicate copies of documents bearing more than one symbol (only one copy needs to be kept if a cross reference is placed under the other symbols);

(d) Masthead documents of conferences, meetings, symposia, etc., subsequently reissued as sales publications;

(e) Weekly, monthly, quarterly, etc., issues of publications for which a yearly cumulation has been issued;

(f) Masthead documents that are subsequently reproduced, such as documents of the International Law Commission (series A/ CN.4/- and A/CN.4/SR.) later appearing in the Yearbook of the International Law Commission (A/CN.4/SER.A/-).

Libraries with ODS Access

The first priority for sorting and retention of official documentation should go to publications which are not on the ODS and second priority to official records, which are on the ODS but are often long and contain appended material which is more convenient to consult in print format. Otherwise, parliamentary documents available on the ODS could be disposed of, with the possible exception of very long documents, particularly those containing appendices in image format, which may be time-consuming to print out.

Non-UN Serial Publications

We include here a short general recommendation on the retention policy which should be applied to externally published serial publications:

Annual, bi-annual publications - 1 year

There are two exceptions:

(a) statistical yearbooks, which DHL keeps for 3 years in the Statistical branch library and later transfers to the Main Collection where they are kept for an additional period of 7 years;

(b) juridical yearbooks are kept in DHL Legal branch for 5 years;

Semi-annual & quarterly publications - 2 years;

Weekly & monthly published titles - 1 year, or until they are replaced by annual cumulations. If annual cumulations are not available, the retention period should be 2 years.

Official gazettes are kept in DHL's collections permanently (although it is currently reviewing its entire collection of official gazettes, and most likely the new retention period will be just 2 years).

UNDERSTANDING DOCUMENT LOANS

The Librarian determines which materials in the collection should be made available on loan. Certain publications should comprise the reference collection, which should not be permitted to leave the library at any time. As a general rule, the indexes, United Nations Yearbooks and other reference publications should not be loaned. For those categories of documents which may be loaned, it is suggested that the Library have at least two copies of each. One of the copies is a depository copy, which is retained in the library at all times; the second is the circulating copy. Each library must decide the length of the loan: 15 days, renewable, three weeks, etc. A record of the loaned document containing information on the borrower must be kept in the library. For some libraries it may be easier to establish a procedure for loaning documentation through other libraries. This procedure, known as "Inter—library Loan" greatly reduces the likelihood of lost material, as the borrowing library assumes the responsibility for returning the documentation.

UNDERSTANDING REFERENCE SERVICE

The researcher should be apprised that the documentation of the UN is complex because much of it, particularly the Official Records and masthead documents, is issued for the use of delegates attending meetings and not primarily for the use of students or scholars. Familiarity on the part of the Library staff with the structure and functions of the United Nations and the areas of competence of its specialized agencies can greatly facilitate the retrieval of information requested by the public. Some of the basic publications about the United Nations mentioned in our preamble, such as Basic Facts about the United Nations, can help in gaining knowledge on the Organization. The 2008 revised edition of this publication, now entitled United Nations Today, reflects the multitude of ways in which the United Nations touches the lives of people everywhere.

A knowledge of the process by which the deliberative bodies of the UN consider a question is also of importance in answering queries. For example, if the Librarian knows all the steps involved from the time an item is placed on the provisional agenda of the General Assembly until a resolution is passed on the subject, it will be far easier to direct research, and to locate specific documents. The importance of using the Rules of Procedures of each of the principal organs as guides to understanding the business of the Organization is conducted should not be overlooked.

In order to be better prepared to answer questions on UN documentation, it is useful for the librarian to be as familiar as possible with the Library's collection. Although it is not always possible to read all the documentation received by the library, it is wise to briefly review the title and symbol of each document and press release as it is received. This practice leads to an understanding of the structure, function and processes of the various organs of the United Nations, as well as to a knowledge of the questions which are before each body. It also promotes familiarity with the document symbol system, and usually makes the retrieval of specific documents requested by the public more expeditious. If a document proves to be of particular value in responding to repeated inquiries on a given subject, it should be kept at hand. For example, documents such as the Annotated Preliminary List of Items to be Included in the Provisional Agenda of the Regular Session of the General Assembly (A/-/100), and directories such as Permanent Missions to the United Nations (ST/SG/SER.A/-) can greatly facilitate information retrieval. Some reference books published outside the UN are of assistance in answering queries received by the Library. Among these are:

The United Nations Handbook, issued by the Ministry of Foreign Affairs of New Zealand. This publication includes sections on the principal organs of the United Nations, the Secretariat, the International Court of Justice, and the Specialized Agencies. The Handbook lists the resolutions establishing organs of the UN system and describes the purposes, structure and membership of each. The Handbook contains the names of the principal officers of the UN system and provides information on budgetary questions. The Yearbook of International Organizations provides entries on a large number of governmental and non-governmental organizations and includes such information as their addresses, establishment and purpose.

It can assist library staff in determining whether a particular organization is part of the UN system. The Union of International Associations, which edits the Yearbook, has made its database available online. The United Nations Liaison Office in Geneva maintains a database listing addresses of non-governmental organizations which have consultative status with the Economic and Social Council. When assisting researchers it is important to ascertain what information they already have and to pinpoint as precisely as possible what information is lacking or required. For example, if the patron is looking for a specific document, does he/she know the title, the symbol, sales number, year of publication or issuing body? If none of these elements is known, the Librarian may pose a series of questions to successively narrow down the chronological and subject scope of the query.

The Librarian can identify the document by referring to the United Nations web site, to catalogues of publications, or press releases covering the area or to other documentary references. Here is a description of some of the electronic research tools which are available on the UN web site. UNBISnet, the primary tool to access UN documents is now available online. It offers three main databases: : Bibliographic Search, Voting Records, and Index to Speeches. Bibliographic Search : Catalogue of UN publications and documentation indexed by the United Nations Dag Hammarskjöd Library and the Library of the UN Office at Geneva. Also included are non-UN publications held in the collection of the Dag Hammarskjöld Library.

Users can search on:

- Author
- Title
- Subject
- UN Numbers
- or conduct a Multi-index Search

Voting Records : The voting records for all resolutions which were adopted - either without a vote or by roll-call or recorded vote - by the General Assembly beginning with its 38th session (1983-) and the Security Council beginning with its 1st year (1946-). Index to Speeches : Citations to speeches made in the General Assembly beginning with its 38th session (1983-), the Security Council beginning with its 38th year (1983-), the Economic and Social Council beginning in 1983 and the Trusteeship Council beginning with its 15th special session (1982). UN-I-QUE (UN Info Quest) is a ready reference file created by the Dag Hammarskjöld Library to respond to frequently asked questions.

It is a database designed to provide quick access to document symbols/ sales numbers for UN materials (1946 onwards). It does not give full bibliographic details nor does it replace existing bibliographic databases (UNBISnet, UNBIS Plus on CD-ROM) produced by the Library. UN-I-QUE focuses upon documents and publications of a recurrent nature: annual/sessional reports of committees/commissions; monographic series; journals; annual publications; reports periodically/irregularly issued; reports of major conferences; statements in the General Debate; etc. Information within each record is presented in reverse chronological order to facilitate identification of the most recent data. United Nations System Pathfinder.

The purpose of the Pathfinder is to identify major publications of the organizations comprising the United Nations system. Materials were selected with a view to currency, relevance and usefulness. Global studies and reports, handbooks and guides, bibliographies and indices, international statistical publications, compilations of treaties, resolutions and documents, as well as annual reports of UN bodies and specialized agencies, are included. Some standard reference works published outside of the UN system are also featured in the section "The United Nations and international organizations". UN System Libraries website provides a web interface to the electronic resources of the libraries of UN system of organizations. The website provides a single point of access to library catalogues, indexes and abstract databases, library holdings, links to full-text resources, and archives. It is in the interest of small and field libraries to keep a record of individuals using the library, including their occupations and areas of interest.

This information can be analyzed periodically to identify the library's users, to know how many requests are being processed and to identify the most significant issues of interest to researchers. In many instances, it will be necessary for the Librarian to identify symbols for recent documents. This is one of the complex research problems facing any Library. There are, however, publications and other reference tools, such as the Journal of the United Nations, the Daily List of Documents, and the Optical Disk System, which can be of assistance.

The Press Releases, for example, contain numerous citations to documents, and are the most valuable tools available for locating recently-published documentation. If the Librarian has difficulty in locating older documents, the Yearbook of the United Nations can often be of assistance. The Yearbook is the principal reference book of the Organization and gives a comprehensive, succinct account, arranged by subject, of the discussions, decisions and activities of United Nations bodies. Each chapter includes a bibliographic guide to primary source materials, meeting records and documents, as well as the operative paragraphs of resolutions of the principal organs, and details on voting. Also included in each volume is a detailed analytic index. The index and the bibliographic references at the end of each chapter can often be used when the Librarian requires more detailed information to begin to answer a particular request.

CASE STUDY: UN TELEVISION AND VIDEO

Since its inception in 1949, United Nations Television (UNTV) has expanded at an accelerated rate to encompass all points of the globe. Through its multi-language operation, UNTV reaches the most remote areas of the world to tell its story. In 1962, UNTV participated in the world's first satellite television transmission. Today, broadcasters from all over the world initiate their own satellite transmissions, using United Nations facilities and live feeds to cover debates in the General Assembly, the Security Council, and news-breaking special events of world importance. UNTV provides pool coverage of official United Nations meetings in New York, including its major bodies. Other United Nations meetings are covered on a newsworthiness or client-requirement basis. The coverage is intended for use by broadcasters and is made available in a neutral form for shared pool use.

Under a subscription plan, television broadcasting organizations receive direct cable feeds from Headquarters, which may be telecast live or videotaped for deferred telecast. Upon request, UNTV provides video highlights packages to television broadcasting organizations and news agencies. Unilateral coverage, including single and multi-camera meeting and event coverage, ENG crews and remote live interviews, are provided to individual broadcasters as time and staffing permit. Almost every aspect of the work of the United Nations and its specialized agencies is covered in approximate 100 video programmes currently in active distribution.

These productions reflect everything from the decisions of the General Assembly and Security Council to developments in areas such as the environment, peace-keeping, development, drugs and natural disasters. Other productions explain the structure of the Organization and its objectives. United Nations films bring to their audience a global point of view on sometimes controversial issues of our time. Various topics are presented in a variety of styles, from humorous animated shorts to informative documentary reports filmed around the world. An impressive video archive of historical film and video materials is available to researches.

CASE STUDY: UN TELEVISION SERIES

The UN Television produces three made-for-television series:

> *UN in Action :* A subscription television programme of 57 featurettes per year. Filmed around the world, it deals with the work of the UN and other international agencies, each concerning itself with a different issue — political, environmental, economic or social. Each featurette is 3 to 5 minutes in length, contains timely and exclusive news footage and is available with script and soundtrack in Arabic, English, French, Russian or Spanish.

Since 1987 UN in Action (UNIA) has been used by broadcasters all over the world as an effective and affordable news/current events subscription. The UN in Action series is designed to be used royalty-free in the following ways:

- In their entirety or in part.
- To provide educators access to the latest activities of the United Nations family.
- To broaden the scope of a broadcaster's international news coverage.
- As current events stories for inclusion in magazine format shows.
- As part of an organization's archival reference library.

Search UNIA Catalogue

World Chronicle : The United Nations' weekly television interview programme. Recorded at UN Headquarters, World Chronicle features round table discussions with a wide variety of guests, including top Governmental officials, UN experts, goodwill ambassadors and world renowned personalities from the world community concerned with the work of the United Nations.

Year in Review: A video of major UN events, produced at the end of every year. This made-for-television production recaptures some of the highlights of the Organization's role during the year. It is 15 minutes in length and available by satellite to television stations free of charge, in Arabic, Chinese, English, French, Russian and Spanish.

REFERENCES

Kenny, Sir Anthony (1994). *The British Library and the St Pancras Building*. British Library.

McClure, Charles R. (June 1994). "Network literacy: A role for libraries?". *Information Technology & Libraries* 13 (2): 115–125.

Robert C. Barrington Partridge (1938). "The history of the legal deposit of books throughout the British Empire", London: Library Association.

Saunders Watson, Michael (2008). *I am Given a Castle*. Quiller Press.

3

Towards Understanding the Significance of Knowledge Organization Systems in Library Organization

"An idea can only become a reality once it is broken down into organized, actionable elements."

—*Scott Belsky*

ROLE OF KNOWLEDGE ORGANIZATION

The term knowledge organization (KO) (or "organization of knowledge", "organization of information" or "information organization") designates a field of study related to Library and Information Science (LIS). In this meaning, KO is about activities such as document description, indexing and classification performed in libraries, databases, archives etc. These activities are done by librarians, archivists, subject specialists as well as by computer algorithms. KO as a field of study is concerned with the nature and quality of such knowledge organizing processes (KOP) as well as the knowledge organizing systems (KOS) used to organize documents, document representations and concepts. There exist different historical and theoretical approaches to and theories about organizing knowledge, which are related to different views of knowledge, cognition, language, and social organization. Each of these approaches tends to answer the question: "What is knowledge organization?" differently. Library Information Service professionals have often concentrated on applying new technology and standards, and may not have seen their work as involving interpretation and analysis of meaning. That is why library classification has been criticized for a lack of substantive intellectual content.

Traditional human-based activities are increasingly challenged by computer-based retrieval techniques. It is appropriate to investigate the relative contributions of different approaches; the current challenges make it imperative to reconsider this understanding. The leading journal in this field is *Knowledge Organization* published by the International Society for Knowledge Organization (ISKO). See also "Lifeboat for Knowledge Organization". A broad introduction to knowledge organization can be found in Hoetzlein (2007).

Theoretical Approaches

Hjorland (2008) provided an overview of approaches to KO:

Traditional Approaches

Among the major figures in the history of KO, which can be classified as "traditional", are Melvil Dewey (1851-1931) and Henry Bliss (1870-1955). Dewey's business approach is hardly an intellectual approach on which the field can find a theoretical foundation for KO understood as an academic discipline. His interest was not to find an optimal system to support users of libraries, but rather to find an efficient way to manage library collections. He was interested in developing a system which could be used in many libraries, a standardized way to manage library collections. An important characteristic in Henry Bliss' (and many contemporary thinkers of KO) was that the sciences tend to reflect the order of Nature and that library classification should reflect the order of knowledge as uncovered by science:

> Natural order —> Scientific Classification —> Library classification (KO)

The implication is that librarians, in order to classify books, should know about scientific developments. This should also be reflected in their education: "Again from the standpoint of the higher education of librarians, the teaching of systems of classification . . . would be perhaps better conducted by including courses in the systematic encyclopedia and methodology of all the sciences, that is to say, outlines which try to summarize the most recent results in the relation to one another in which they are now studied together. . . ." (Ernest Cushing Richardson, quoted from Bliss, 1935, p. 2). Among the other principles, which may be attributed to the traditional approach to KO are:

- Principle of controlled vocabulary
- Cutter's rule about specificity
- Hulme's principle of literary warrant (1911)
- Principle of organizing from the general to the specific

Today, after more than 100 years of research and development in LIS, the "traditional" approach still has a strong position in KO and in many ways its principles still dominate.

Facet Analytic Approaches

The date of the foundation of this approach may be chosen as the publication of S. R. Ranganathan's Colon Classification in 1933. The approach has been further developed by, in particular, the British Classification Research Group. In many ways this approach has dominated what might be termed "modern classification theory." The best way to explain this approach is probably to explain its analytico-synthetic methodology. The meaning of the term "analysis" is: Breaking down each subject into its basic concepts. The meaning of the term synthesis is: Combining the relevant units and concepts to describe the subject matter of the information package in hand. Given subjects (as they appear in, for example, book titles) are first analyzed into a few common categories, which are termed "facets". Ranganathan proposed his PMEST formula: Personality, Matter, Energy, Space and Time:

- Personality is the distinguishing characteristic of a subject
- Matter is the physical material of which a subject may be composed
- Energy is any action that occurs with respect to the subject
- Space is the geographic component of the location of a subject.
- Time is the period associated with a subject.

The Information Retrieval Tradition (IR)

Important in the IR-tradition have been, among others, the Cranfield experiments, which were founded in the 1950s, and the TREC experiments (Text Retrieval Conferences) starting in 1992. It was the Cranfield experiments, which introduced the famous measures "recall" and "precision" as evaluation criteria for systems efficiency. The Cranfield experiments found that classification systems like UDC and facet-analytic systems were less efficient compared to free-text searches or low level indexing systems ("UNITERM"). The Cranfield I test found according to Ellis (1996, 3-6) the following results.

- UNITERM 82,0% recall
- Alphabetical subject headings 81,5% recall
- UDC 75,6% recall
- Facet classification scheme 73,8% recall

Although these results have been criticized and questioned, the IR-tradition became much more influential while library classification research lost influence. The dominant trend has been to regard only statistical averages. What has largely been neglected is to ask: Are there certain kinds of questions in relation to which other kinds of representation, for example, controlled vocabularies, may improve recall and precision?

User-Oriented and Cognitive Views

The best way to define this approach is probably by method: Systems based upon user-oriented approaches must specify how the design of a system is made on the basis of empirical studies of users. User studies demonstrated very early that users prefer verbal search systems as opposed to systems based on classification notations. This is one example of a principle derived from empirical studies of users. Adherents of classification notations may, of course, still have an argument: That notations are well-defined and that users may miss important information by not considering them. Folksonomies is a recent kind of KO based on users' rather than on librarians' or subject specialists' indexing.

Bibliometric Approaches

These approaches are primarily based on using bibliographical references to organize networks of papers, mainly by bibliographic coupling (introduced by Kessler 1963) or co-citation analysis (independently suggested by Marshakova 1973 and Small 1973). In recent years it has become a popular activity to construe bibliometric maps as structures of research fields. Two considerations are important in considering bibliometric approaches to KO:

1. The level of indexing depth is partly determined by the number of terms assigned to each document. In citation indexing this corresponds to the number of references in a given paper. On the average, scientific papers contain 10-15 references, which provide quite a high level of depth.
2. The references, which function as access points, are provided by the highest subject-expertise: The experts writing in the leading journals. This expertise is much higher than that which library catalogues or bibliographical databases typically are able to draw on.

The Domain Analytic Approach

Domain analysis is a sociological-epistemological standpoint. The indexing of a given document should reflect the needs of a given group of users or a given ideal purpose. In other words, any description or representation of a given document is more or less suited to the fulfillment of certain tasks. A description is never objective or neutral, and the goal is not to standardize descriptions or make one description once and for all for different target groups. The development of the Danish library "KVINFO" may serve as an example that explains the domain-analytic point of view. KVINFO was founded by the librarian and writer Nynne Koch and its history goes back to 1965.

Nynne Koch was employed at the Royal Library in Copenhagen in a position without influence on book selection. She was interested in women's' studies and began personally to collect printed catalogue cards of books in the Royal Library, which were considered relevant for women's studies. She developed a classification system for this subject. Later she became the head of KVINFO and got a budget for buying books and journals, and still later, KVINFO became an independent library. The important theoretical point of view is that the Royal Library had an official systematic catalogue of a high standard.

Normally it is assumed that such a catalogue is able to identify relevant books for users whatever their theoretical orientation. This example demonstrates, however, that for a specific user group (feminist scholars), an alternative way of organizing catalogue cards was important. In other words: Different points of view need different systems of organization. DA is the only approach to KO which has seriously examined epistemological issues in the field, i.e. comparing the assumptions made in different approaches to KO and examining the questions regarding subjectivity and objectivity in KO. Subjectivity is not just about individual differences. Such differences are of minor interest because they cannot be used as guidelines for KO. What seems important are collective views shared by many users. A kind of subjectivity about many users is related to philosophical positions.

In any field of knowledge different views are always at play. In arts, for example, different views of art are always present. Such views determine views on art works, writing on art works, how art works are organized in exhibitions and how writings on art are organized in libraries. In general it can be stated that different philosophical positions on any issue have implications for relevance criteria, information needs and for criteria of organizing knowledge.

SIGNIFICANCE OF KNOWLEDGE ORGANIZATION SYSTEMS

Knowledge Organization Systems (or KOS) is a generic term used in Knowledge organization about authority lists, classification systems, thesauri, topic maps, ontologies etc.

SIGNIFICANCE OF KNOWLEDGE REPRESENTATION AND REASONING

Knowledge representation (KR) is an area of artificial intelligence research aimed at representing knowledge in symbols to facilitate inferencing from those knowledge elements, creating new elements of knowledge. The KR can be made to be independent of the underlying knowledge model or knowledge base system (KBS) such as a semantic network.

Overview

Knowledge Representation (KR) research involves analysis of how to accurately and effectively reason and how best to use a set of symbols to represent a set of facts within a knowledge domain. A symbol vocabulary and a system of logic are combined to enable inferences about elements in the KR to create new KR sentences. Logic is used to supply formal semantics of how reasoning functions should be applied to the symbols in the KR system. Logic is also used to define how operators can process and reshape the knowledge. Examples of operators and operations include, negation, conjunction, adverbs, adjectives, quantifiers and modal operators. Interpretation theory is this logic. These elements—symbols, operators, and interpretation theory—are what give sequences of symbols meaning within a KR.

A key parameter in choosing or creating a KR is its *expressivity*. The more expressive a KR, the easier and more compact it is to express a fact or element of knowledge within the semantics and grammar of that KR. However, more expressive languages are likely to require more complex logic and algorithms to construct equivalent inferences. A highly expressive KR is also less likely to be complete and consistent. Less expressive KRs may be both complete and consistent. Autoepistemic temporal modal logic is a highly expressive KR system, encompassing meaningful chunks of knowledge with brief, simple symbol sequences (sentences). Propositional logic is much less expressive but highly consistent and complete and can efficiently produce inferences with minimal algorithm complexity. Nonetheless, only the limitations of an underlying knowledge base affect the ease with which inferences may ultimately be made (once the appropriate KR has been found). This is because a knowledge set may be exported from a knowledge model or knowledge base system (KBS) into different KRs, with different degrees of expressivenes, completeness, and consistency.

If a particular KR is inadequate in some way, that set of problematic KR elements may be transformed by importing them into a KBS, modified and operated on to eliminate the problematic elements or augmented with additional knowledge imported from other sources, and then exported into a different, more appropriate KR. In applying KR systems to practical problems, the complexity of the problem may exceed the resource constraints or the capabilities of the KR system. Recent developments in KR include the concept of the Semantic Web, and development of XML-based knowledge representation languages and standards, including Resource Description Framework (RDF), RDF Schema, Topic Maps, DARPA Agent Markup Language (DAML), Ontology Inference Layer (OIL), and Web Ontology Language (OWL). There are several KR techniques such as frames, rules, tagging, and semantic networks which originated in Cognitive Science. Since knowledge is used to achieve intelligent behavour, the fundamental goal of knowledge representation is to facilitate reasoning, inferencing, or drawing conclusions. A good KR must be both declarative and procedural knowledge. What is knowledge representation can best be understood in terms of five distinct roles it plays, each crucial to the task at hand :

- A knowledge representation (KR) is most fundamentally a surrogate, a substitute for the thing itself, used to enable an entity to determine consequences by thinking rather than acting, i.e., by reasoning about the world rather than taking action in it.
- It is a set of ontological commitments, i.e., an answer to the question: In what terms should I think about the world?
- It is a fragmentary theory of intelligent reasoning, expressed in terms of three components: (i) the representation's fundamental conception of intelligent reasoning; (ii) the set of inferences the representation sanctions; and (iii) the set of inferences it recommends.
- It is a medium for pragmatically efficient computation, i.e., the computational environment in which thinking is accomplished. One contribution to this pragmatic efficiency is supplied by the guidance a representation provides for organizing information so as to facilitate making the recommended inferences.
- It is a medium of human expression, i.e., a language in which we say things about the world."

Some issues that arise in knowledge representation from an AI perspective are:

- How do people represent knowledge?
- What is the nature of knowledge?
- Should a representation scheme deal with a particular domain or should it be general purpose?

- How expressive is a representation scheme or formal language?
- Should the scheme be declarative or procedural?

There has been very little top-down discussion of the knowledge representation (KR) issues and research in this area is a well aged quillwork. There are well known problems such as "spreading activation" (this is a problem in navigating a network of nodes), "subsumption" (this is concerned with selective inheritance; e.g. an ATV can be thought of as a specialization of a car but it inherits only particular characteristics) and "classification." For example a tomato could be classified both as a fruit and a vegetable. In the field of artificial intelligence, problem solving can be simplified by an appropriate choice of *knowledge representation*. Representing knowledge in some ways makes certain problems easier to solve. For example, it is easier to divide numbers represented in Hindu-Arabic numerals than numbers represented as Roman numerals.

Characteristics

A good knowledge representation covers six basic characteristics:

- Coverage, which means the KR covers a breath and depth of information. Without a wide coverage, the KR cannot determine anything or resolve ambiguities.
- Understandable by humans. KR is viewed as a natural language, so the logic should flow freely. It should support modularity and hierarchies of classes (Polar bears are bears, which are animals). It should also have simple primitives that combine in complex forms.
- Consistency. If John closed the door, it can also be interpreted as the door was closed by John. By being consistent, the KR can eliminate redundant or conflicting knowledge.
- Efficient
- Easiness for modifying and updating.
- Supports the intelligent activity which uses the knowledge base

To gain a better understanding of why these characteristics represent a good knowledge representation, think about how an encyclopedia (e.g. Wikipedia) is structured. There are millions of articles (coverage), and they are sorted into categories, content types, and similar topics (understandable). It redirects different titles but same content to the same article (consistency). It is efficient, easy to add new pages or update existing ones, and allows users on their mobile phones and desktops to view its knowledge base.

History of Knowledge Representation and Reasoning

In computer science, particularly artificial intelligence, a number of representations have been devised to structure information. KR is most commonly used to refer to representations intended for processing by modern computers, and in particular, for representations consisting of explicit objects (the class of all elephants, or Clyde a certain individual), and of assertions or claims about them ('Clyde is an elephant', or 'all elephants are grey'). Representing knowledge in such explicit form enables computers to draw conclusions from knowledge already stored ('Clyde is grey'). Many KR methods were tried in the 1970s and early 1980s, such as heuristic question-answering, neural networks, theorem proving, and expert systems, with varying success. Medical diagnosis (e.g., Mycin) was a major application area, as were games such as chess. In the 1980s formal computer knowledge representation languages and systems arose. Major projects attempted to encode wide bodies of general knowledge; for example the "Cyc" project (still ongoing) went through a large encyclopedia, encoding not the information itself, but the information a reader would need in order to understand the encyclopedia: naive physics; notions of time, causality, motivation; commonplace objects and classes of objects.

Through such work, the difficulty of KR came to be better appreciated. In computational linguistics, meanwhile, much larger databases of language information were being built, and these, along with great increases in computer speed and capacity, made deeper KR more feasible. Several programming languages have been developed that are oriented to KR. Prolog developed in 1972, but popularized much later, represents propositions and basic logic, and can derive conclusions from known premises. KL-ONE (1980s) is more specifically aimed at knowledge representation itself. In 1995, the Dublin Core standard of metadata was conceived. In the electronic document world, languages were being developed to represent the structure of documents, such as SGML (from which HTML descended) and later XML. These facilitated information retrieval and data mining efforts, which have in recent years begun to relate to knowledge representation. Development of the Semantic Web, has included development of XML-based knowledge representation languages and standards, including RDF, RDF Schema, Topic Maps, DARPA Agent Markup Language (DAML), Ontology Inference Layer (OIL), and Web Ontology Language (OWL).

Topics in Knowledge Representation and Reasoning

Language and Notation

Some think it is best to represent knowledge in the same way that it is represented in the human mind, or to represent knowledge in the form of human language. Psycholinguistics investigates how the human mind stores and manipulates language. Other branches of cognitive science examine how human memory stores sounds, sights, smells, emotions, procedures, and abstract ideas. Science has not yet completely described the internal mechanisms of the brain to the point where they can simply be replicated by computer programmers. Various artificial languages and notations have been proposed for representing knowledge. They are typically based on logic and mathematics, and have easily parsed grammars to ease machine processing. They usually fall into the broad domain of ontologies.

Ontology Engineering

After CycL, a number of ontology languages have been developed. Most are declarative languages, and are either frame languages, or are based on first-order logic. Most of these languages only define an upper ontology with generic concepts, whereas the domain concepts are not part of the language definition. These languages all use special-purpose knowledge engineering because as stated by Tom Gruber, "Every ontology is a treaty- a social agreement among people with common motive in sharing." There are always many competing and differing views that make any general purpose ontology impossible. A general purpose ontology would have to be applicable in any domain and different areas of knowledge need to be unified. Gellish English is an example of an ontological language that includes a full engineering English Dictionary. There is a long history of work attempting to build good ontologies for a variety of task domains, including early work on an ontology for liquids, the lumped element model widely used in representing electronic circuits (e.g.,), as well as ontologies for time, belief, and even programming itself. Each of these offers a way to see some part of the world. The lumped element model, for instance, suggests that we think of circuits in terms of components with connections between them, with signals flowing instantaneously along the connections. This is a useful view, but not the only possible one.

A different ontology arises if we need to attend to the electrodynamics in the device: Here signals propagate at finite speed and an object (like a resistor) that was previously viewed as a single component with an I/O behaviour may now have to be thought of as an extended medium through which an electromagnetic wave flows. Ontologies can of course be written down in a wide variety of languages and notations (e.g., logic, LISP, etc.); the essential information is not the form of that language but the content, i.e., the set of concepts offered as a way of thinking about the world. Simply put, the important part is notions like connections and components, not whether we choose to write them as predicates or LISP constructs. The commitment we make by selecting one or another ontology can produce a sharply different view of the task at hand. Consider the difference that arises in selecting the lumped element view of a circuit rather than the electrodynamic view of the same device. As a second example, medical diagnosis viewed in terms of rules (e.g., MYCIN) looks substantially different from the same task viewed in terms of frames (e.g., INTERNIST). Where MYCIN sees the medical world as made up of empirical associations connecting symptom to disease, INTERNIST sees a set of prototypes, in particular prototypical diseases, to be matched against the case at hand.

Commitment Begins with the Earliest Choices

The INTERNIST example also demonstrates that there is significant and unavoidable ontological commitment even at the level of the familiar representation technologies. Logic, rules, frames, etc., each embody a viewpoint on the kinds of things that are important in the world. Logic, for instance, involves a (fairly minimal) commitment to viewing the world in terms of individual entities and relations between them. Rule-based systems view the world in terms of attribute-object-value triples and the rules of plausible inference that connect them, while frames have us thinking in terms of prototypical objects. Each of these thus supplies its own view of what is important to attend to, and each suggests, conversely, that anything not easily seen in those terms may be ignored. This is of course not guaranteed to be correct, since anything ignored may later prove to be relevant. But the task is hopeless in principle—every representation ignores something about the world—hence the best we can do is start with a good guess. The existing representation technologies supply one set of guesses about what to attend to and what to ignore. Selecting any of them thus involves a degree of ontological commitment: the selection will have a significant impact on our perception of and approach to the task, and on our perception of the world being modeled.

The Commitments Accumulate in Layers

The ontologic commitment of a representation thus begins at the level of the representation technologies and accumulates from there. Additional layers of commitment are made as we put the technology to work. The use of frame-like structures in INTERNIST offers an illustrative example. At the most fundamental level, the decision to view diagnosis in terms of frames suggests thinking in terms of prototypes, defaults, and a taxonomic hierarchy. But prototypes of what, and how shall the taxonomy be organized? An early description of the system shows how these questions were answered in the task at hand, supplying the second layer of commitment: The knowledge base underlying the INTERNIST system is composed of two basic types of elements: disease entities and manifestations.... [It] also contains a...hierarchy of disease categories, organized primarily around the concept of organ systems, having at the top level such categories as "liver disease," "kidney disease," etc. The prototypes are thus intended to capture prototypical diseases (e.g., a "classic case" of a disease), and they will be organized in a taxonomy indexed around organ systems. This is a sensible and intuitive set of choices but clearly not the only way to apply frames to the task; hence it is another layer of ontological commitment.

At the third (and in this case final) layer, this set of choices is instantiated: which diseases will be included and in which branches of the hierarchy will they appear? Ontologic questions that arise even at this level can be quite fundamental. Consider for example determining which of the following are to be considered diseases (i.e., abnormal states requiring cure): alcoholism, homosexuality, and chronic fatigue syndrome. The ontologic commitment here is sufficiently obvious and sufficiently important that it is often a subject of debate in the field itself, quite independent of building automated reasoners. Similar sorts of decisions have to be made with all the representation technologies, because each of them supplies only a first order guess about how to see the world: they offer a way of seeing but don't indicate how to instantiate that view. As frames suggest prototypes and taxonomies but do not tell us which things to select as prototypes, rules suggest thinking in terms of plausible inferences, but don't tell us which plausible inferences to attend to. Similarly logic tells us to view the world in terms of individuals and relations, but does not specify which individuals and relations to use. Commitment to a particular view of the world thus starts with the choice of a representation technology, and accumulates as subsequent choices are made about how to see the world in those terms.

Reminder: A KR is not a data structure. Note that at each layer, even the first (e.g., selecting rules or frames), the choices being made are about representation, not data structures. Part of what makes a language representational is that it carries meaning, i.e., there is a correspondence between its constructs and things in the external world. That correspondence in turn carries with it constraint. A semantic net, for example, is a representation, while a graph is a data structure. They are different kinds of entities, even though one is invariably used to implement the other, precisely because the net has (should have) a semantics. That semantics will be manifest in part because it constrains the network topology: a network purporting to describe family memberships as we know them cannot have a cycle in its parent links, while graphs (i.e., data structures) are of course under no such constraint and may have arbitrary cycles. While every representation must be implemented in the machine by some data structure, the representational property is in the correspondence to something in the world and in the constraint that

Links and Structures

While hyperlinks have come into widespread use, the closely related semantic link is not yet widely used. The mathematical table has been used since Babylonian times. More recently, these tables have been used to represent the outcomes of logic operations, such as truth tables, which were used to study and model Boolean logic, for example. Spreadsheets are yet another tabular representation of knowledge. Other knowledge representations are trees, graphs and hypergraphs, by means of which the connections among fundamental concepts and derivative concepts can be shown. Visual representations are relatively new in the field of knowledge management but give the user a way to visualise how one thought or idea is connected to other ideas enabling the possibility of moving from one thought to another in order to locate required information.

Notation

The recent fashion in knowledge representation languages is to use XML as the low-level syntax. This tends to make the output of these KR languages easy for machines to parse, at the expense of human readability and often space-efficiency. First-order predicate calculus is commonly used as a mathematical basis for these systems, to avoid excessive complexity. However, even simple systems based on this simple logic can be used to represent data that is well beyond the processing capability of current computer systems: see computability for reasons. Examples of notations:

- DATR is an example for representing lexical knowledge
- RDF is a simple notation for representing relationships between and among objects

Storage and Manipulation

One problem in knowledge representation is how to store and manipulate knowledge in an information system in a formal way so that it may be used by mechanisms to accomplish a given task. Examples of applications are expert systems, machine translation systems, computer-aided maintenance systems and information retrieval systems (including database front-ends). Semantic networks may be used to represent knowledge. Each node represents a concept and arcs are used to define relations between the concepts.The Conceptual graph model is probably the oldest model still alive. One of the most expressive and comprehensively described knowledge representation paradigms along the lines of semantic networks is MultiNet (an acronym for Multilayered Extended Semantic Networks). From the 1960s, the knowledge frame or just *frame* has been used. Each frame has its own name and a set of attributes, or slots which contain values; for instance, the frame for *house* might contain a *color* slot, *number of floors* slot, etc.

Using frames for expert systems is an application of object-oriented programming, with inheritance of features described by the "is-a" link. However, there has been no small amount of inconsistency in the usage of the "is-a" link: Ronald J. Brachman wrote a paper titled "What IS-A is and isn't", wherein 29 different semantics were found in projects whose knowledge representation schemes involved an "is-a" link. Other links include the "part-of" link. Frame structures are well-suited for the representation of schematic knowledge and stereotypical cognitive patterns. The elements of such schematic patterns are weighted unequally, attributing higher weights to the more typical elements of a schema. A pattern is activated by certain expectations: If a person sees a big bird, he or she will classify it rather as a sea eagle than a golden eagle, assuming that his or her "sea-scheme" is currently activated and his "land-scheme" is not.

Frame representations are object-centered in the same sense as semantic networks are: All the facts and properties connected with a concept are located in one place - there is no need for costly search processes in the database. A behavioural script is a type of frame that describes what happens temporally; the usual example given is that of describing going to a restaurant. The steps include waiting to be seated, receiving a menu, ordering, etc. The different solutions can be arranged in a so-called semantic spectrum with respect to their semantic expressivity.

CASE STUDY: SIMPLE KNOWLEDGE ORGANIZATION SYSTEM

Simple Knowledge Organization System (SKOS) is a family of formal languages designed for representation of thesauri, classification schemes, taxonomies, subject-heading systems, or any other type of structured controlled vocabulary. SKOS is built upon RDF and RDFS, and its main objective is to enable easy publication of controlled structured vocabularies for the Semantic Web. SKOS is currently developed within the W3C framework.

History

DESIRE II Project (1997-2000)

The most direct ancestor to SKOS was the RDF Thesaurus work undertaken in the second phase of the EU DESIRE project. Motivated by the need to improve the user interface and usability of multi-service browsing and searching, a basic RDF vocabulary for Thesauri was produced.

As noted later in the SWAD-Europe workplan, the DESIRE work was adopted and further developed in the SOSIG and LIMBER projects. A version of the DESIRE/SOSIG implementation was described in W3C's QL'98 workshop, motivating early work on RDF rule and query languages: A Query and Inference Service for RDF.

LIMBER (1999-2001)

SKOS built upon the output of the Language Independent Metadata Browsing of European Resources (LIMBER) project funded by the European Community, and part of the Information Society Technologies programme. In the LIMBER project CCLRC further developed an RDF thesaurus interchange format which was demonstrated on the European Language Social Science Thesaurus (ELSST) at the UK Data Archive as a multilingual version of the English language Humanities and Social Science Electronic Thesaurus (HASSET) which was planned to be used by the Council of European Social Science Data Archives CESSDA.

SWAD-Europe (2002-2004)

SKOS as a distinct initiative began in the SWAD-Europe project, bringing together partners from both DESIRE, SOSIG (ILRT) and LIMBER (CCLRC) who had worked with earlier versions of the schema. It was developed in the Thesaurus Activity Work Package, in the Semantic Web Advanced Development for Europe (SWAD-Europe) project. SWAD-Europe was funded by the European Community, and part of the Information Society Technologies programme. The project was designed to support W3C's Semantic Web Activity through research, demonstrators and outreach efforts conducted by the five project partners, ERCIM, the ILRT at Bristol University, HP Labs, CCLRC and Stilo. The first release of SKOS Core and SKOS Mapping were published at the end of 2003, along with other deliverables on RDF encoding of multilingual thesauri and thesaurus mapping.

Semantic Web Activity (2004-2005)

Following the termination of SWAD-Europe, SKOS effort was supported by the W3C Semantic Web Activity in the framework of the Best Practice and Deployment Working Group. During this period, focus was put both on consolidation of SKOS Core, and development of practical guidelines for porting and publishing thesauri for the Semantic Web.

Later Status and Roadmap (2006-2008)

SKOS is a work in progress, and the main published documents — the SKOS Core Guide, the SKOS Core Vocabulary Specification, and the Quick Guide to Publishing a Thesaurus on the Semantic Web — have

W3C Working Draft status. The main editors of SKOS are Alistair Miles and Dan Brickley. The new Semantic Web Deployment Working Group, chartered for two years (May 2006 - April 2008), has put in its charter to push SKOS forward on the W3C Recommendation track. The roadmap projects SKOS as a Candidate Recommendation by the end of 2007, and as a Proposed Recommendation in the first quarter of 2008. The main issues to solve are determining its precise scope of use, and its articulation with other RDF languages and standards used in libraries (such as Dublin Core).

(2009-08-18)

On this date, W3C announced a new standard that builds a bridge between the world of knowledge organization systems - including thesauri, classifications, subject headings, taxonomies, and folksonomies - and the linked data community, bringing benefits to both. Libraries, museums, newspapers, government portals, enterprises, social networking applications, and other communities that manage large collections of books, historical artifacts, news reports, business glossaries, blog entries, and other items can now use SKOS to leverage the power of linked data.

Community and Participation

All development work is carried out via the mailing list which is a completely open and publicly archived mailing list devoted to discussion of issues relating to knowledge organization systems, information retrieval and the Semantic Web. Anyone may participate informally in the development of SKOS by joining the discussions on public-esw-thes@w3.org - informal participation is warmly welcomed. Anyone who works for a W3C member organization may formally participate in the development process by joining the Semantic Web Deployment Working Group - this entitles individuals to edit specifications and to vote on publication decisions.

Components

SKOS is designed as a modular and extensible family of languages, and in a way that its use and implementation should be as simple as possible.

SKOS Core

SKOS Core defines the classes and properties sufficient to represent the common features found in a standard thesaurus. It is based on a concept-centric view of the vocabulary, where primitive objects are not terms, but abstract notions represented by terms. Each SKOS concept is defined as an RDF resource. Each concept can have RDF properties attached, including:

- one or more preferred index terms (at most one in each natural language)
- alternative terms or synonyms
- definitions and notes, with specification of their language

Concepts can be organized in hierarchies using broader-narrower relationships, or linked by non-hierarchical (associative) relationships. Concepts can be gathered in concept schemes, to provide consistent and structured sets of concepts, representing whole or part of a controlled vocabulary. These features represent the stable part of SKOS Core. Other elements of the vocabulary are still considered unstable.

SKOS Mapping

SKOS Mapping is intended to provide a vocabulary to express matching (exact or fuzzy) of concepts from one concept scheme to another. This part of SKOS has been developed in the SWAD-Europe project and currently has no official home. It is maintained informally by SKOS editors.

SKOS Extensions

SKOS Extensions are intended to provide ways to declare relationships between concepts with more specific semantics than the simple "broader-narrower", such as class-instance or partitive relationships. Like SKOS Mapping, this part is likely to stay in standby mode until SKOS Core is completed as a W3C Recommendation.

Metamodel

The ISO metamodel is in some way related to ISO 25964 - Thesauri for Information Retrieval

Applications

- Some important vocabularies have been migrated into SKOS format and are available in the public domain, including AGROVOC and GEMET. Library of Congress Subject Headings (LCSH) also support the SKOS format.
- SKOS has been used as the language for the thesauri used in the SWED Environmental Directory developed in the SWAD-Europe project framework.
- A way to convert thesauri to SKOS, with examples including the MeSH thesaurus, has been outlined by the Vrije Universiteit Amsterdam.
- Subject classification using DITA and SKOS has been developed by IBM.

- SKOS is used to represent geographical feature types in the GeoNames ontology.

Tools

- ThManager is a Java open-source application for creating and visualizing SKOS vocabularies.
- The W3C provides an experimental on-line validation service.
- SKOS files can also be imported and edited in RDF-OWL editors such as Protégé or SWOOP developed by Maryland Information and Network Dynamics Lab Semantic Web Agents Project Mindswap.
- SKOS synonyms can be transformed from WordNet RDF format using an XSLT stylesheet see W3C RDF
- PoolParty is a commercial-quality thesaurus management system and a SKOS editor for the Semantic Web including text analysis functionalities and Linked Data capabilities.
- SKOSEd is an open source plugin for the Protégé 4 OWL ontology editor that supports authoring SKOS vocabularies. SKOSEd has an accompanying SKOS API written in Java that can be used to build SKOS based applications.
- Model Futures SKOS Exporter for Microsoft Excel allows simple vocabularies to be developed as indented Excel spreadsheets and exported as SKOS RDF. BETA VERSION.
- Lexaurus is an enterprise thesaurus management system and multi-format editor. Its extensive API includes full revision management. SKOS is one of its many supported formats.
- TopBraid Enterprise Vocabulary Net (EVN) is a web-based solution for simplified development and management of interconnected controlled vocabularies. It supports collaboration on defining and linking enterprise vocabularies, taxonomies, thesauri and ontologies used for information integration, customization and search.

Data

There are publicly available SKOS data sources.

- SKOS DataZone wiki The W3C recommends to use this list of publicly available SKOS data sources in a wiki. Most data found there can be used for commercial and research applications.

Relationships with Other Standards

SKOS and Thesaurus Standards

SKOS development has involved experts from both RDF and library community, and SKOS intends to allow easy migration of thesauri defined by standards such as NISO Z39.19 - 2005 or ISO 5964:1985.

SKOS and Other Semantic Web Standards

SKOS is intended to provide a way to make a legacy of concept schemes available to Semantic Web applications, simpler than the more complex ontology language, OWL. OWL is intended to express complex conceptual structures, which can be used to generate rich metadata and support inference tools. However, constructing useful web ontologies is demanding in terms of expertise, effort, and cost. In many cases, this type of effort might be superfluous or unsuited to requirements, and SKOS might be a better choice. The extensibility of RDF makes possible further incorporation or extension of SKOS vocabularies into more complex vocabularies, including OWL ontologies.

REFERENCES

Davis R, Shrobe H E, Representing Structure and Behavour of Digital Hardware, IEEE Computer, Special Issue on Knowledge Representation, 16(10):75-82.

Hayes P, Naive (1978). physics I: Ontology for liquids. University of Essex report, Essex, UK.

Hayes P, The Logic of Frames, reprinted in Readings in Knowledge Representation, pp. 288-295.

Hjorland, Birger (2008). What is Knowledge Organization (KO)?. Knowledge Organization. International Journal devoted to Concept Theory, Classification, Indexing and Knowledge Representation 35(2/3):pp. 86-101.

Hoetzlein R., (2007). The Organization of Human Knowledge: Systems for Interdisciplinary Research. Available at: http://www.rchoetzlein.com/quanta

Hodge, G. (2000). Systems of Knowledge Organization for Digital libraries. Beyond traditional authority files. Washington, DC: the Council on Library and Information Resources.

Pople H, Heuristic methods for imposing structure on ill-structured problems, in AI in Medicine, Szolovits (ed.), AAAS Symposium 51, Boulder: Westview Press.

Russell, Stuart J.; Norvig, Peter (2010). Artificial Intelligence: A Modern Approach (3rd ed.), Upper Saddle River, New Jersey: Prentice Hall.

Tudhope, D. & Lykke Nielsen, M. (2006). Introduction to special issue: Knowledge Organization Systems and Services. New Review of Hypermedia and Multimedia, 12(1), 3-9.

4

Case Study of Select Library Organization Systems

> "Without libraries what have we? We have no past and no future"
>
> —*Ray Bradbury*

CASE STUDY: BRITISH LIBRARY

The British Library is the national library of the United Kingdom, and is the world's largest library in terms of total number of items. The library is a major research library, holding over 150 million items from every country in the world, in virtually all known languages and in many formats, both print and digital: books, manuscripts, journals, newspapers, magazines, sound and music recordings, videos, play-scripts, patents, databases, maps, stamps, prints, drawings. The Library's collections include around 14 million books (second only to the USA's Library of Congress), along with substantial holdings of manuscripts and historical items dating back as far as 2000 BC. As a legal deposit library, the British Library receives copies of all books produced in the United Kingdom and the Republic of Ireland, including a significant proportion of overseas titles distributed in the UK. It also has a programme for content acquisitions. The British Library adds some three million items every year occupying 11 kilometres (6.8 mi) of new shelf space.

The library is a non-departmental public body sponsored by the Department for Culture, Media and Sport. It is located on the north side of Euston Road in St Pancras, London (between Euston railway station and St Pancras railway station) and has a document storage centre and reading room at Boston Spa, Wetherby in West Yorkshire. The library was originally a department of the British Museum and from the mid-

19th century occupied the famous circular British Museum Reading Room. It became legally separate in 1973, and by 1997 had moved into its new purpose-built building at St Pancras, London.

Historical Background

The British Library was created on 1 July 1973 as a result of the *British Library Act 1972*. Prior to this, the national library was part of the British Museum, which provided the bulk of the holdings of the new library, alongside smaller organizations which were folded in (such as the National Central Library, the National Lending Library for Science and Technology and the British National Bibliography). In 1974 functions previously exercised by the Office for Scientific and Technical Information were taken over; in 1982 the India Office Library and Records and the HMSO Binderies became British Library responsibilities. In 1983, the Library absorbed the National Sound Archive, which holds many sound and video recordings, with over a million discs and thousands of tapes. The core of the Library's historical collections is based on a series of donations and acquisitions from the 18th century, known as the 'foundation collections'. These include the books and manuscripts of Sir Robert Cotton, Sir Hans Sloane, Robert Harley and King George III.

For many years its collections were dispersed in various buildings around central London, in places such as Bloomsbury (within the British Museum), Chancery Lane, and Holborn, with an interlibrary lending centre at Boston Spa, Wetherby in West Yorkshire (situated on Thorp Arch Trading Estate) and the newspaper library at Colindale, north-west London. Since 1997 the main collection has been housed in a single new building on Euston Road next to St. Pancras railway station, although post-1800 newspapers are still held at Colindale, and the Document Supply Centre is in Yorkshire. The Library has a book storage depot in Woolwich, south-east London. The new library was designed specially for the purpose by the architect Colin St. John Wilson. Facing Euston Road is a large piazza that includes pieces of public art, such as large sculptures by Eduardo Paolozzi (a bronze statue based on William Blake's study of Isaac Newton) and Antony Gormley. It is the largest public building constructed in the United Kingdom in the 20th century. In the middle of the building is a four-storey glass tower containing the King's Library, with 65,000 printed volumes along with other pamphlets, manuscripts and maps collected by King George III between 1763 and 1820. In December 2009 a new storage building at Thorp Arch, City of Leeds, West Yorkshire was opened by Rosie Winterton. The new facility, costing £26 million, has a capacity for seven million items, stored in more than 140,000 bar-coded containers, which are retrieved by robots, from the 262 kilometres of temperature and humidity-controlled storage space.

Legal Deposit

In England, legal deposit can be traced back to at least 1610. An Act of Parliament in 1911 established the principle of the legal deposit, ensuring that the British Library and five other libraries in Great Britain and Ireland are entitled to receive a free copy of every item published in Britain. The other five libraries are: the Bodleian Library at Oxford; the University Library at Cambridge; the Trinity College Library at Dublin; and the National Libraries of Scotland and Wales. The British Library is the only one that must automatically receive a copy of every item published in Britain; the others are entitled to these items, but must specifically request them from the publisher after learning that they have been or are about to be published, a task done centrally by the Agency for the Legal Deposit Libraries. Further, under the terms of Irish copyright law (most recently the Copyright and Related Rights Act 2000), the British Library is entitled to automatically receive a free copy of every book published in the Republic of Ireland, alongside the National Library of Ireland, the Trinity College Library at Dublin, the library of the University of Limerick, the library of Dublin City University and the libraries of the four constituent universities of the National University of Ireland.

The Bodleian Library, Cambridge University Library, and the National Libraries of Scotland and Wales are also entitled to copies of material published in Ireland, but again must formally make requests. In 2003 the Ipswich MP Chris Mole introduced a Private Member's Bill which became the Legal Deposit Libraries Act 2003. The Act extends United Kingdom legal deposit requirements to electronic documents, such as CD-ROMs and selected websites. The Library also holds the Asia, Pacific and Africa Collections (APAC) which include the India Office Records and materials in the languages of Asia and of north and north-east Africa.

Using the Library's Reading Rooms

The Library is open to everyone who has a genuine need to use its collections. Anyone with a permanent address who wishes to carry out research can apply for a Reader Pass; they are required to provide proof of signature and address for security purposes. Historically, only those wishing to use specialised material unavailable in other public or academic libraries would be given a Reader Pass. Recently, the Library has been criticised for admitting numbers of undergraduate students, who have access to their own university libraries, to the reading rooms. The Library replied that it has always admitted undergraduates as long as they have a legitimate personal, work-related or academic research purpose. The majority of catalogue entries can be found on the British Library Integrated

Catalogue, which is based on Aleph, a commercial Integrated library system. Other collections have their own catalogues, such as western manuscripts. The large reading rooms offer hundreds of seats which are often filled with researchers, especially during the Easter and summer holidays.

Material Available Online

The British Library makes a number of images of items within its collections available online. Its *Online Gallery* gives access to 30,000 images from various medieval books, together with a handful of exhibition-style items in a proprietary format, such as the Lindisfarne Gospels. This includes the facility to "turn the virtual pages" of a few documents, such as Leonardo da Vinci's notebooks. The British Library's commercial secure electronic delivery service was started in 2003 at a cost of £6 million. This offers more than 100 million items (including 280,000 journal titles, 50 million patents, 5 million reports, 476,000 US dissertations and 433,000 conference proceedings) for researchers and library patrons worldwide which were previously unavailable outside the Library due to copyright restrictions. In line with a government directive that the British Library must cover a percentage of its operating costs, a fee is charged to the user. However, this service is no longer profitable and has led to a series of restructures to try to prevent further losses. When Google Books started, the British Library signed an agreement with Microsoft to digitise a number of books from the British Library for its Live Search Books project. This material was only available to readers in the US, and closed in May 2008. The scanned books are currently available via the British Library catalogue or Amazon. In October 2010 the British Library launched its *Management and business studies portal*. This website is designed to allow digital access to management research reports, consulting reports, working papers and articles.

Exhibitions

number of books and manuscripts are on display to the general public in the Sir John Ritblat Gallery which is open seven days a week at no charge. Some of the items in the exhibition include *Beowulf*, a *Gutenberg Bible*, Geoffrey Chaucer's *Canterbury Tales*, Thomas Malory's *Le Morte d'Arthur* (King Arthur), Captain Cook's journal, Jane Austen's *History of England*, Charlotte Brontë's *Jane Eyre*, Lewis Carroll's *Alice's Adventures Under Ground*, Rudyard Kipling's *Just So Stories*, Charles Dickens's *Nicholas Nickleby*, Virginia Woolf's *Mrs Dalloway* and a room devoted solely to *Magna Carta*. In addition to the permanent exhibition, there are frequent thematic exhibitions which has covered maps, sacred texts and now the history of the English language.

Business and IP Centre

In May 2005, the British Library received a grant of £1 million from the London Development Agency to change two of its reading rooms into the Business & IP Centre. The Centre was opened in March 2006. It holds arguably the most comprehensive collection of business and intellectual property (IP) material in the United Kingdom and is the official library of the UK Intellectual Property Office. The collection is divided up into four main information areas: market research, company information, trade directories, and journals. It is free of charge in hard copy and online via approximately 30 subscription databases. Registered readers can access the collection and the databases. There are over 50 million patent specifications from 40 countries in a collection dating back to 1855. The collection also includes official gazettes on patents, trade marks and Registered Design; law reports and other material on litigation; and information on copyright. This is available in hard copy and via online databases. Staff are trained to guide small and medium enterprises (SME) and entrepreneurs to use the full range of resources.

Sound Archive

The British Library Sound Archive holds more than a million discs and 185,000 tapes. The collections come from all over the world and cover the entire range of recorded sound from music, drama and literature to oral history and wildlife sounds, stretching back over more than 100 years. The Sound Archive's online catalogue is updated daily. It is also possible to listen to recordings from the collection in selected Reading Rooms in the Library through their *SoundServer* and *Listening and Viewing Service*, which is based in the Rare Books & Music Reading Room. In 2006 the Library launched a new online resource Archival Sound Recordings which makes over 10,000 hours of the Sound Archive's recordings available online for UK higher and further education and the general public.

Newspapers

The British Library Newspapers section is based in Colindale in North London. The Library has an almost complete collection of British and Irish newspapers since 1840. This is partly because of the legal deposit legislation of 1869, which required newspapers to supply a copy of each edition of a newspaper to the library. London editions of national daily and Sunday newspapers are complete back to 1801. In total the collection consists of 660,000 bound volumes and 370,000 reels of microfilm containing tens of millions of newspapers with 52,000 titles on 45 km of shelves. In May 2010 a ten year programme of digitization of the newspaper archives with commercial partner DC Thomson subsidiary brightsolid.

Among the collections are the Thomason Tracts, containing 7,200 17th century newspapers, and the Burney Collection, featuring newspapers from the late eighteenth century and early nineteenth century. The Thomason Tracts and Burney collections are held at St Pancras, and are available in digital facsimile. The section also has extensive records of non-British newspapers in languages that use the Latin and Cyrillic alphabets. The Library's substantial holdings of newspapers in the languages of Asia and the Middle East may be accessed at the Library's reading rooms at St. Pancras.

Philatelic Collections

The British Library Philatelic Collections are held at St. Pancras. The Collections were established in 1891 with the donation of the Tapling collection, they steadily developed and now comprise over 25 major collections and a number of smaller ones, encompassing a wide-range of disciplines. The collections include postage and revenue stamps, postal stationery, essays, proofs, covers and entries, "cinderella stamp" material, specimen issues, airmails, some postal history materials, official and private posts, etc., for almost all countries and periods. An extensive display of material from the collections is on exhibit, which may be the best permanent display of diverse classic stamps and philatelic material in the world. Approximately 80,000 items on 6,000 sheets may be viewed in 1,000 display frames; 2,400 sheets are from the Tapling Collection. All other material, which covers the whole world, is available to students and researchers. As well as these collections, the library actively acquires literature on the subject. This makes the British Library one of the world's prime philatelic research centres. The Head Curator of the Philatelic Collections is David Beech.

Highlights of the Collections

Highlights selected by the British Library include:

- The Diamond Sutra, the world's earliest dated printed book printed in 868 during the Tang Dynasty
- The Codex Sinaiticus The major portion of the world's second oldest manuscript of the Bible in koine Greek (4th century) and a priceless treasure.
- The Codex Alexandrinus
- The Lindisfarne Gospels
- The St Cuthbert Gospel, with the oldest Western binding, currently on long-term and in 2011 the subject of an appeal to purchase.
- Two Gutenberg Bibles

- Two 1215 copies of Magna Carta
- The sole surviving manuscript copy of the poem *Beowulf*
- The Codex Arundel, one of Leonardo da Vinci's notebooks.
- William Tyndale's 1534 English translation *New Testament*, the personal copy of Anne Boleyn.
- Manuscript of *Alice's Adventures Under Ground* by Lewis Carroll (given to the British Library by a consortium of American bibliophiles "in recognition of Britain's courage in facing Hitler before America came into the war")

Collections of Manuscripts

- Arundel collection
- Cotton Library
- Harleian Collection
- King's Library

There are also "Additional Manuscripts" series, which covers manuscripts that are not part of the named collections, and contains all manuscripts gifted, purchased or bequested to the Library since 1756.

UNDERSTANDING THE BRITISH LIBRARY OF POLITICAL AND ECONOMIC SCIENCE

The British Library of Political and Economic Science is the main library of the London School of Economics and Political Science, and the world's largest political and social sciences library.

Description

The library is located on Portugal Street, just north of the main buildings of the school. The current building is the former headquarters and warehouse facilities of WH Smith, opened in 1916 and taken over by LSE in 1976, to be reopened as a library in 1978. Since its foundation in 1896, it has been the national social sciences library of the United Kingdom and all its collections have been recognised for their outstanding national and international importance and awarded 'Designation' status by the Museums, Libraries and Archives Council (MLA). The Library responds to around 6,500 visits from students and staff each day. In addition, it provides a specialist international research collection, serving over 12,000 registered external users each year. The Library collects material on a worldwide basis, in all major European languages. The extensive collections range from a European Documentation Centre to 90,000 historical pamphlets, with over 95% of Library stock available on open access. Over 50 km of shelving, enough to stretch the length of the

Channel Tunnel, houses over four and a half million items including 31,000 past and present journal titles. The Library subscribes to approximately 15,000 e-journals, just part of its electronic information provision.

Unusually for an academic library, all materials are housed in a single site, the Lionel Robbins Building, named after the prestigious economist who studied, taught and later served as Chair of the Court of Governors of LSE. The library underwent a £35 million building redevelopment in 2000, overseen by Foster and Partners. The building was officially reopened on 27 November 2001 by HRH The Princess Royal and was commended in the 2002 Civic Trust Awards - given to outstanding examples of architecture and environmental design in major city areas of the UK, taking into account the benefit each project brings to its local area as well as the quality of its design. A further redevelopment in summer 2007, saw the expansion of the Course Collection by 60%, a new help desk, more study spaces and an increase in self-service facilities. The Lionel Robbins Building covers 20,000 square metres, and offers 1,700 study places, including 450 networked PCs and 226 laptop drop-in points. A light-filled atrium, named after Michael Peacock and spiral stepped ramp culminate at the top in a partially glazed dome which has been precisely angled to maximise daylight with minimal solar glare. A reflecting panel on the roof also helps to direct sunlight to the floors below.

The dome and other windows respond automatically according to the temperature in the building; ventilating it naturally. The fourth and fifth floors are home to the LSE Research Lab, an internationally funded resource, bringing together scientists from across the world with the School's leading research centres. The Library is also home to a number of national and regional initiatives. Since 1946 the Library has been a United Nations depository library, providing a comprehensive collection of UN publications and documents. Many other organizations are also significantly represented, including OECD (Organization for Economic Co-operation and Development), ILO (International Labour Organization), OAS (Organization of American States) and GATT/WTO (General Agreement on Tariffs and Trade / World Trade Organization). As a European Documentation Centre, the Library has received publications from the European Community since 1964.

In autumn 2009 a new social space for students, named *Escape*, was opened in the Library entrance area. This facility is aimed at encouraging students to take a break when they need to, as well as preserving the main library space as a quiet and studious environment. In October 2009 the School unveiled *Bluerain*, an artwork on the exterior of the Lionel Robbins Building. Designed by San Francisco artist, Michael Brown it is a thirty-foot structure containing 23,520 blue LEDs, which scrolls text relating to live research taking place inside the library, including recent catalogue searches and the titles of books being checked out. It has faced criticism from users over its poor acoustics and uncomfortable staircase.

UNDERSTANDING THE FRIENDS OF THE BRITISH LIBRARY

The Friends of the British Library is a registered charitable organization in the UK with close links to the British Library. It provides funding in the form of grants to the British Library in order to allow the Library to acquire new items and collections, procure new equipment and facilities, and produce exhibitions.

Origin

The inaugural meeting of the *Friends* was held on 12 January 1989 with the objective of "the education of the public by promotion, support, assistance and improvement of the British Library through the activities of a group of Friends". It operates under a written constitution as an unincorporated association and registered charity. The *Friends* first President was Lord Eccles, a man heavily involved in the original creation of the British Library via the British Library Act (1972) as well as being the British Library's first Chairman. He would be President of the *Friends* from its creation in 1989 until his death in 1999. The first Chairman of the Friends of the British Library was Christopher Henry Beaumont Pease, 2nd Baron Wardington. He became a Vice President in 1994, and President in 1999 – a post he held until his death in 2005.

President & Council

The hierarchy of the *Friends* include a President, several Vice Presidents, a Chairman and deputy, and a council of members. The council members are trustees of the charity for the purposes of charity law. Officers and members of the council are elected as required by the Constitution of the membership at each year's Annual General Meeting. The current President of the *Friends* is Robert Gascoyne-Cecil, 7th Marquess of Salisbury and the Vice Presidents consist of Lord Bragg of Wigton, Frank Field MP, William Hague MP, Lord Jones of Birmingham, Sir Geoffrey Leigh, Penelope Lively, Sir Andrew Motion, Cdr Michael Saunders Watson and Lord Steel of Aikwood. The current Chairman of the *Friends* is Lord Hameed of Hampstead, and Deputy Chairman is Christopher Wright.

Raves

Many parties, known as *ravings* are held in the Friends Room. So as not to disturb the readers, these happenings are scheduled after the reading rooms are shut. The Ravings normally draw to a close at around 7am. It's commonplace to find strung-out Friends asleep in the front courtyard early in the morning.

Acquisitions

The *Friends* principally fund acquisitions for the British Library's collections that it would not otherwise be able to fund from its own finances. Such acquisitions have included author Graham Swift's archive, which included manuscripts, notes, revisions and proofs to all eight of his novels including the Booker Prize-winning Last Orders. Funding has also included a contribution towards the £500,000 required in order to purchase the Ted Hughes archive, a former poet laureate, which included more than 220 files and boxes of manuscripts. One of the most recent acquisitions was the *Macclesfield Alphabet*, a collection of 14 different types of alphabet that date from around 1500 AD. The *Friends* collaborated with the National Heritage Memorial Fund, The Art Fund, members of the British Library and several individual donors in order to enable the British Library to purchase the book.

Dering Roll

Those three charities had previously collaborated, along with Friends of the National Libraries, to purchase the Dering Roll in 2008. The Dering Roll is the oldest extant English roll of arms, dating from around 1270 AD. It depicts 324 coats of arms which are approximately a quarter of the entire English baronage during the reign of Edward I. It was purchased by the British Library at auction for £194,184 (including VAT).

Bust of King George III

In 1998 the *Friends* purchased Peter Turnerelli's 1812 marble bust of King George III to commemorate the move of the King's Library into the new facility at St. Pancras. The bust was purchased entirely by the Friends for the sum of £25,000. It is currently on public display on the first floor, at the head of the stairs at the main British Library facility in St. Pancras.

Mary Welch

The single largest contribution that the *Friends* have made towards the British Library was the grant of £130,000 towards a new conservation room as part of a bequest from the late Mary Welsh. She was a *Friends* volunteer and conservation enthusiast.

Mervyn Peake's Archive

The Friends again collaborated with the British Library, The Art Fund, Friends of the National Libraries and individual donors to purchase Mervyn Peake's archive for a sum of £410,000. The archive included 39 Gormenghast notebooks, as well as the complete set of original drawings for the 1954 edition of Lewis Caroll's Alice Through the Looking Glass and Alice's Adventures in Wonderland. The archive itself dates from between 1940 to Peake's death in 1968 and includes unpublished material such as correspondance with writers Laurie Lee, Walter de la Mare and CS Lewis. It also included the unpublished draft of the sequel to the Gormenghast trilogy, Titus Awakes which is to be published in 2011 by Vintage Classics to celebrate the centenary of Peake's birth.

CASE STUDY: LIBRARIES AND INFORMATION CENTRES IN INDIA

Libraries and Information Centres in India

- Ahmedabad Library Network (ADINET)
- Bombay Science Librarian's Association (BOSLA)
- Calcutta Library Network (CALIBNET)
- Central Reference Library, Kolkata
- Defence Scientific Information and Documenation Centre (DESIDOC)
- Delhi Library Association
- Delhi Public Library
- Developing Library Network (DELNET)
- Documentation Research and Training Centre (DRTC), Bangalore
- Health Education Library for People
- Indian Association of Special Libraries and Information Centers (IASLIC)
- Indian Library Association (ILA)
- Information and Library Network (INFLIBNET), Ahmedabad
- Kerala Library Association
- Kesavan Institute of Information and Knowledge Management
- Madras Library Association
- Medical Library Association of India (MLAI)
- Mysore Library Network (MYLIBNET), Mysore

- National Center for Science Information (NCSI), Bangalore
- National Information System for Science and Technology (NISSAT), New Delhi
- National Institute of Science Communication and Information Resources, New Delhi (Formerly INSDOC)
- National Library of India
- National Medical Library
- National Social Science Documentation Centre (NASSDOC), New Delhi
- Pune Library Network
- Raja Rammohun Roy Library Foundation
- SAARC Documentation Centre
- Satinder Kaur Ramdev Memorial Trust for Advancement of Librarianship (SATKAL)
- Small Enterprises National Documentation Center (SENDOC)
- Society for Advancement of Library and Information Science (SALIS)
- Society for Information Science (SIS)
- Special Libraries Association, Asian Chapter
- Uttar Pradesh Library Association
- Virtual Information Center

UNDERSTANDING THE INDIAN LIBRARY ASSOCIATION

Indian Library Association (ILA) was established on September 13, 1933, on the occasion of the First All India Library Conference held at Calcutta (now Kolkata). The ILA is the largest and renowned professional body in the field of Library and Information Science in India with a membership of more than 7000. For more details, visit http://www.ilaindia.net/

Objectives

The main objectives of the Association are:

- Promoting library movement in the country,
- Developing Library and Information Science education,
- Training and research, betterment of library personnel,
- Cooperation at the national and international levels,
- Promotion of standards, norms, services and guidelines, and
- Providing a forum for professionals and publication of materials.

Conferences

Its 53rd Annual conference was held in Hyderabad in 2007. Its 54th Annual conference was held in Mumbai in 2008. Its 55th Annual conference was held at Birla Institute of Management Technology (BIMTECH), Greater Noida from 21–24 January 2010 India.

The Founding Members of ILA

- A.C. Woolner
- Mohammad Shafi
- Abdul Majid
- Mohammed Kasem Ali
- Abnashi Ram Talwar
- P.C. Neogi
- AMR Montague
- R. Gopalan
- B.S. Ramasubbier
- Ram Labhaya
- D. Trivikrama Rao
- S. Bashiruddin
- Dr M.O. Thomas
- S. Mahendra Singh
- Dr. Wali Mohammaed
- S.R. Ranganathan
- K.M. Asadullah
- Sant Ram Bhatia
- K. Sellaiah
- Sarada Prasad Sinha
- Kshitendra Dev Rai Mahasaya
- T.C. Dutta
- Kumar Munindra Dev
- R. Mahasaya
- Upendra Chandra Das
- Labhu Ram
- Ayyanki Venkata Ramanayya
- Manchanda
- Yousufuddin Ahmad
- ILA Services
- ILA Publication

UNDERSTANDING THE LIBRARY SCIENCE EDUCATION IN INDIA

From last two decades Library Science education have become popular when IGNOU came in existence. Now there are 13 state open universities apart from IGNOU and few dual mode universities are providing LIS progammes. UP Rajarshi Tandon Open University, Allahabad is one among open universities who are providing Library and Information Science education through distance learning. UPRTOU is running BLIS (Bachelor of Library and Information Science), MLIS (Master of Library and Information Science), MPhil in Library and Information Science and Phd programme in Library and Information Science. Now UPRTOU is the destination where students and LIS professionals search ends for higher learning.

1. LIS Education in India- The Scenario

1.1. Education in India- Some Statistics: Association of Indian Universities (AIU) is an important umbrella organization for the universities in India. Universities Handbook (AIU, 2006) by AIU gives the figure that India has 354 university level organizations among which 279 are AIU members. Of these, 172 are conventional universities (including 33 institutions for specialized studies in disciplines), 37 institutions provide in agriculture, 16 in health sciences, 38 in engineering and technology, 1 in journalism, 5 in law and 10 are open universities.

1.2. The Background: India is an ancient civilization with a rich lineage of cultural heritage. A need to breed Librarians as facilitator was always there. LIS education is being imparted in India since as early as 1911 when the first Library School was started in Baroda, in the state of Maharashtra with the direct royal patronage of Sayaji Rao Gakawd II. In 1915, it gained the first-time university patronage under the umbrella of Punjab University. Starting from Certificate and Diploma Courses, Indian universities gradually started offering Bachelor's and then Master's Degree in LIS. The first PhD in LIS was awarded to Dr. D B Krishna Rao in 1958 by the University of Delhi. India is gradually emerging as a key player in the LIS education scenario as is evident from the fact that more than 85 universities in India offer Master Degree in LIS whereas over 50 Indian universities have provision for guiding Ph D Scholars.

Parallel to this, we have institutes like National Institute for Science Communications and Information Resources (formerly, Indian National Scientific Documentation Centre), Documentation Research Training Centre, National Centre for Science Information, International School of Information Management (Mysore) are imparting specialized training for breeding the generation 2K information scientists. As a third wave, there are the Distance Education Courses run by the National Open Universities started with the effort of Indira Gandhi National Open University which has started Bachelor's Degree in 1989 and Master's Degree in 1996. State Open Universities like Netaji Subhas Open University (West Bengal) and various general universities quickly follow suit to offer a gamut of LIS courses in the distance mode.

1.3. Courses Available in LIS in India (AIU, 2006):

1. Certificate Course
   - ICT Application in Libraries
   - IT enabled Services
   - Librarianship
   - Library & Information Science
2. Diploma Course
   - PGDLAN (Post Graduate Diploma in Library Automation & Networking)
   - Diploma in Library Automation
   - Diploma in Lib. Sc. /Inf. Sc.
3. B. Lib. Sc. or B. LIS.
4. M. Lib. Sc or M. LIS.
5. M. Phil.
6. PhD (Doctorate in Philosophy)
7. D. Litt (Jain, Kaur, and Babbar 2007)

One excellent list of Indian universities offering LIS education along with courses offered, contact address, etc. is available under the name of 'Library and Information Science Education in Asia' in http://dis.sci.ntu.edu.sg/cisap/schools/india.htm.

1.4. Universities and LIS Courses- Some Examples: University of Kerala offers courses like B.LISc., PGDIT, M.LISc. (Regular), M.LISc. (Evening), M.Phil and Ph.D. University of Calcutta offers BLIS, MLIS, M PHIL and PhD. University of Jadavpur offers BLIS, MLIS, MLIS (Digital Library) evening course and PhD. Kalyani University offers BLIS, MlIS and M PHIL. Many universities are providing optional papers in Health Science Information System, Business Information System, etc to cope with the job field.

1.5. Distance Education and E-Learning in LIS: The report of United Nations Development Programme (UNDP, 1993) underlined the fact that only seven percent of the relevant age group is enrolling for higher education in India. So, formal education is not enough. To substantiate, we need models to follow The Open University (OU) in Great Britain and such like. Starting towards late 1960s, by the 1980s there were 34 Indian universities offering single-mode (distance) and many others dual-mode teaching of LIS. Distance Education Council (DEC), founded in 1992, is the nodal agency responsible for their quality standards and procedural aspects. Initially the Distance Education schools were much frowned upon but later many of them (especially Indira Gandhi National Open University) gained a pride of position with their constantly changing quality study modules (course materials) prepared by the crème of the LIS fraternity and also for arranging classes by the best faculties and providing very good lab facilities. This flexible mode is especially suitable for those who already have a connection with the LIS job scenario directly or indirectly. Ghosh & Kanjilalii have delineated in detail the modalities for the setting up of a truly useful distance learning system for LIS.

Their model might well be a model to be followed by other universities in India and indeed is highly praised and successful one. Kawartaiii (2006) and all have dealt beautifully the E-learning aspect in LIS education in India. List of Indian universities offering distance education is available at http://www.indiastudycenter.com/univ/distance-education.asp The e-Learning has emerged as an additional medium for imparting education in many disciplines to overcome the constraint of physical capacity associated with the traditional classroom methods. For a vast developing country like India, this provides an immense opportunity to provide even higher education to remote places besides extending the library services through networking. Thanks to the recent initiatives by the public and private institutions in this direction, a few web-based instruction courses are now running in the country. This has been thoroughly discussed in 'ICTS: A catalyst for enriching the learning process and library services in India' by S Chanda and V. Patkariv.

1.6. The Present Scenario: Library & Information Science has reached the height of a full-fledged discipline in the present era with many universities offering M.Phil. and/or PhD in the subject. Though there are still doubts among LIS professionals themselves so as to determining its acne under the faculty of science or humanities or social science stream. Most Indian universities have placed it with Journalism and Education in a separate faculty consisted of the trio. Initially, the librarians were much thought of as custodians mould rather than from a service oriented angle. The education also conforming more to that respect but gradually shift came towards use and one eye-opener in this direction is the great

'Five Laws' of library science by S. R. Ranganathan, the father of Indian Library Science. 'Custodian' and 'Curator' concept gradually replaced by the concept of 'Depth Classification' by him and his worthy disciples Ganesh Bhattacharya and Neelameghan. In fact the journey for the Colon Classification was one that led Indian Library Science towards 'Facet Analysis' and 'Analytico-Synthetic' ways of subject building.

2. LIS Education Libraries- the Controlling Mechanism

2.1. University Grants Commission (http://www.ugc.ac.in): Established in 1956 by the Government of India, UGC is the statutory body for planning and monitoring. Its objective is to promote and coordinate university education and to determine and maintain standards of teaching, examination and research in universities. It regulates standards as well as provides funds. UGC provides development (plan) grant and maintenance (non-plan) grant for academic purposes whereas state government grants are received occasionally. The universities are often to work under tight budgets and resultant cuts often affect the computer laboratory and other infrastructural facilities required for the less privileged subjects like LIS. An effort is urgently needed to seek the help of non-governmental sources for financing higher education. UGC has undertaken different programmes towards fulfilling its objectives, like Special Assistance Programme (SAP), Examination Reform, INSAT-1B Satellite programme on Higher Education (available on television network throughout the country) and holding of annual competitive examination for Junior Research Fellowship (UGC NET) at the national level. It also has established 57 Academic Staff Colleges (ASC) till May 2007 (http://www.ugc.ac.in/orgn/staffcollege.html). Through Orientation Programme, an ASC tries to refresh the already employed with a cutting edge of recent trends in his subject.

2.2. Information and Library Network (INFLIBNET) Centre (http://www.inflibnet.ac.in): It is an Autonomous Inter-University Centre (IUC) of University Grants Commission involved in creating infrastructure for sharing of library and information resources and services among Academic and Research Institutions. INFLIBNET works collaboratively with Indian university libraries to shape the future of the academic libraries in the evolving information environment. Two important activities of it are creation of SOUL (Software for University Libraries) and UGCINFONET Digital Library Consortium. The electronic resources subscribed under the Consortium are available on subscription to the universities and other academic institutions. SOUL has been used in building up a great project IndCat. IndCat is the Online Union Catalogue of Indian Universities of books, theses and journals available in major university libraries in India. The union database contains bibliographic description, location and holdings information for books, journals and theses in all subject areas available in more than 112 university libraries across the country.

Database	*No. of Records*	*No of Universities*
Books	10697998	112
Theses	220206	238
Current Serials	22471	200
Serial Holdings	50164	89

The saddest thing is that despite this gigantic endeavor of INFLIBNET of unifying India in LIS terms (especially considering the vastness and multilingual plurality of our country), SOUL is still to be incorporated in the LIS syllabus of the Universities and yet to take top seat in the library function of many universities. Likewise much other library software- is it proprietary like LibSys, VTLS or open source and/or free like Koha are yet to be a part of the LIS curricula though questions regarding that software often form a crucial part of most job interviews.

2.3. Absence of an All-India Body: There are bodies like Indian Council of Agricultural Research, Indian Council of Medical Research, Council of Scientific and Industrial Research, Indian Council of Social Science Research, etc to supervise over different disciplines. Also there are Indian Administrative Service, Indian Statistical Service, Indian Forest Service, etc. to nurture the cadres of a particular genre. Sadly though, we are yet to get an Indian Library & Information Service for us. If constituted, it would surely help in transparency and better employability of potential LIS candidates. Furthermore, it would encourage in the smooth flow of quality professionals throughout India and would help all employers (and institutes) to find appropriate quality personnel to fill up their vacant positions.

3. LIS Education: The Problems

3.1. Medium of Instruction and Employability of LIS students: Perhaps as a legacy of almost 200 years of British colonial rule, higher education in India is still dependent mostly on English language. Our LIS is no exception especially in Masters and Research level though certificate, diploma and sometimes graduation (B LIS) is done through the local Indic language. Though now some LIS books are available in Indic languages, still LIS students with English language option gets wider coverage of quality LIS books written by LIS experts from India and abroad. There are other serious considerations associated with this choice of medium. Today's Indian LIS job world has become more sophisticated where communication skills matter much and it also helps the candidates to seek job anywhere in India and also abroad whereas students coming from rural India and/or from non-English-medium schooling background, fare not so well in the job market. Their options are confined to the sector speaking only the Indic language(s) they are comfortable with. Unfortunately, this aspect has so far been neglected by the curriculum development bodies. This language factor is perpetuating the gaps between the haves and have-nots in the field of LIS.

3.2. Problem of Nomenclature and Determination of Discipline: Traditionally prone towards Arts, and sometimes Social Science, LIS discipline is turning more and more towards Science stream with the inclusion of subjects like Information Technology, Communication Technology, Statistics and sometimes many mathematical formulations also. There are doubts and uncertainties about its exact position and status. Many universities have positioned it - along with other multidisciplinary subjects like Journalism and Education - under a separate faculty from ARTS, Science and Commerce. This obscurity sometimes prevents the entry of more brilliant students into the fold of LIS.

3.3. Asymmetrical Treatment of the Subject under Different Universities: There are so many discrepancies among different universities about treating the subject. Some universities requires 10+2+3 schooling before entering BLIS, some used to prefer till 1990s, a Masters (10+2+3+2) degree before entering the same course. Some requires Honours (i.e. Major) in the Bachelor's Degree level whereas others will do without. Some universities offer two years Masters Course (as is done for all other subjects in all the universities) but some LIS Masters course is of 1 year duration. Some universities have a quota for admitting Certificate Course holders while others have no such preference. All these ambiguities make it impossible for easy and uniform entry of quality intake. Some of the universities have only the traditional subjects (cataloguing, classification, library management, information sources, etc.) in BLIS whereas some has papers like Library Automation and Networking (theory and practice), Document Description (a new name for Cataloguing that reflects the changing nature of the subject) that truly reflect the effect of market demand. An important point to observe here is the young departments are more prone to take on the changes whereas the older ones are more hesitant towards radical transition. Whereas 'Information Sources, Services and Users' have been clubbed into one paper, many universities have separated them into different papers on 'User Study', etc.

3.4. Ill-equipped Infrastructural Facilities: By nature, LIS departments needs print materials, CDROM based materials, audio-video tapes and a very good departmental as well as central library to provide these in adequate amounts. They need practical classes in well-equipped lab with adequate nodes for every student with provision for digital learning through Internet and other Web based materials. Many of them still lack in good labs with adequate nodes, regular maintenance and up gradation and faculties knowledgeable and willing to provide hands-on. Sadly, LIS departments do not have Technical Assistants to help in lab set up. It's difficult even for well-meaning faculties to give their best, teacher-student ratio being a burden.

4. LIS Education-the Employability

4.1. Placement Opportunities for Passed out Students: Unlike other professional courses like Medical, Engineering, etc. LIS course providers rarely offer any placement opportunity. At the most, some advertisements for positions cut and pasted on a notice board are provided by some LIS departments. Some student-friendly faculties sometimes act as a liaison between a student and a job. Career Counseling and job placements are yet to be included within the periphery of LIS teaching obligations and/or curricula. One placement avenue frequently followed is to explore the connections made by the teachers of the concerned departments and another is the contacts of the well-placed alumnus. The later is more effectively followed when there are active alumni associations connected with the departments.

4.2. Industry-LIS Interface: Apprenticeship generally does not constitute a part of the curricula. This lacuna provides harmful in many ways:

1. Dearth of frequent Industry-LIS interaction leaves the LIS departments unaware of the requirements and happenings of the current job-market bosses.
2. The students lose the opportunity for knowing the cutting edge of the stocks-in-trade and thereby increasing their own employability.
3. The Departments lose the opportunity of revamping their curricula, teaching methods and orientation towards market demands.

4.3. Information Literacy as a part of LIS Curriculum in India: American Library Association (1989) has defined the concept of Information Literacy as a set of abilities requiring individuals to recognize when information is needed, have ability to locate, evaluate and use effectively the needed information. Even in India, information is growingly being acknowledged as a key component of an Information Society that is leading towards a knowledge-based society. In fact along with community centers, media and some others, libraries have the primeval role to play in the field of lifelong literacy. Karisiddappa & othersv (2004, IFLA) have discussed about the inclusion of Information Literacy in the LIS curricula. The paper on "Information Sources and Services" demands that students get to nurture their capabilities for preparing their individual/group search strategies and aided by the guidance of an innovative faculty and/or library professional create their own information-seeking acumen that helps them on all their future unique dealings with information. It will also to help them to educate and train the user community in optimum utilization of the information for development.

5. The Efforts towards Solving the Problems

5.1. Efforts of University Grants Commissionvi: Since its inception in 1956, the University Grants Commission has tried to overhauling the arena of LIS education vis-à-vis services. The first two committees (1959 and 1965) saw the eminent Indian LIS scholar S. R. Ranganathan as its mentor. Both Committees set as its purview infrastructure & service of LIS in Indian universities and colleges. After that almost 20 years passed away with thriving of LIS education against many odds as manifested in the studies held by Mangla and Singh and collocated by Sarkhelvii (Sarkhel, 2006)

- Unplanned proliferations of library schools
- Lots of variations in syllabi and no norms or standards are maintained in regard to course contents
- Lack of consensus regarding duration of the LIS courses at various levels
- Student-teacher ratio
- Lack of uniformity in
  - Selection criteria for admission
  - Intake
  - Class periods
  - Teaching methodology
  - Distribution of marks
  - Methods of evaluation and
  - Research programmes
- Inadequate infrastructure in respect of
  - Space
  - Faculty members

  - Information Technology Laboratory
  - Library and
  - Teaching aids
- Inadequate training facilities to update the professional competence of in-service teachers
- Existing UGC refresher courses failed to provide needed expertise and skills to meet the growing complexities of information environment
- Lack of internal quality assurance and accreditation mechanism.

5.2. Curriculum Development Committee and its model curriculum for LIS (UGC Model Curriculum: Library & Information Science 2001)viii: To allay these malfunctioning, to instill quality considerations and to impart 'Unity in diversity' among the deviant syllabuses adopted by LIS Departments in different parts of the country, University Grants Commission after a considerable gap of about 18 years formed and declared the report of the Kaula Committee on Curriculum Development in Library and Information Science in 1993. It was seen from practice that there are problems of exactly adopting any one stipulated curricula by a LIS department is going against the specific demands and uniqueness of a LIS Department. So, to provide a flexible framework as well as to satisfy the need of a standardized curriculum- the concept of 'model curriculum' came into being in 2001 in the report of the Karisiddappa Committee on Curriculum Development in Library and Information Science. It stated the learning objectives of each module, the syllabi is divided into distinct units, the whole thing revolves around a balance of theory and practice (60:40 ratio) LIS Curriculum is generally changed by every Indian university once in every few years to accommodate the new ideas generated in the field. This also helps in purging the redundant ideas and imbibing the new ideals.

5.3. Quality Control Mechanisms: University Grants Commission is the statutory body that looks over the funds and functions of the Indian universities. It has set up The National Assessment and Accreditation Council (NAAC) for evaluative assessment of the courses and curricula as offered by the Indian universities on the basis of a set of criteria on a regular interval on Institutional & Departmental performance. Different grades are offered as a result that signifies the concerned LIS Department's degree of conformity with the Model Curriculum. But so far no LIS Department has been reported so far (Sarkhel, 2006).

6. International Scenario

6.1. Effort of IFLA: IFLA through its 'IFLA Education and Training

Section' and 'IFLA Division Education and Research' is working hard towards removal of obstacles and facilitating access in LIS education in the world through the induction of international collaboration in the field of education and research. In this context, we must consider Tammaro'six words regarding how the LIS people should be trained in the Web 2.0 Environment and also how important the equivalency of LIs degree conferred by universities of the different countries in the world. Prof. Aira Lepik has also dealt with a section of international Collaboration in IFLA Norway conference in the paper 'The Nordic-Baltic cooperation in doctoral education: the case of NORSLIS'x.

6.2. The Bologna Processxi, xii, xiii and Related Efforts in India: The Bologna process aims at creating a European educational space characterized by transparency and promoting mobility of academic staff and students, as well as professionals within the LIS Sector in order to promote employability and facilitate integration. It aims the academic cooperation in European LIS education as evidenced in the cooperative efforts like facilitating exchange of staff and students among members, developing cooperation on research projects, encouraging support from stronger to weaker members, and also encouraging mutual recognition of curricula or parts thereof. Some experimental models have been derived -examples are the cooperation between Tallinn University in Estonia and University of Parma in Italy and another is a Scottish University and University of Parma in Italy.

Indian efforts towards academic cooperation with other countries in LIS field are also found. We cite an example here: Kolkata International Book Fair (held in end January every year) is an important activity in the Indian calendar. This year's theme country was Scotland. Through the collaborative efforts of British Council Library Kolkata, LIS-professional association IASLIC, Calcutta University, Calcutta University Department of Library & Information Science Students Association (CUDELSAA), etc.; a series of lectures were arranged by eminent Scottish LIS professionals in different universities and associations. Likewise evidence of academic cooperation may be found in India in:

- Fulbright scholar programmes in LIS that work between USA and India,
- Commonwealth Fellow programmes that work between UK and India,
- arranging special lectures by eminent professors of other universities,
- arranging special lectures by eminent scholars & practicing

librarians- those who are not in the teaching positions, thereby increasing university-(LIS) Industry Liaison,

- inviting eminent LIS professors/scholars as resource persons to conduct classes in Refresher Courses,
- inviting eminent non-LIS professors/scholars as resource persons to conduct classes in Orientation Courses, thereby opening platform for interdisciplinary interaction,
- Frequent interaction is happening between Indian LIS Professionals with Malaysia, Singapore, etc.

7. LIS Education- Areas for Consideration

7.1. Skills Required of LIS professionals in the Indian Employment Market: Along with the professional degree (Bachelor's/Master's, etc.), today's market scenario necessitates acquiring a whole range of skills by the potential employee (Kwartaxiv, 2006)

- Library related activities - Network Administration/Coordination
- Information services and supports - Network service
- Information brokerage - Office automation
- Information systems services - Telecommunication
- End-user training - Information system design
- Information product evaluation - Information Technology planning
- Usability analysis - Data security
- Information Analysis and - Internet Resources
- Consolidation - Internet site architecture
- Online searching

7.2. Recommendations for Consideration in LIS Curriculaxv: The following concepts/services may be considered as to be part of the practical classes/apprenticeship programmes:

1. Proper propagation of educational programmes offered by IGNOU through Panchayeti Raj systems to remote villagers
2. Using the CLICs (Community Kiosks) effectively
3. Children's Library
4. Subject Librarianship
5. Information Commons
6. Outreach Services
7. Technical Writing Classes/Workshops
8. Evidence-based librarianship

9. Case Studies
10. Documenting Heuristic Knowledge
11. Appropriate apprenticeship programmes are also to be arranged so as to develop leadership qualities (Mahapatra, 2006)xvi through exploring 'information handling; communication, crisis management, team building and decision making'.

8. LIS Education, Marketability and Positive Players

8.1. Positive Role Played by the Discussion Forums: Discussion Forums like LIS Forum (by NCSI, Bangalore) is frequented by many professionals and provide a valuable platform for interaction on many relevant issues including LIS education. IATLIS forum also offers teaching-related information. Digital Library Research Group (DLRG) run by Prof. ARD Prasad and others at Documentation Research Training Centre, Bangalore is a valuable source from IT and Digital Library related issues that concern the teaching of LIS. Except these major three, there are some other specialized groups that cater to the need of the LIS education related information.

8.2. The Crucial Role played by Indian Association of Teachers in Library & Information Science (IATLIS): Since 1990s, India is witnessing an economic as well as cultural awakening where she tries to envelop the world through its liberalization, globalization and market-centered progression. Despite debates among left and right wing political forces regarding pros and cons of these steps, many of these changes have made tremendous impact in our LIS employment market in the form of increased opportunities in India and abroad. To take significant part in this march towards the knowledge economy, LIS Departments should make a continual assessment of the market demands and periodic evaluation and modification of their curricula. National Library Associations may take an active role in this endeavor.

In fact, Indian Association of Teachers in Library & Information Science (IATLIS) is continually working towards this goal with the following programmes and more: Building Curriculum with a Difference: A Vision for LIS Education in the 21st Century: XXIII IATLIS National Conference, held at Department of Library and Information Science, *Punjabi University, Patiala from 23-25 November, 2006.Dharwad, IATLIS, 2006* (Chairmen: C R Karisiddappa and B D Kumbar). IATLIS organized National Workshop on LIS Teachers and the Digital Future during 17th to 19th January 2007 (Director: Dr. Harish Chandra). 46 participants from 17 states attended the programme. Changing Face of LIS Education: Learning Styles and Teaching Methodologies: XXV IATLIS National Conference, 2008, Organized by Department of Library & Information Science, Panjab

University, Chandigarh, November 27-29, 2008. There are some similar efforts in Asia where some Indian LIS experts took part: Asia-Pacific Conference on Library & Information Education & Practice, 2009: preparing Information Professionals for International Collaboration, 6-8th March 2009, at Tsukuba, Japan

8.3. National Knowledge Commission- the Ray of Hope for LIS Education and for Libraries: It is indeed a giant step forward integrating demand and supply of information- a boon to the masses. While inaugurating The National Knowledge Commission (NKC), Prime Minister of India Dr. Manmohan Singh told that the time has come to create a second wave of institution building, and of excellence in the fields of education, research and capacity building to make us better prepared for the 21st Century. National Knowledge Commission (NKC) under the chairmanship of Mr. Sam Pitroda envisaged Knowledge Society as the Goal for India. As NKC sees it- along with many other countries of the world India is to join in the march of Knowledge Society. Knowledge Society needs information professionals well equipped with the zeal of documenting, preserving, sharing, and in short, facilitating the use of information in whichever way possible for the growth and development of our country. Towards that end, LIS curricula must incorporate into it the concepts of ICT-D (Information & Communication Technology for Development), Web for Development, Information Literacy, etc. There should also be a tremendous thrust so as to preserve and disseminate the indigenous knowledge not only in the S & T sector but also in the field of literature, social science and also every little tit-bit that is important to portray our culture. The Terms of Reference of National Knowledge Commission Working Group on Libraries are:

1. To redefine the objectives of the country's Library and Information Services sector;
2. To identify constraints, problems and challenges relating to the sector;
3. To recommend changes and reforms to address the problems and challenges to ensure a holistic development of information services in all areas of national activity;
4. To take necessary steps to mobilize and upgrade the existing library and information systems and services, taking advantage of the latest advances in Information Communication Technology (ICT);
5. To explore possibilities for innovation and initiate new programme relevant to our national needs, especially to bridge the gap between the information rich and the information poor within society;

6. To suggest means of raising standards and promoting excellence in Library and Information Science education including re-orientation and training of working professionals;
7. To assist in setting up facilities to preserve and give access to indigenous knowledge and the nation's cultural heritage;
8. To set up adequate mechanisms to monitor activities for securing the benefits of acquisition and application of knowledge for the people of India;
9. To examine any other issues that may be relevant in this context.

The National Knowledge Commission (NKC) Working Group on Libraries gave ten recommendations for a journey towards Knowledge Society -

1. Set up a National Mission on Libraries
2. Prepare a National Census of all Libraries
3. Revamp Library and Information Science education, training and research facilities. The proposed Mission on Libraries must assess as soon as possible the manpower requirements of the country in the area of Library and Information Science management, and take necessary steps to meet the country's requirement through Library and Information Science education and training. To keep the sector abreast of latest developments, necessary encouragement should be given to research after evaluating the research status in this field. Establishing a well equipped institute (Indian Institute of Library and Information Science) for advanced training and research in library and information science and services would provide the necessary impetus to this task.
4. Re-assess staffing of libraries
5. Set up a Central Library Fund
6. Modernize library management
7. Encourage greater community participation in library management
8. Promote Information Communication Technology (ICT) applications in all libraries
9. Facilitate donation and maintenance of private collections
10. Encourage public - private partnerships in development of library and information services

Despite being a well-paid job in terms of remuneration, job-security, etc., LIS professionals still face an identity crisis due to perceived lack of glamour/sophistication attached with this profession. The effort is therefore for reaching the sublime height of a faculty position which somehow redeems its lack of glory covering it with an enviable and exalted status of being 'Teacher'. Once entered, a few seek the new pastures of higher learning & research, but mostly tend to gloat over their privy position and indulge in the laid-back attitudes of having reached the journey's end. The real fight is to convince them that the road just begins there. For it is up to them to imbibe a new generation of LIS scholars towards a path of learning where they can mingle the academic brilliance and professional intelligence into some visionary delight. NKC has raised a lot of hope in the heart of the LIS professionals that with the fervent activities of NKC under the dynamic leadership of Mr. Sam Pitroda, importance of libraries and LIS professionals are heavily underlined and re-defined once again. Along with the educators, we LIS professionals have been asked to facilitate this inclusive society where knowledge as power is accessible to all. The creation of the proposed Indian Institute of Library and Information Science by National Knowledge Commission is supposedly going to be the break through towards which every Indian library professional is looking forward.

LIBRARIES AND THE NATIONAL RESEARCH AND EDUCATION NETWORK

Libraries operate as part of the technological infrastructure that supports the National Research and Education Network (NREN), acting as an electronic safety net for the American public to guarantee basic access to electronic information. Public libraries are in particular capable to take on this role, as they already serve such a role in a print-based society. They not only provide electronic information and network connectivity but also provide training and education to the public on how to access and use network information. One of the most profound consequences of the NREN for librarians, library users, and the general education and research community is the "virtual library". Consortia of public libraries use the NREN to connect their online catalogues. This cooperation enables the "universal borrowing card" subsequently allowing library users to move between public libraries as just one. Extensive lobbying by the American Library Association (ALA) helped to add language referring to libraries to the NREN bill.

History of NREN

The National Research and Education Programme often referred to by the terms "National Information Highway", "National Information Infrastructure", Information Superhighway", "High-Performance and high-speed network", and "Gigabit test bed", is a programme to support improvements and enhancements to the existing Internet. The National Research and Education Network have been under discussion since 1987 and was proposed in 1969 as an experiment under the sponsorship of the United States Advance Research Projects Agency (ARPA), an agency of the Department of Defense. The NREN was officially established with the passage of the High Performance Computing Act signed into law by President Bush on December 9, 1991.

Purpose

The main purpose and fundamental emphasis is to maintain the United States leading place in high-performance or high-speed computing. The NREN is intended to be a gigabit network that is able to move one billion bits (binary digits) of data per second, or the equivalent of 30,000 pages of text. The intention was to connect a moderate number of diverse and geographically dispersed computers with the intention of acquiring experience in techniques for offering remote login access from one computer to another through a series of intermediate computers. The initial practical application, even though not originally planned, was the electronic mail.

Objectives

1. Establish a gigabit network for the research and education community and foster its use.
2. Develop advanced networking technologies and accelerate their development.
3. Stimulate the availability, at a reasonable cost, of the required services from the private sector.
4. Catalyze the rapid deployment of a high speed general purpose digital communications infrastructure for the nation.

Prototypes of the NREN

1. ARPANET

Founded in 1969 by the Defense Advanced Research Projects Agency (DARPA) of the Department of Defense.

2. MILNET

The military section of the ARPANET, turned into a separate network on 1983.

3. BITNET

An academic network founded in 1980.

4. NSFNET

The National Science Foundation Network, established in 1985, known as the domestic "spinal column" of the Internet and often called the "interim NREN".

ANNEX: SOME NOTABLE LIBRARIES OF THE WORLD

This is a list of notable libraries. It includes both notable public lending libraries and research libraries.

1. Advocates' Library, Edinburgh, Scotland
2. Ann Arbor District Library, Ann Arbor, Michigan
3. Archive for Research in Archetypal Symbolism
4. Astan Quds Razavi's Central Library, Mashhad, Iran
5. Baltimore County Public Library, Baltimore, Maryland
6. Bayerische Staatsbibliothek, Munich, Bavaria, Germany
7. Beinecke Rare Book and Manuscript Library, New Haven, Connecticut
8. Biblioteca Nacional de España, Madrid
9. Biblioteca Nacional de Portugal, Lisbon
10. Biblioteca Nazionale Centrale Firenze, Firenze
11. Biblioteca Nazionale Centrale Roma, Rome
12. Bibliotheca Alexandrina, Egypt
13. Bibliothèque nationale de France, Paris
14. Birmingham Central Library, England
15. Bizzell Memorial Library, University of Oklahoma, Norman, Oklahoma
16. Bodleian Library, Oxford
17. Boston Public Library, U.S.
18. Botanical Research Institute of Texas Library, Fort Worth, Texas
19. British Library, London
20. Brooklyn Public Library, U.S.
21. Burton Barr Central Library, Phoenix, Arizona
22. Cambridge University Library
23. Carolina Rediviva at Uppsala University

24. Catholic National Library, Farnborough, Hampshire
25. Center for Jewish History, Manhattan
26. Cerritos Millennium Library in Cerritos, California
27. Charles V. Park Library at Central Michigan University, Mount Pleasant, Michigan
28. Chekhov Library in Taganrog
29. Chetham's Library in Manchester
30. Chicago Public Library, Chicago, Illinois, U.S.
31. Cincinnati Public Library, Cincinnati, Ohio
32. City of Playford Library Service in Adelaide, Australia
33. CISTI, Ottawa
34. Clinton-Macomb Public Library, Clinton Township, Michigan
35. College of DuPage Library, Glen Ellyn, Illinois
36. Columbia Public Library, Columbia, Missouri
37. Columbus Metropolitan Library, Columbus, Ohio
38. Contra Costa County Library, Pleasant Hill, California
39. Cornish Studies Centre, Redruth, Cornwall, UK
40. Cuyahoga County Public Library, Cleveland, Ohio
41. Danish Royal Library in Copenhagen, Denmark
42. Deutsche Bücherei Leipzig, Leipzig
43. Dr Williams's Library, Bloomsbury, London
44. Duchess Anna Amalia Library, Weimar, Germany
45. Enoch Pratt Free Library, Baltimore, Maryland
46. Family History Library, Salt Lake City, Utah
47. Folger Shakespeare Library, Washington, DC
48. Francis Skaryna Belarusian Library and Museum, London, United Kingdom
49. Frank Melville Jr. Memorial Library, State University of New York at Stony Brook, Stony Brook, New York
50. Free Library of Philadelphia, Philadelphia
51. Glasgow University Library, Scotland
52. Grande Bibliothèque du Québec, Montreal
53. Haskell Free Library and Opera House
54. Hilandar Research Library, Ohio State University

55. Hong Kong Central Library, Causeway Bay, Hong Kong Island
56. Houston Public Library, Texas
57. Huntington Library, San Marino, California
58. Jenkins Law Library, Philadelphia
59. John Rylands Library
60. Kedermister Library
61. Kenton County Public Library, Kentucky
62. Koninklijke Bibliotheek, Netherlands
63. Leiden University Library, Leiden, Netherlands
64. Library of Alexandria, ancient Egypt
65. Library of Congress, Washington, D.C.
66. Library of Parliament, Ottawa
67. Library of Sir Thomas Browne
68. Library of the Russian Academy of Sciences
69. Lied Library, University of Nevada, Las Vegas
70. Lilly Library, Indiana University Bloomington, Indiana
71. London Library
72. Los Angeles Central Library
73. Louisville Free Public Library, Louisville, Kentucky
74. Louisville Public Library, Louisville, Ohio, USA
75. Luís Ángel Arango Library, Bogotá, Colombia
76. Malek National Library, Tehran, Iran
77. Malcolm A. Love Library (San Diego State University), San Diego, California
78. Marathon County Public Library (MCPL), Wausau, Wisconsin
79. Mário de Andrade Library in São Paulo
80. Marsh's Library in Dublin
81. Mark O. Hatfield Library, at Willamette University
82. Michigan State University Libraries
83. Milli Kütüphane (National Library of Turkey, Ankara)
84. Minneapolis Public Library, Minneapolis, Minnesota
85. Mitchell Library, Glasgow
86. Moorland-Spingarn Research Center
87. Morton Grove Public Library, Morton Grove, Illinois

88. Multnomah County Library, Multnomah County, Oregon
89. National Agricultural Library
90. National Diet Library, Tokyo and Kyoto, Japan
91. National Library of Australia, Canberra
92. National Library of Brazil, Rio de Janeiro
93. National Library of Canada
94. National Library of China
95. National Library of India, Kolkata
96. National Library of Iran, Tehran
97. National Library of Ireland, Dublin
98. National Library of New Zealand, Wellington
99. National Library of Medicine
100. National Library of Pakistan, Islamabad, Pakistan
101. National Library of Russia in St Petersburg
102. National Library of Scotland, Edinburgh
103. National Library of Serbia, Belgrade
104. National Library of Wales, Aberystwyth
105. National Library, Singapore
106. New Orleans Public Library
107. New York Public Library, New York, New York
108. Newberry Library, Chicago, Illinois
109. Openbare Bibliotheek Amsterdam, Netherlands
110. Oregon State Library, Salem, Oregon
111. Park Ridge Public Library, Park Ridge, Illinois
112. Peckham Library
113. Pepys Library, Magdalene College, Cambridge
114. Pikes Peak Library District,Colorado Springs, Colorado
115. Plainfield Public Library District, Plainfield, Illinois
116. Public Library of Charlotte and Mecklenburg County
117. Regenstein Library, University of Chicago, Chicago, Illinois
118. Robarts Library, University of Toronto, Canada
119. Royal Library of Sweden
120. Ruskin Library at Lancaster University, UK
121. Russian State Library in Moscow

122. Salt Lake City Public Library
123. San Antonio Public Library
124. Schlesinger Library
125. Seattle Central Library
126. South San Francisco Public Library
127. Southfield Public Library, Southfield, Michigan
128. SS. Cyril and Methodius National Library, Sofia, Bulgaria
129. State Library of New South Wales, Sydney
130. State Library of Victoria, Melbourne
131. Texas A&M University Libraries, College Station, Texas
132. Topeka & Shawnee County Public Library, Topeka, Kansas
133. Toronto Public Library, Toronto
134. Toronto Reference Library, Toronto
135. Twinsburg Public Library
136. U. Grant Miller Library, Washington & Jefferson College
137. UC Berkeley Library
138. UCLA Library
139. University of Sydney Library, Sydney
140. Valley Library, Oregon State University
141. Vancouver Public Library, Vancouver
142. Vatican Library in Vatican City
143. W.E.B. Du Bois Library, University of Massachusetts Amherst
144. Wellcome Library, London
145. Williams Research Center, New Orleans, Louisiana
146. University of Coimbra General Library, Coimbra, Portugal
147. Windhoek Public Library in Windhoek, Namibia
148. Winnipeg Public Library
149. Wren Library, Trinity College, Cambridge
150. Yale University Library, Yale University
151. Yiu Tung Public Library, Shau Kei Wan, Hong Kong Island, Hong Kong.

REFERENCES

Dainton, Fred (2001). *Doubts and Certainties.* Sheffield Academic Press.

Day, Alan Edwin (1998). *Inside the British Library*. Library Association Publishing (UK).

Dorrell, Ed. "Students 'inundate' LSE with complaints over Foster library". Architects Journal.

Kenny, Sir Anthony (1994). *The British Library and the St Pancras Building*. British Library.

McClure, Charles R. (June 1994). "Network literacy: A role for libraries?". *Information Technology & Libraries* 13 (2): 115–125.

Nichols, Thomas (1870). *A handy-book of the British Museum: for every-day readers*, Cassell, Petter, and Galpin, p. 396.

Reitz, Joan M. (2004). *Dictionary for Library and Information Science*, Libraries Unlimited, p. 103.

Richard J. Goodram (1990). *The Virtual Library: collections on demand* (Memex Research Institute White Paper #2). Chico: California State University, p. 1.

Robert C. Barrington Partridge (1938). "The history of the legal deposit of books throughout the British Empire", London: Library Association.

Saunders Watson, Michael (2008). *I am Given a Castle*. Quiller Press.

Smith, Dorothy (December 1992). "The NREN—The next library revolution?". *Alki* 8 (3): 5–8.

Walkowitz, Daniel J.; Knauer, Lisa Maya (2009). *Contested Histories in Public Space: Memory, Race, and Nation*, Duke University Press, p. 103.

5

Select Additional Factors in Library Organization and Use

> "A public library is the most enduring of memorials, the trustiest monument for the preservation of an event or a name or an affection; for it, and it only, is respected by wars and revolutions, and survives them"
>
> —*Mark Twain*

LIBRARY BILL OF RIGHTS

The Library Bill of Rights is the American Library Association's statement expressing the rights of library users to intellectual freedom and the expectations the association places on libraries to support those rights. The Association's Council has adopted a number of interpretations of the document applying it to various library policies.

The Library Bill of Rights

The Library Bill of Rights, as adopted by the American Library Association in 1939, revised in 1948, and amended in 1961, 1967, and 1980, reads:

"I. Books and other library resources should be provided for the interest, information, and enlightenment of all people of the community the library serves. Materials should not be excluded because of the origin, background, or views of those contributing to their creation.

II. Libraries should provide materials and information presenting all points of view on current and historical issues. Materials should not be proscribed or removed because of partisan or doctrinal disapproval.

III. Libraries should challenge censorship in the fulfillment of their responsibility to provide information and enlightenment.

IV. Libraries should cooperate with all persons and groups concerned with resisting abridgment of free expression and free access to ideas.

V. A person's right to use a library should not be denied or abridged because of origin, age, background, or views.

VI. Libraries which make exhibit spaces and meeting rooms available to the public they serve should make such facilities available on an equitable basis, regardless of the beliefs or affiliations of individuals or groups requesting their use."

History

Originally written by Forrest Spaulding, director of the Des Moines Public Library, in 1938, the Library Bill of Rights was adopted by the American Library Association in 1939, and has been revised several times since. Its original adoption was introduced with the statement, "Today indications in many parts of the world point to growing intolerance, suppression of free speech, and censorship affecting the rights of minorities and individuals," a reference to the emergence of totalitarian states during that time. During the Cold War period, the Library Bill of Rights supported opponents of censorship of materials interpreted as communist propaganda. In 1948, the association adopted a major revision of the document, which strengthened it significantly to address the new wave of censorship attempts that marked the beginning of the Second Red Scare, and was subsequently attacked in newspapers as "leftist," a "red front," and a "Communist organization."

A 1967 revision shortened the document and removed rhetorical flourishes, also removing the qualification "of sound factual authority," which it was felt could have been used to justify censorship; also, "age" (along with background, origin, and views) was added to the attributes that should not be a basis for denying access to information. The document was revised again in 1980. In 1996, the American Library Association reaffirmed the inclusion of age as an attribute that should not be the basis for denying access to information. This occurred after the American Library Trustee Association (ALTA) brought a request for this to the ALA Council.

Criticism

Shirley Wiegand, professor emeritus of law at Marquette University, asserts that the Library Bill of Rights uses rhetoric disconnected from the legal understanding of "rights", such as "Bills of Rights", and "rights" themselves, are legally enforceable and backed by well-developed arguments. The Library Bill of Rights has no such force or backing, because it is simply a statement of principles. Wiegand argues that the Library Bill of Rights (and the accompanying rhetoric) needs to be supplanted by a code well-grounded in the case law and language of the First Amendment and its accompanying legal principles. Something similar to the Library Bill of Rights could be retained as an accompanying "aspirational creed", such as a revised form of the ALA Code of Ethics, but it would need to provide more practical guidance.

David Woolwine of Hofstra University has criticized the philosophical underpinnings of the Library Bill of Rights, specifically objecting to the use of utilitarianism and "rights discourse" in defense of the principles. The "moral calculus" of the utilitarian argument that free access of information produces the greatest good for the greatest number can also be used to argue in support of restrictions for the purposes of safety and national security. Rights discourse relies on the assertion of rights with minimal referencing, while neglecting detailed argumentation. Woolwine asserts that utilitarianism and rights discourse need to be replaced by a synthesis of *modern* and *post-modern* philosophy to coherently and soundly justify the principles of the Library Bill of Rights.

MASTER OF LIBRARY AND INFORMATION SCIENCE

The Master of Library and Information Science (MLIS) is the master's degree that is required for most professional librarian positions in the United States and Canada. The MLIS is a relatively recent degree; an older and still common degree designation for librarians to acquire is the Master of Library Science (MLS), or Master of Science in Library Science (MSLS) degree. The MLIS and MLS degrees are widely considered to be equivalent. In some universities, these degrees are denoted as MLISc or MLSc, as in the case of M.S. for MSc. But in most commonwealth universities, both bachelor's programme and master's programme has been merged to provide MLIS/MLISc degree. Admission to MLIS programmes normally requires holding a bachelor's degree in any academic discipline, and library schools encourage applications from people with diverse academic backgrounds. In the United Kingdom it is more common for a vocational degree in library and information science to bear the standard designation M.A. or M.Sc.

Schools

The MLIS or MLS degree is usually acquired from an accredited library school. The American Library Association accredits programmes across the U.S. and Canada.

Curriculum

The MLIS/MLS curriculum can vary widely. Typically, both practical and theoretical components are included, often along with a practicum or internship. Course work may entail traditional library topics, such as reference work, Cataloguing, school libraries, or archiving. There may also be a focus on information science and computer science topics, such as database and website design, as well as information architecture (thus leading to the "I" in MLIS). Other skills taught may include management or pedagogy.

LIBRARY ATMOSPHERICS

Library atmospherics is a term used to describe particular aspects of library design. It refers to the micro-level design of library common areas to create a desired emotional effect in library visitors.

Purpose and Practice

The practice of library atmospherics is the manipulation of a library's physical environment to provoke particular emotional responses in library users, typically to improve the experience of the library environment in order to secure and promote increased patronage of the library. The study of library atmospherics is a particularly important development for library marketing, influencing how library users view library services, collections, buildings, systems, and the broader role of the library in society.

Atmospheric Variables in Library Design

Atmospheric variables include sight, sound, scent, and the general feel of both the exterior architecture and interior design of the library. Examples of these atmospheric variables within the library structure include colour schemes, acoustics, ventilation, lighting, electronic support, furniture, upholstery, and shelving fixtures. The exterior atmospherics of a library are just as important to the feel of entrance walkways, landscaping, and parking lots. The value of considering library atmospherics has been demonstrated by the ways in which design variables influence patrons' experience approaching, entering, within, and exiting, the library. Jeffrey Scherer has indicated that lighting schemes, for example, influence perception, mood and even the outward behavour of library patrons.

Library atmospherics require designers to take into consideration that the more varied the patron population, the more complex the atmospheric decisions that need to be made. Libraries that provide services to a varied target audience can utilise the study of library atmospherics as a successful marketing tool, by considering and incorporating different atmospheric designs to encourage certain groups of library users to particular parts of the physical library environment. This kind of target-area marketing requires close integration with stock selection and management.

Technological Atmospheric Variables

Some libraries offer public access to a range of electronic equipment, including public-access computers, fax machines, photocopiers, ATMs, and self-service checkout units. These technological variables create a need for varied environments within the library building in order to take account of different needs expressed by patrons - a silent-study area should not also house a group of photocopiers.

Noise Criteria

Noise criteria (NC) translates complex acoustical characteristic into a single quantitative value. NC level 35 is generally considered acceptable for most library functions, with NC level 40 acceptable in the busier areas (for comparison, NC 20-25 is considered acceptable for concert halls). NC values consider the background noise level traditionally heard from building systems including heating, air conditioning, ventilation, fan units and noise through windows. With increasing numbers of electrical equipment to be found in libraries, increasingly on unmediated public access, consideration of noise must be incorporated into the practice of library atmospherics.

Computers and Lighting

The presence of computers in libraries has greatly impacted lighting issues within library environments. As the library becomes more reliant on information existing primarily or solely in digital form, it is increasingly important to understand the role played in library atmospherics by considered uniformity in comfort levels and by efficiency in use of lighting levels.

Generally speaking, when people are working on computers their eyes move from the screen, to the background and to adjacent visual attractions. Each time the eye moves, it adjusts to the new lighting level. If the degree of adaptation between visual tasks is too great, eye strain, fatigue and stress result.

Similarly, a significant cause of eye strain for computer users is reflected light from poorly-placed light fixtures on glass screens. Glare and brightness ratios provide guidelines for lighting schemes within libraries to minimise eye strain.

Considering these ratios in balancing different light sources can be complicated considering a library's various uses, from computer-screen use and microfiche, to reading and browsing, but is important in creating a productive and safe library atmosphere for all patrons.

PUBLIC LIBRARY ADVOCACY

Public library advocacy is support given to a public library for its financial and philosophical goals or needs. Most often this takes the form of monetary or material donations or campaigning to the institutions which oversee the library. Originally, library advocacy was centered on the library itself, but current trends show libraries positioning themselves to demonstrate they provide "economic value to the community."

History

Letter-Writing Campaigns

Letter writing campaigns are chiefly intended to inform law makers, library officials, and citizens about the ramifications of decisions regarding public libraries and to promote library-related causes. Letter writing has been a valuable form of communication among public library advocates. A well-timed and hand-crafted email or strategically sent letter can be a potent mechanism used to sway the decisions of elected officials and the masses. Letters are practical because they can be distributed to many individuals and can serve as representation for public library advocates who cannot attend crucial meetings or rallies.

Programmes

Public libraries frequently use programming to increase awareness of the valuable services and resources that they offer to the community.

Some of these programmes offer information and educational resources for library advocates and librarians while others are directed towards increasing public knowledge of library services and resources.

- Library Card Sign-up Month is celebrated in September as a part of The Smartest Card campaign. During Library Card Sign-up Month, the library card is frequently promoted as the most important card that individuals can have in their wallets. Library Card Sign-Up Month is a popular programme across the United States. The ALA logo for the Smartest Card campaign is, "The Smartest Card. Get it. Use it. @ your library".
- "Turning the Page: Building Your Library Community" is an advocacy education and training programme funded by the Bill and Melinda Gates Foundation. Courses are available

both online and in person and are designed to give library advocates access to the training, skills, and resources to better advocate for their library's funding needs."

- Toolkits: Frontline Advocacy is an ALA toolkit that provides librarians and library workers with the advocacy tools and support they need to advocate for their own libraries and the profession. It is intended for public, school, academic, and special libraries. The Frontline Advocacy for Public Libraries Toolkit offers a variety of helpful resources including information about blogging, speech making, and data collecting. Advocating in a Tough Economy is a response to difficult economic situations when the library is simultaneously increasing patronage while losing tax based funding. Its toolkit contains, "resources and tools, including news clips, op-eds, and statistics to help library supporters make the case for libraries in tough economic times." The CLA also provides a Copyright Grassroots Advocacy Kit to address Bill C-32, An Act to amend the Copyright Act. The contents of this kit are "a list of 8 key messages, a sample form letter to your MP, a guide for holding an in-person meeting, and a link to find contact information for your MP. The kit also contains background information, including the latest CLA Position Statement "Protecting the Public Interest in the Digital World: the views of the Canadian Library Association/Association canadienne des bibliothèques on Bill C-32, An Act to amend the Copyright Act." The Australian Library and Information Association offers the Every Member An Advocate kit beginning in September 2010 to complement their Every Member An Advocate workshops, which offers advocacy tools and approaches in all sectors.
- Banned Books Week takes place every year during the last week of September and brings attention to the library's mission of supporting intellectual freedom and the importance of the First Amendment. "Observed since 1982, this annual ALA event reminds Americans not to take this precious democratic freedom for granted." Since 2006, the Canadian Library Association has surveyed library resources and policies challenges. In September 2010, libraries in the United Kingdom joined together to celebrate intellectual freedom by creating and publicizing Banned Books activities. Amnesty International, a human rights organization "directs attention to the plight of individuals who are persecuted because of the writings that they produce, circulate or read."
- El Día de los Niños is a celebration of children, families and

reading that is held on April 30. This celebration "emphasizes the importance of advocating literacy for children of all linguistic and cultural backgrounds."

- "Every Child Ready to Read @ Your Library" is a joint project of the Public Library Association and the Association for Library Service to Children Programmes, which helps provide parents with tools to help them in, "their critical role as their child's first teacher."
- Summer reading programmes meet in many public libraries to support education and literacy while children are on summer breaks from school. Benefits of a Summer Reading Programme include "encouragement that reading become[s] a lifelong habit", "[influencing] reluctant readers [to] be drawn in by the [library's] activities", "[helping] children keep their [academic] skills up [during the summer break]", and "[generating] interest in the library and books." Summer Reading Programmes generate important parent and child involvement with libraries and literacy.
- Canadian Library Month is sponsored by the Canadian Library Association/Association canadienne des bibliothèques.

Public Demonstrations

Most public demonstrations for libraries take one of three forms – rallies, protests, and read-ins.

Rallies

Rallies in support of public libraries are usually positive events designed to bring people together and raise awareness of issues facing public libraries. They are generally organized by professional library staff or by organizations like the American Library Association. Effective rallies are well-organized and paint a clear and compelling picture of the issues facing a library and specific actions to be taken to reach specific goals. Typical rally activities include musical performances and public speeches. Rally organizers will frequently distribute fliers containing brief statements of facts supporting the objective of the rally that are designed to be quickly digested by interested passers-by. Rally participants typically signify solidarity by wearing the same t-shirt or dressing in similar colors. Rally organizers will often have stickers, leaflets, or other promotional items to give to participants and passers-by to help publicize the issue at hand. On June 29, 2010 more than 1600 supporters showed up for the Library Advocacy Day Rally organized by the American Library Association. Speakers included authors, members of Congress, and the ALA Executive Director.

Public Protest

Whereas rallies are generally a positive event to achieve a goal, protests are usually held in reaction to a negative event, such as drastic changes in library services, staff lay-offs, or branch closings. They are often organized by Friends groups, community members, or library unions and are usually last-ditch efforts to stop a proposed action. Most public protests for libraries involve picketing the legislative body that made the final or proposed decisions, in hopes that a large public outcry will cause elected officials to reconsider. Others involve picketing outside a library branch or in a place with high traffic to draw the public's awareness to the issues at hand.

Read-Ins

A particular type of public demonstration almost exclusively used to support libraries, read-ins can take two different forms. The simplest one is when supporters of a library simply meet en masse and read their own books. Usually this type of read-in is held at or near the supported library or the targeted legislative body. Indianapolis library lovers organized a read-in during July 2010 to protest drastic budget cuts that would have closed 6 branches. The other type of read-in involves volunteers reading aloud for a specified amount of time, usually 24 hours. These are also often held near the targeted legislative body or the supported library. Volunteers usually read books of their choice for their allotted time span, and then are replaced by another volunteer reading a different book. New York activists held this type of read-in June 2010 as part of their "We Will Not Be Shushed" campaign to stave off proposed budget cuts.

Meetings with Elected Officials

Some advocates may decide to appeal to those in power to help with library issues and trends.

Locating Officials

If an advocacy group is searching for relevant officials to contact, the ALA has a listing.

Library Advocacy Day

The Library Advocacy Day is an annual spring event where library supporters flock to Washington D.C. to meet with congressional offices.

Types of Advocates

Grassroots Campaigns

Grassroots advocates participate in movements or campaigns to promote or support libraries that are frequently led by library staff or members of the local community. These groups are not necessarily part of an organization like Friends of Libraries and are often run independently. Activities can include: demonstrations; promotion through letter-writing, email, or word-of-mouth; fund-raising; and social networking. Various resources are available for those who want to lobby for support of their local library. Elsevier Training Desk provides a Lobbying Grassroots Checklist and the American Library Association offers help with framing a message to use when advocating for the library, among other resources. Another tool in grassroots advocacy is Save Libraries. "Save Libraries is a grassroots effort to compile information and advocacy resources for libraries that are facing devastating budget cuts" and offers resources, tools, and information regarding library advocacy.

> *"The need for public support of libraries never diminishes. In critical times, advocacy moves right to the top of the priority list of support activities. Having a solid advocacy programme is essential to any library."*

Friends of the Library

Friends of the Library are non-profit organizations whose members have banded together with the common goal of helping a specific library. They often volunteer their time or resources on behalf of that library. Friends groups are very diverse, including Friends of state libraries, individual libraries, library systems, teen Friends, and even Friends foundations. The first "Friends of the Library" group was founded in Paris in 1913 as a support group for the Bibliothèque Nationale. and was approved by the state in 1927. In October 1995, the name of the group was changed from la Société des Amis de la Bibliothèque Nationale (Friends Society of the National Library) to l'Association des Amis de la BnF (Association of Friends of the BnF). Friends of public libraries have traditionally raised money through book sales, bake sales, and similar fundraisers. Moneys raised from these efforts often go toward library programmes, supplies and collections. Friends can also be instrumental in lobbying politicians and informing the public about legislation that may be beneficial or detrimental to their library. In 1979, the Friends of Libraries U.S.A. (FOLUSA) was created to formalize the loose national network of Friends groups increasing their potential to promote libraries. FOLUSA joined with the American Library Trustee Association (ALTA) in 2008 to form a new American Library Association (ALA) division, the Association for Library Trustees, Advocates, Friends, and Foundations (ALTAFF). ALTAFF provides many resources for Friends groups seeking to advocate for their libraries in new ways.

Advocacy Organizations in the United States

American Library Association

The American Library Association (ALA) is one of the largest national associations which advocates for public libraries. ALA was founded in 1876 and since then has given libraries a more unified way to discuss, plan, and develop cooperative initiatives. "Advocacy for library support at local, state, and national levels throughout the twentieth century was orchestrated by the ALA and the National Commission on Libraries and Information Services, with countless hours contributed by members of associations" ALA has an Office for Library Advocacy that "supports the efforts of advocates seeking to improve libraries of all types by developing resources, a peer-to-peer advocacy network, and training for advocates at the local, state and national level".

In 2001, ALA started its public awareness campaign initiative called The Campaign for America's Libraries to further help promote the value of libraries and librarians. "Thousands of libraries of all types – across the country and around the globe - use the Campaign's @ your library brand. The Campaign is made possible in part by ALA's Library Champions".

The Public Library Association

In 1944, the Division of Public Libraries was formed within ALA and merged with the Library Extension Division in 1950 to become the Public Library Division. This division was reorganized and became the Public Library Association (PLA) in 1958. Today, it is the overarching association for most public librarians in the United States, and its main aim is to "strengthen public libraries and their contribution to the communities they serve".

The Institute of Museum and Library Services

The Institute of Museum and Library Services (IMLS) is one of the main sources of federal support for the United States' 123,000 libraries and 17,500 museums. According to the IMLS website, the Institute's mission is to "create strong libraries and museums that connect people to information and ideas. The Institute works at the national level and in coordination with state and local organizations to sustain heritage, culture, and knowledge; enhance learning and innovation; and support professional development". Through this agency, "libraries and museums have converged as cultural heritage institutions with a renewed commitment to collaborative engagement within local and world communities".

The Chief Officers of State Library Associations

The Chief Officers of State Library Associations (COSLA) is an independent organization (that engages in some forms of advocacy for public libraries) of the chief officers of state and territorial agencies and is "designated as the state library administrative agency and is responsible for statewide library development. Its purpose is to identify and address issues of common concern and national interest; to further state library agency relationships with federal government and national organizations; and to initiate cooperative action for the improvement of library services to the people of the United States".

State Associations

Each state has a state library agency which distributes federal library funds received from the IMLS. "There are fifty-seven state and regional library association chapters affiliated with the American Library Association, each including at least a committee or section that addresses public library issues. Generally these associations hold an annual conference, as well as ongoing workshops and programmes. The five largest chapters are: Texas, Ohio, New York, Illinois, and Indiana". State Library Associations "support the establishment of public libraries, and stand out as catalysts for a great deal of the motivation for public library cooperation". State library agencies began to be founded in the 1890s and have since worked to encourage public library development, and "have come to play an increasingly larger role in enhancing library cooperation, extension, and collaboration".

International Advocacy Organizations

The Canadian Library Association/Association canadienne des bibliothèques advocates to the federal government on the issues of public policy and funding, with particular interest for the areas of literacy, privacy, and access to information for print-disabled Canadians. In France, the Association of Friends of the BnF(l'Association des Amis de la BnF) is led by a Board of Directors who are elected by the General Assembly for renewable terms of three years. Although the International Federation of Library Associations and Institutions (IFLA) does not have a distinct advocacy group or committee within their organization, their Public Libraries Section is intended to provide "an active international forum for the development and promotion of public libraries which serve the whole community in the context of the information society and ensure free and equal access to information at the local level". The IFLA does, however, participate in the Campaign for the World's Libraries (@your Library), launched in 2001, with the American Library Association and libraries across the world "to showcase the unique and vital roles played by public, school, academic and special libraries worldwide".

The campaign aims "to raise awareness about the variety of programmes and services offered; to increase use of libraries at schools, at colleges and universities, in government, at work, and in daily community life; to increase funding for libraries; to involve librarians as stakeholders on public policy issues such as intellectual freedom, equity of access and the digital divide; to encourage librarianship as a profession". The Italian Library Association's work group on advocacy strives to build on the work done by the IFLA in Italian libraries in the areas of public relations, librarian professional development, and demonstration of the benefit of libraries to the cultural and educational aspects of society. The Library and Information Association of South Africa (LIASA) was founded in 1997 and is a"professional non-profit organization [sic], uniting and representing all institutions and people working in libraries and information services in South Africa. It strives to unite, develop and empower all people in the library and information field into an organization [sic] that provides dynamic leadership in transforming, developing and sustaining library and information services for all people in South Africa". A branch is located in each province of the country, and one of the interest groups is dedicated to public and community libraries and lists advocacy for libraries and librarians as two of its objectives in its constitution. Voices for the Library is a grass-roots initiative to promote Public Library Services in the United Kingdom.

Subjects of Advocacy

Local

Advocacy for public libraries at the local level has been demonstrated to be an effective partial defense against library cuts and closings. Local library governing bodies are at the mercy of state and local governments with regard to funding and thus are often required to make decisions based on factors other than what is best for the community where the library is located. As a result, advocacy at the local level often requires a three-pronged plan of attack requiring a lobbying effort at the state, local, and library governing body level. There are several ways individuals can act as advocates at the local level. These include:

- speaking to local groups about library needs and issues;
- talking to friends about the library, its role in the community, and its needs;
- writing letters to the editor of the local newspaper and to local and state representatives;
- speaking at local governmental and library board budget hearings; and
- contributing to a library publication and having the publication sent to local and state representatives.

There are many online resources for those interested in learning who their representatives at the local and state levels are. These include the

American Library Association Issues and Advocacy page as well as the Library of Congress Newspaper and Current Periodical Reading Room.

State

Public library advocacy may be a collective voice from public libraries and their supporters throughout an entire state and may be directed toward state government bodies or the state's general population. Allocation of taxpayer money to support vital community programmes, including public libraries, in the United States is the responsibility of state and local governments rather than the federal government; however, ever since the 1980s when the power to allocate tax dollars for such services was handed down to state and local governments, competition for tax dollars has become fierce and has caused budget problems in a number of states. With state budget issues and the fact that "statewide legislation cannot usually be passed through the efforts of one library alone," a public library will often work with library associations or with other libraries within the state to have its voice heard and gain financial and legislative support.

State library associations play a major role in advocating the importance of public libraries and the services they offer. Such associations in the United States are affiliated with the American Library Association (ALA) and are thus considered ALA chapters representing all libraries within their respective geographic coverage. State library associations facilitate connections between libraries and state government. Their websites provide contact information about and links to state legislators. Many of these websites also use Capwiz, an online advocacy tool that provides a means to learn about and communicate with elected officials as well as awareness of relevant issues in government and of relevant news in the media.

To ensure awareness of legislation that may affect libraries, a state library association may hire a lobbyist who will keep a close eye on legislation in the state capitol, influence legislators on behalf of libraries statewide, and keep the association updated on what is happening in state government. The lobbyist, however, cannot be solely responsible for the lobbying effort; thus, state library associations often organize legislative committees headed by librarians from different parts of each state. State library associations also work with state libraries, whose budgets directly affect local libraries, to maintain their awareness of important amendments and bills; this cooperation is especially essential in states where state libraries are prohibited from influencing legislation.

Statewide library events also serve to advocate public libraries. On February 11, 2004, Bookmobile Day was held in Frankfort, Kentucky, in which 70 bookmobiles arrived at the state capitol to celebrate 50 years of bookmobile and outreach services throughout the state and to reinforce the importance of public library services to all Kentuckians. A number of state library associations, including those in Missouri, California, Massachusetts, and the state of Washington, hold Library Legislative Day, an advocacy event inviting library supporters statewide to meet and speak with state legislators. On Library Snapshot Day, another advocacy event, "... libraries of all types across a state, region, system or community [show] what happens in a single day in their libraries. ... This initiative provides an easy means to collect statistics, photos and stories that [enable] library advocates to prove the value of their libraries to decision-makers and increase public awareness." As of October 2010, as many as 34 states have held a Library Snapshot Day in their libraries.

National

National advocates like the American Library Association advocate for library issues to the United States Congress. The American Library Association gets involved with the national debate to ensure that all people have access to the information and services they need. ALA has used librarians to testify before Congress about civil liberties and national security, and they also advocate federal legislation that preserves and promotes fundamental library values by lobbying Congress, partnering and working with others "inside the Beltway" and beyond, and engaging in grassroots advocacy on behalf of the public.

Legislation that ALA has advocated for the public:

- Children's Internet Protection Act (CIPA)
- Consumer Product Safety Improvement Act
- Education and Literacy Legislation
- Library Services and Technology Act (LSTA)
- The USA PATRIOT Act

The Library Business Association meets with elected officials to share with them some of the key issues of interest to the library business community, such as library funding legislation. The Public Library Association advocates for the public library and has a training programme called Turning the Page for national advocacy that has been funded by the Bill and Malinda Gates Foundation.

Successes

South Carolina Public Libraries

In June 2010, South Carolina library advocates and their allies got

Governor Mark Sanford's vetoes 31 and 92 of state aid to libraries overturned in less than one week. Governor Sanford's vetoed $4,653,933 in state aid to public libraries and $1,172,758 in stimulus funds to public libraries. "In his veto message, Sanford said he had decided 'that fully funding local libraries does not rise to the level of many of our other core services such as law enforcement and health care'. Sanford said that libraries are also supported by lottery funds, and suggested that counties raise other money for the libraries". Librarians and advocates got on the phone and the computer, contacting their legislators using the state's version of CapWiz. South Carolina State Library Director David Goble states that "in less than 2 hours of receiving news of the Governor's veto, public library leadership was taking action. In less than 24 hours, a significant and effective effort by public library directors, patrons, trustees, friends groups, citizens, etc. was well underway.

The issue was being discussed in the media (print and TV) within 5 days (including a weekend). The $5,826,691 will come and it will go. The spirit of collaboration and the sense of accomplishment are ours forever. The effectiveness of our efforts is clearly demonstrated in the numbers of votes received in support of overriding the vetoes". When the representatives got up to speak, the first words were, "the libraries are needed because people need their Internet connection in order to get back to work," Goble also reported.

"On June 16th, the South Carolina House of Representatives voted to override the Governor's veto 31 – State Aid to Public Libraries - 110 to 5, and veto 92 – ARRA Stimulus funds - 77 to 33. The next day, June 17th, the Senate followed suit and overrode veto 31, 41-3. Twelve days later the Senate overrode veto 92, 36-4." They voted to override both vetoes that would have cut South Carolina public library funding.

New York Public Library

In 2009, the New York Public Library faced city budget cuts of $37 million. The funding cuts would have meant the closure of numerous branch libraries, a reduction of library services hours, and staff layoffs. NYPL has successfully retained $23 million in subsidies and raised $144,000 through an advocacy campaign entitled "Don't Close the Book on Libraries." NYPL implemented a variety of advocacy efforts to fight the budget cuts. A key aspect of the campaign was a message that online users saw when entering the library's main Web site. The message read, "Keep your library open. We need your help! Record numbers of New Yorkers are relying on The New York Public Library in these difficult economic times." The library asked patrons to make a donation of $5 or more and protest the budget cuts by contacting the city representatives.

The library also utilized a variety of other online tools to support the campaign. NYPL asked celebrities to create a YouTube video that encouraged people to participate in advocating for the library. Some of the celebrities included Bette Midler, Amy Tan, Jeff Daniels, and Mike Nichols. Facebook, Twitter and other social networking sites were also used to inform people of the campaign and ask them to contribute in any way possible.

The most unique advocacy effort was a Ghostbusters skit performed in the library by Improv Everywhere, a group that "causes scenes of chaos and joy in public places." The performers created a video of the act which features a link to the NYPL's website. In addition to library users donating money and contacting local officials, the New York Public Library also received "spontaneous support" for their campaign. This unanticipated and unsolicited support included a NYC photographer who created art in support of NYPL, teenagers who created and distributed buttons for NYPL, and a patent attorney who started a Facebook group, "Save the NYPL" with 600 members, and a store featuring "Save the NYPL" t-shirts, the profits of which were donated to the library. Although the NYPL reduced its service hours to five days per week, all branches have been retained at this point. This success was realized through the advocay of "130,000 New Yorkers and others who wrote letters, donated more than $144,000 online, called elected officials, and raised their voices on the steps of City Hall" as well as "children who created artwork and the seniors who passed our flyers." An article by Tom Murphy states that, "The NYPL is a community service and it is right and just that the community can be involved in saving it."

Findlay-Hancock County Public Library

In the summer of 2009, the Findlay-Hancock County Public Library in Findlay, Ohio discovered that state legislators were planning to cut its funding by about $1.2 million over the next two years. Including the loss of funding due to the general economic downturn, Library Director Jeff Winkle expected the total decrease in funding to be around $725,000 per year. The Library Board reacted immediately to the expected budget cuts by reducing library hours, number of staff, staff benefits, and materials. In an attempt to recoup the lost funding, the Library Board decided to request the inclusion of a $500,000 levy on the next ballot, which would garner approximately $700,000 in added revenue per year and allow the library to reinstate the previous library hours and staffing levels. It was uncertain whether the levy – costing the owner of a $100,000 home about $16 per year - would be supported by the community. In April 2010, a month before the county was to vote on the levy, a plea for library support was printed in the local paper:

> "For the first time in its 120 years of serving the community, the Findlay-Hancock County Public Library needs our help…We urge voters to support the levy, which is needed to offset recent cuts in state funding… A library, like schools, safety forces, and the hospital, is one of the pillars of a community, and helps define who we are…The community has always supported the library with our business, now we need to support it by giving it a small, but needed, boost in funding. We all will benefit from the investment."

The Citizens for Findlay-Hancock County Public Library raised $8,575 in contributions from the Friends of the Library and local and non-local individuals to campaign for the levy. Campaign publicity included yard signs, banners, radio and newspaper ads, flyers, postcards, bookmarks, and door hangers advocating that locals vote yes on the levy. A website was created to provide information about the levy and allow supporters to download a "Vote YES For Our Library" graphic. On May 4, 2010, the final verdict on the levy was a firm yes by 64% of voters. ""I'm just so grateful to everyone who supported this levy," library Director Jeff Winkle said after the election results came in. "We're looking forward to getting back to full services.""

El Paso County Library

When El Paso County, Texas faced a $20 million shortfall in 2004, the manager of the county library in the small town of Fabens reduced her budget by 31%. Members of the Commissioners' Court saw this decrease as insufficient, voting to close the library in August 2004. Upon hearing the news, the local library collective, EPAL (El Paso Area Libraries) met to organize a library support rally. They used the ALA (American Library Association) "Save America's Libraries" toolkit and followed the model rally agenda to plan the event. The rally was held in the Fabens Middle School cafeteria. Over 500 people, representing all ages and backgrounds, attended including the three county commissioners. The rally was covered by nearly all El Paso area media outlets. Citizens spoke out about their support for their library including 15-year old Karina Cacho: "We wouldn't have anywhere to go to do homework or use the Internet" if the library closed.

At the public hearing two weeks later, the commissioners voted to fund the salaries of the staff for one year, with the condition that the library transition into an existing organization and/or create a joint-use model to ensure the maintenance of future library services. EPAL provided $21,000 for materials & supplies for the year and facilitated the change to a new location. The crowd of over 400 people who attended the commissioners meeting, some with homemade signs urging long-term library funding, were boisterous and passionate about the library programmes they supported. EPAL then actively researched many options by holding a community meeting with representatives from the County Commissioners, school district heads, and other major contributors in the community. This meeting garnered much support for the library and helped in finding the new home for the library within the Fabens Independent School District. As of October 2005, the library has a new home at one of the schools in the Fabens Independent School District. The county agreed to provide transition funds for the move. Fabens ISD funds the salary for the librarian. EPAL agreed to help, along with other fundraisers, to provide funds for materials, supplies, and other needs. The new Fabens ISD Community Library opened during National Library Week 2006 (first Monday in April).

Phoenix Public Library

At the beginning of 2010, the Phoenix Public Libraries were faced with a difficult situation. The city council began proposing budget cuts for public safety organizations, including the Phoenix Fire Department and the Phoenix Police Department. This was the first time the city proposed cuts to these vital organizations. In an attempt to retain the jobs held at the police and fire departments, police union representative, Mark Spencer, suggested in an interview to create more cuts to the libraries stating that police officers should not lose their jobs until every librarian position has been cut. The community wrote in to *The Arizona Republic* arguing that libraries are in part responsible for creating safer and friendlier communities. The proposed cuts would ultimately close six of the 15 branches within the city and cut 73.5 positions. In addition, all branches would be closed on Fridays. The overall library budget would be cut 21.4%.

This is including the 2.4% that would be considered efficiency savings. The closing of this many branches for a city the size of Phoenix, AZ could severely hurt the quality of services provided. For a population of 1.5 million, the 15 branches were already overcrowded. According to the Phoenix Public Library website, between July 1, 2009 and June 30, 2010 more than 4.7 million people used the library facilities, 14.4 million materials were checked out, and more than 29 million visits were made to the library's website. As of February 4, 2010, the city council enacted a 2% food tax that would create an additional $50 million in revenue.

One month later, the food tax was passed, and the branches were kept from closing. This is not an entirely happy ending, however, as the library system still faced budget cuts. As an answer to closing entire branches, 27.8 positions would be cut throughout the remainder of the fiscal year as well as concessions in employee benefits and pay. In addition, each branch would cut one day of operation a week. The efforts of the community to save the library cannot be ignored. Many wrote to newspapers like the one mentioned above. There was also much support for and participation in organizations such as Friends of the Phoenix Public Library, who raised awareness of the budget cuts and the effects they would have on the community. All of these efforts forced the city council to reevaluate the planned budget cuts.

San Francisco Public Library

In November 2007, the Friends of the San Francisco Library were successful in getting voters to pass Proposition D. The passing of Prop D renewed the Library Preservation Fund that "enabled the library to increase operating hours by 53% and expanded the budget for books and materials by almost 400%. In addition, Prop D grants the City the authority to issue revenue bonds and to ensure that the Branch Library Improvement Programme can continue to renovate San Francisco's neighborhood libraries." In 1988, the advocates "realized their long time goal of a new Main Library by championing Proposition A, a bond issue that would fund $109.5 million to build a new Main Library, which opened its doors on April 18, 1996." In 2000, Friends advocates also "led a $106 million bond measure to build and refurbish 24 neighborhood branch libraries city-wide. As with the Main, public bonds will not pay for equipment or furnishings inside the branches. To meet this need, Friends is charged with raising $16 million through the Neighborhood Library Campaign."

Bridgeport Public Library

When the city of Bridgeport, Connecticut looked for ways to address its $10 million budget deficit in 2008, Mayor Bill Finch suggested cutting the Bridgeport Public Library budget by $1.1 million, arguing that "[l]ibraries are not essential services." It was not the first time the BPL budget had come under fire. The library was already suffering the effects of a budget eroded throughout the 1990s, with buildings badly in need of repair and dispirited workers shifted from location to location as a stopgap for severe staffing shortages. "The Connecticut Post" reported in 2009 that the library had seen its budget reduced by 16 percent over the past two years. It was Finch's drastic proposal that ultimately spurred Scott Hughes, the library director, to action. Hughes fought to take the matter of library funding directly to the public. Citing a long-obscure tax law, he sued the city to allow a library-budget referendum be put directly to voters on the next ballot. In August, 2009, Superior Court Judge David Tobin sided with Hughes, and the referendum was set to go forward the following November. Prior to the election, Hughes enlisted more than

100 volunteers to rally support for the referendum through phone calls and neighbor education. On November 3, 2009, the referendum - which guaranteed the equivalent of $1 million every year to the library - passed 2683 votes to 1455. It amounted to roughly 44 percent more than the budget in place and brought per capita support from $35 to $50. As a long term effect, the library system now has a reliable source of income that cannot be changed by City Council vote.

Western Australia Public Libraries

In 2008–2009, the Western Australia State Government provided additional funding to public libraries but then decreased that amount in 2009–2010 by 40%. Steps were made for the Local Government Association to represent the libraries to the State Government, but this was insufficient. Instead, a grassroots campaign was started; it was supported by the Australian Library and Information Association but led by Public Libraries Western Australia and Western Australian librarians. Postcards and a letter template to send to politicians and bumper stickers were created and shared with the public. The media picked up the story in both print and radio. Although Culture Minister John Day did not approve the full amount that was asked for, the budget that was approved represented a significant increase that could sustain the Western Australian Public Libraries.

Failures

While many libraries benefit from advocacy many more suffer from a lack of advocacy or insufficient support.

Lincoln Library

In June 2009, faced with a large deficit to the city budget, Mayor Tim Davlin of Springfield, Illinois began proposing service cuts to the library, police, and firefighters. At this time, the possibility of closing branches or the whole library system was discussed to help make up for a $7 to $ 9 million deficit. Library patrons quoted in a news article from *The State Journal-Register* found the idea of closing the library “pretty awful” and “unthinkable”. In this same article Bob Doyle, executive director of The Illinois Library Association, stated that library use across the nation had increased by 20 to 30 percent due to the recession, indicating the increased need for library services. The Lincoln Public Library system consisted of a main library and two branches, the Southeast and the West branches. Between fiscal year 2008 and 2009, the library had seen an increase in all aspects of library services including a 13% increase in the number of programmes offered and an 18% increase in programme attendance. Mayor Davlin even described the loss of services as a blow to “literacy and a societal goal of providing educational access to our citizens." But the shortfall was too great and some form of cuts seemed imminent.

In January 2010, Mayor Davlin announced his new budget for fiscal year 2011, which began March 2010, with many cost saving measures. This included the closure of the Lincoln Libraries branches. Within several weeks of the budget announcement the branches were closed with little resistance from the public or politicians. Because the city leased the building where the Southeast branch was located all books and materials had to be removed by March 1, 2010. In a February 11 press release, the city announced the closing of the branches and the sale of much of the Southeast branch's collection. While some of the collection was transferred to the main branch much of the collection was put on sale for the public or other organizations. During these closures, several alderman expressed their sadness at losing library services but maintained hope that these closures would be temporary.

In the Lincoln Library Bulletin newsletter for March/April 2010 library director Nancy Huntley recapped the recent library cuts. She stated that the materials from the Southeast branch were sold at a Friends book sale or given to local schools. These materials were able to benefit the community, but dispersing the library collection makes the cuts seem more permanent. Perhaps summing up the situation best she wrote, "It takes a long time to build a library and a very short time to dismantle it; one is done with hope and promise, the other with sadness and regret."

Indianapolis-Marion County Public Library

In 2009, the Indianapolis-Marion County Public Library spent $46 million on operations, but the 2011 budget was reduced by approximately $2.5 million. Tom Shevlot, President of the library board, said that this would only be a temporary fix, and the library will have to establish a long-term plan to keep costs down. A few of the cuts include:

- A 20% cut ($1 million) in the acquisitions budget
- Elimination of more than twenty staff members
- No longer sending out notices to patrons
- Closing branches during the summer
- Fees for borrowing DVDs
- Fees for the replacement of lost library cards

"A little more than 80 percent of library revenue comes from property taxes, which were recently capped by Indiana law." In April 2010, the library board proposed to close six of the twenty-two branches in order to meet the projected deficit. After an out-pouring of public support, city officials commissioned the High Performance Government Team to come up with alternatives to closing branches. This team suggested cutting hours in lieu of closing branches. In August 2010, the IMCPL board voted to cut the 26 percent of the system's hours from 1,324 to 980 at Central Library and the 22 branches. The Central Library is now closed every Thursday with hours reduced on other days throughout the week, beginning October 3, 2010. Branches will be closed either Fridays or Saturdays. Fewer than half of the library branches will have Sunday hours. While the library has seen its support grow during 2010, it still needs more assistance from the community or branches may be closed in the future.

Siskiyou County Library

Siskiyou County, California administrator Brian McDermott announced in May 2010 that due to a $3.7 million deficit the entire library would be closed down forever by June 30. By closing the main library and its 10 branches, the county would save $716,000. This northern California county with 46,000 residents is roughly the size of Connecticut and is very rural, and though it once boomed thanks to gold and lumber, it now suffers from 17% unemployment. Siskiyou libraries are not unfamiliar with budget cuts; in 2000, there were 20 staff members covering 11 buildings, and by 2010 there were only 12 employees. Lisa Musgrove, the library director, proposed a plan that would allow for at least four of the libraries to remain open and bring staff counts down to six with a handful of volunteers. This proposal was rejected by the county supervisors but gave Musgrove 6 months to find alternative funding for the library.

In the meantime, the library was given $140,000 from emergency funds to keep four branches open with a skeleton crew through December 2010. Volunteers stepped in to keep all of the branches open, although hours were significantly cut short at all locations.

Consultants proposed a new library system that involved 2 to 4 branch locations, a centralized warehouse, book dispensing kiosks, book "drop points," and a reading room. This would cut the library budget to $165,000 per year. The decision for the proposal will not be made until the November 2010 election. However, even if the plan is approved, the county supervisors foresee even more choppy waters for the following year's budget.

New Jersey Knowledge Initiative

The New Jersey Knowledge Initiative was a statewide library business and technology programme which provided entrepreneurs, small business owners and students access to top science and technology journals and key business information which endured a drastic reduction in funding in

2008 under Governor Corzine. This forced cancellation of contracts with medical and scientific databases. Governor Chris Christie's FY 2011 budget proposal slashed statewide library funding by 74%, including the entire appropriation for NJKI databases. The New Jersey State Library has campaigned tirelessly for a restoration of funding, pointing out that the benefits to small businesses, universities and students represent a 13 to 1 return on the dollars invested, and that many beneficiaries cannot afford direct access to these databases at their own expense. Small businesses, among the greatest beneficiaries of the programme, have not advocated for restoration of the funding, opting instead to support Governor Christie's call for reduced government spending and lower taxes. Had small businesses joined the state library, local public libraries, academic libraries and universities in advocating for restoration of the NJKI, the outcome might have been different.

Montgomery County Public Libraries

From 2008 to 2010, the Maryland Montgomery County Public Libraries' budget was cut by 30%, from $40 million to $28 million. This has led to cuts in hours, staffing, materials, and services. In July 2010, MCPL implemented new hours at all locations. Though the changes represented an overall cut in hours, they also served to make hours consistent between branches. The budget for library materials also suffered, being reduced by 45%. This translated to some electronic resources being dropped, fewer new reference materials, fewer magazine subscriptions, and reduction in the availability of popular titles. The library lost 60 staff positions during FY 2010 and expects to lose another 80 in FY 2011. In part because of the reduced staffing, many services are also being reduced or eliminated. MCPL was unable to participate in a statewide summer reading programme this year. The cost of the programme is usually covered by Friends of the Library Montgomery County, but with reduced staff the library was unable to run the state programme. MCPL has also suspended bookmobile service for at least two years, possibly longer depending on what sort of service they decide to implement once the funding is in place. Despite these setbacks, MCPL soldiers on. Several renovation/construction projects are underway, and over 900 people participated in an online programme survey in June. The library communicates with its users in a variety of media, including blogs and topical RSS feeds, monthly director's reports, Twitter, and Facebook.

Hood River County Libraries

Residents of Hood River County, Oregon lost local access to a public library in July 2010 when their three libraries closed for lack of funding. Located about 60 miles east of Portland, the library system had been in continuous operation for nearly 100 years. The closure resulted from the failure of Measure 14-37 in the May 2010 election, which would have created a new library tax district. Voters defeated the measure by 54 percent to 46 percent. An editorial in *The Oregonian* explained the outcome this way: "... like many other counties, Hood River County is in serious financial trouble. And the library is one place it can cut." Ironically, the closures came just seven years after voters approved a bond measure to expand the system's flagship library. Taxpayers will continue to repay that debt until it retires in 2015. The libraries may not be closed for good. Measure 14-39 in the November 2010 election will provide voters another chance to create a library tax district. If the measure passes, a newly elected library board will decide how and when to reopen the libraries. That could be as late as early 2012.

REFERENCES

Banned Books Week (2010). Celebrating the Freedom to Read. Retrieved October 5, 2010, from American Library Association: http://www.ala.org/ala/issuesadvocacy/banned/bannedbooksweek/index.cfm

CLA Copyright Grassroots Advocacy Kit. (2010). Canadian Library Association. Retrieved November 3, 2010.

CLA IFC. (2010). Challenges to Canadian Library Resources and Policies in 2009: Report of the Annual Survey of the Advisory Committee on Intellectual Freedom. Retrieved November 1, 2010, from Canadian Library Association: http://www.cla.ca/Content/NavigationMenu/CLAatWork/Committees/Challenges_to_Canadi.htm Canadian Library Association

Miller, Ellen G. (2009). "Hard Times = A New Brand of Advocacy." Georgia Library Quarterly. 46:1.

Sannwald, William (1998). "Espresso and Ambiance: What Public Libraries Can Learn from Bookstores." *Library Administration & Management* 12:4: 200-11.

Scherer, Jeffrey (2005). "Lights and Libraries." *Library Hi Tech* 17:4: 358-371.

Thomison, Dennis (1978). *A History of the American Library Association: 1876-1972*. Chicago: American Library Association.

Wiegand, S.A. (1996). "Reality Bites: The Collision of Rhetoric, Rights, and Reality in the Library Bill of Rights." *Library Trends 45, (1)*, 76-86.

Woolwine, David E. (2007). "Libraries and the Balance of Liberty and Security." *Library Philosophy and Practice (E-Journal)*, Libraries at University of Nebraska-Lincoln.

Wrightson, Denelle and John M. Wrightson (2005). "Acoustical Considerations in Planning and Design of Library Facilities." *Library Hi Tech* 17:4: 358-371.

6

Role of Data and Data Retrieval

The signals retrieved are data in one form or another. The distinction is sometimes made between data retrieval and document retrieval. A "data retrieval system" is one in which specific data are retrieved-the specific information requested in the inquiry. In fact, the term "document retrieval" is ambiguous. It can refer simply to systems in which a document is retrieved. Ordinarily, however, it is used to refer to a retrieval system in which the data retrieved are the description and address of one or more documents; and it is these documents that will contain the data desired. For example, suppose one wanted a list of strong and irregular German verbs. A data retrieval system that enabled one to retrieve such a list directly would have to permit one to use a search command such that the list of strong and irregular verbs would appear.

in a document retrieval system this would not happen. Instead, one would specify the need for a book on German grammar, specifying either a particular known work or any German grammar. This response does not, in itself, inform us about strong and irregular verbs. However, it is a reasonable assumption that, if we were to examine the book, it would contain a list of strong and irregular German verbs and their principal parts. In finding them, however, we may well use another information retrieval system, the index. Looking in the index under either "irregular" or "strong" indicates that, in this case, a list can be found starting on page 274.

There is, it would seem, a basic distinction between a data retrieval system designed to provide *directly* what one thinks one wants and a document retrieval—or, better, a "reference retrieval"—system that merely points one toward the desired data in one or more steps. However, difficulties arise. Suppose, for example, instead of wanting a list of strong and irregular German verbs, we had wanted to know the title of a

German grammar by Luscher and Schapers— or, indeed, of any German grammar. The inquiry could have been formulated in the same way and posed to the same bibliographic retrieval system in the same way. The exact same response might well have been received as that given above. The difference is that the desired datum has been retrieved, without further searching being needed. In this example, the exact same system used in the same manner constitutes both a data retrieval system and a reference retrieval system. The only difference is in the intention of the user. This being so, we need to reexamine the distinction more closely. If it is not to be abandoned, then the following options remain:

(a) We can classify such a retrieval system as being a data retrieval system or a document retrieval system on the basis of the intention of the person using it; or

(b) We can define retrieval systems according to whether they are capable of functioning as a reference retrieval *as well as* a data retrieval system. This capability would appear to extend to any system in which the data stored are capable implicitly or explicitly of indicating further sources of data. From this perspective, we can consider data retrieval systems as a limited, primitive category within the larger class of retrieval systems.

Although the example used was bibliographical, other sorts are possible. The example, in museum documentation, the reference is likely to be to an actual artifact rather than to a book. More generally in data retrieval systems, the inclusion of some kind of reference to further documentation is likely to be provided whether explicitly or implicitly, even if only to indicate the source, authority, or definition of the data retrieved.

Retrieval Languages I: Notation

Describing things is a linguistic problem. Even concepts in formal logic have to be defined linguistically at some stage. One readily recognised distinction in descriptive labels is between "natural" language and "artificial" languages. For example, in a bookshop texts on economics are likely to be shelved by a sign bearing the label "ECONOMICS." The very same books in a public library might bear the sign "330," the symbol denoting Economics in the artificial notation of the Dewey Decimal Classification.

From the point of view of achieving an acceptable *address,* the labeling doesn't matter very much so long as it is intelligible and accurate. Also, from the point of view of achieving acceptable *definition,* the choice of notation, language, or meta-language doesn't matter very much as long as the description is sufficiently precise and intelligible for the purposes intended. It is common for a major distinction to be made between "classification schemes" based on artificial notations (such as Dewey) and natural language indexes. Both will be reviewed.'

Natural Language Systems

In natural language indexing systems, words or terms from the language of choice are used as descriptors. The simplicity is highly attractive. However, as increasing numbers of terms are used, various problems emerge.

Since terms in natural languages overlap in meaning and in appearance, some kind of control is usually imposed. Examples of these include homographs: two or more words spelled the same way but different in meaning. For example, the word CHARACTER means different things to a playwright, a typewriter mechanic, a theologian, and an architect. Similarly, information about a TANK that would interest a general would not necessarily help a plumber. In these cases, the terms need to be expanded or differentiated in some way, or else inappropriate signals are likely to be retrieved.

Different words for the same concept or entity (synonyms) cause other problems. A retrieval system with information under AGRICULTURE might yield nothing in a search under FARMING. Straightforward one-to-one relationships can be handled by imposing further control. Typically, one term becomes the "preferred" term and the other term is used only for redirection. "For FARMING see AGRICULTURE." In practice, more difficult to handle are near-synonyms where the overlap is incomplete, e.g., AGRICULTURE and LAND USE. A list of subject headings, or thesaurus, enumerating terms and relationships between them and other terms is used. The process of control is usually known as vocabulary control or authority control.

Another complexity has to do with hierarchical relationships where material on a topic, such as dairying, can be found not only in books specifically on dairying listed under the heading DAIRYING, but also within more general books on agriculture listed under AGRICULTURE. Alternatively, there might be no general work on agriculture but books dealing with aspects of agriculture such as dairying, horticulture, aquaculture, and so on. Retrieval systems vary in the extent and manner in which they contain references to narrower (more specific) topics and to broader (more general) ones.

So far, only simple definitions have been considered. In practice, the topics of inquiry often require some complexity in description. Consider, for example, "TEACHING METHODS IN AUSTRIAN UNIVERSITIES FROM 1918 TO 1939." Natural language indexing systems can handle such combinations ("coordinations") of concepts in either of two ways. In a manual system, it is convenient to compose ("precoordinate") a single (but complex) entry following agreed conventions concerning the order of the aspects (more technically "facets") of the concept. In a traditional library subject catalog one would expect to find a book on this topic listed under a heading of the following form "AUSTRIA, *Higher education,* 1918-1939. Teaching methods" and probably only under that heading.

If this precoordination were not done, one would need to look at each item listed under AUSTRIA, under *higher education*, under 1918-1939, and under *teaching methods* and select only those items which had been entered under *all* those labels. Technically, this is known as "postcoordination" since the expression of the relationship the coordination— is done at the time of the inquiry, after the time of indexing. It is obviously laborious.

In computer-based systems, where the computer can take on the chore of doing the "coordinating," it is customary not to express the coordination at the time of indexing. Various appropriate index terms would be assigned. In a postcoordinate search, the searcher enumerates the index terms that are expected to be helpful in identifying desired material, and the computer assumes the task of finding the books which have been assigned whatever combination of terms the searcher has specified.

One might also be able to specify the historical period though, in this case, it would probably be quite convenient to browse among the items retrieved by the above terms. These coordinate relationships can be ambiguous, since the mere occurrence of words may be insufficient to define the topic. A textbook example is the difference between a "venetian blind" and a "blind Venetian." Similarly with the three words "bites," "dog," and "man"—"dog bites man" is not the same syntactical relationship or meaning, nor is it as newsworthy, as "man bites dog."

These relationships can properly be described as syntactical in exactly the same way that syntax denotes grammatical relationships. On the whole, syntactical relationships tend to be ignored in indexing languages, but there are notable exceptions, such as relational indexing.

An often overlooked attribute of natural language indexing systems is that each system is natural to a particular time, place, and cultural environment. Subject headings used in the *British National Bibliography* are different from those assigned for a comparable purpose by the U.S. Library of Congress. Special groups of any kind—professional, social, technical, cultural, regional—will tend to use their own particular vocabularies. A natural language indexing system appropriate to one group is likely to be more or less unnatural and inappropriate to another. This limited applicability is also true to a lesser degree in the case of indexing languages with artificial notation in that they too reflect the conceptual arrangements (even though not the language) of a particular group.

Classification Schemes with Artificial Notation

Since they are intended to perform a similar role, it is not surprising that classification schemes with artificial notation tend to have characteristics similar to those of "natural" language systems.

1. Synonyms should also be avoided since, having established a label for a concept, subsequent labels for the same concept need not be created.
2. Homographs (words with identical spelling but different meaning) are avoided since the concepts are identified and distinguished prior to the assignment of the labels.
3. Hierarchical relationships need to be handled in the same sort of way. The relationships are typically embodied in the notation, e.g.,

   942 History of England

   942.7 History of Northwestern England

   942.76 History of Lancashire

   942.769 History of Lancaster
4. With complex topics such as "teaching methods in Austrian Universities, 1918-1939," the same solutions are available as with "natural" language, e.g. 378.1709436 in the Dewey Decimal Classification. Since most existing classification schemes are designed for human rather than computer use, complex precoordinate labels are used.

Precoordination, however, is not a necessary characteristic of classification schemes with artificial notation any more than it is with natural language indexing schemes. It is true that most existing schemes *are* precoordinate, but in recent decades most thinking about classification has been based on analysis into a number of "facets," which, in combination, define the topic concerned. This faceted approach, which is detectable in revisions to existing schemes such as the Universal Decimal Classification (UDC), lends itself to postcordinate searching by computer, because the elements which have been "precoordinated" remain identifiable could, therefore, be used for a postcoordinate search also.

Similarities and Dissimilarities

As the foregoing discussion illustrates, natural language indexing systems and classification schemes with artificial notation are substantially similar in structure, controls, and uses. A natural language indexing system with a fully worked-out relationship between topics will require the same degree of analysis and control as a classification scheme for the same range of topics. From this perspective, it seems helpful to regard them both as part of the generic category of indexing systems. The difference in notation is just one of the differences between them and not necessarily the most important.

Other diferences are as follows:

1. Since the construction of a classification scheme with an artificial notation implies analysis of the relationships between topics, such schemes ordinarily have a great deal of "syndetic" control, i.e., rules concerning the preferred choice of indexing term and the relationships between terms. The development of syndetic control is not a necessary part of using natural language indexing systems, although it may be desirable. Consequently, the amount of syndetic control varies in practice from essentially none to very detailed control. Intuitively, it seems needed; in practice, there is some question as to whether the benefits justify the costs.
2. A classification scheme with artificial notation will need a natural language index to it—a "relative index"—if it is to be conveniently used.
3. Classification schemes with artificial notation permit the designer to arrange topics that are similar or related to be collocated. In natural language indexing systems, the juxtaposition of concepts will depend on accidents of spelling in the language concerned.
4. The labels used in classification schemes with artificial notation tend to be shorter, though there can be considerable variations in this. For example, "Bibliography of the Economic History of Hungary" would be "330.9439016" in the Dewey Decimal Classification but "ML,E2" in the Bliss Bibliographic Classification.

The foregoing discussion indicates that indexing systems vary in several ways: in fineness of detail; in degree of vocabulary control; in syndetic structure; and in choice between pre- and postcoordination. The principal conclusions from tests of retrieval systems are that, despite these variations and the ingenuity of their designers, there is little difference between them in effectiveness, even though they tend to retrieve different material even when the same inquiries are posed in identical circumstances.

Multiple Retrieval Systems

The ability of a retrieval system to retrieve signals (which, according to the intentions of the user, can be regarded either as the data desired or pointers toward the data desired) can be illustrated by considering some the many examples of retrieval mechanisms in a library.

One user might treat the subject arrangement of the documents on the shelves (arranged according to the Dewey Decimal Classification, perhaps) as a retrieval mechanism and go directly to the shelves associated with the Dewey number(s) expected to contain the signals (books) desired.

A second user might approach the library catalog and examine subject headings and note the bibliographical data recorded on the cards there. That may be all that the user wanted if verifying a bibliographical citation and willing to rely on card catalog data instead of inspecting the documents themselves.

A third user might do exactly the same as the second user but the data recorded on the cards do not constitute the goal, only the directions to the document on the shelves.

A fourth user might go to the librarian and express the inquiry verbally. The librarian, acting as a retrieval system, would endeavor to convert the inquiry into the terms of the library system and deliver the data required, whether this is a whole document or merely a mention of specific data from within a book. When a document is found, further retrieval mechanisms—index, table of contents—may be used to identify more specifically what is wanted. Dictionaries, encyclopedias, and bibliographies—all examples of retrieval mechanisms—may well be used independently or in conjunction with other means of searching. It is clear that many examples of retrieval systems occur in libraries and that they can be used independently or sequentially.

Retrieval Languages

In the previous sections we restricted our attention to subject indexes using natural languages or artificial notation. This provided a convenient introduction to some semantic and syntactical aspects. However, it is important to emphasize that "subject" access is only one example of retrieval. Documents and data can have "contextual" attributes assigned to them for the purpose of retrieval, such as author, publisher, and date of creation. Indeed, in academic libraries, more use is made of author entries in the catalogs than of subject entries. The principal means of arrangement and approach for archival materials is their administrative provenance. As noted, attributes of authorship and provenance can also have connotations of subject content.

A citation, by means of which an author refers in one document to another document, implies a relationship between the two and constitutes *prima facie* evidence that if one document is relevant to an inquiry, so might the other be. Citation indexes can be viewed as a form of subject index even though the attribute that forms the basis for retrieval is citedness rather than a description of what the document is about. The argument is that the usual custom in scholarly research is to cite closely related work. Such citation is, therefore, indicative of a close relationship, usually in subject matter. Hence, the citation of one article by another generally implies similar subject matter. Since the description is in the form of a citation, not in the inconstant terminology of subject indexes, a citation index has some advantages when it comes to the use of articles in foreign languages or on subjects without standardised terminology. This is reminiscent of our argument, that a document description can be a surrogate description of a subject inquiry.

This point has been stressed because of our assertion that retrieval is primarily a linguistic process, drawing on:

(a) *semantics:* the study of the elements of a language from the point of view of meaning;

(b) *syntax:* the study of the formal interactions that exist between the elements of language; and

(c) *pragmatics:* the study of the relationships between signs of linguistic expressions and their uses.

Since retrieval systems are based on indexing "languages" which share (more or less) the attributes of ordinary languages, they derive from the culture of their context and their study can be asserted to be a form of linguistic study. We can note that this assertion assumes that linguistics does or can include the study of "artificial" languages. How far this assertion can be pushed is a matter for debate. It is suggested that all retrieval systems could be included on the grounds that all depend on indexing "languages," that all indexing languages depend on the assignment of attributes and on the labeling of these attributes, and that a proper understanding of these systems depends on semantic, syntactical, and pragmatic analysis. This is more easily understood in the case of "word"-based subject indexes than in others, but we speculate that it is also true of all "non-word" indexes using artificial notation, all contextual indexes, all citation indexes, and even systems based on the statistical association of attributes of data or documents.

Concepts, Objects and Definability

So far, we have simply assumed that a "descriptor," whether drawn from natural language or concocted in some artificial notation, can suffice to describe concepts. This is not the case. A descriptor can act as a label. It may also serve as an address. It may define the topic, more or less, but it is unlikely in all cases to provide sufficient definition to describe completely the topic in relation to other topics. The extent to which definition is needed will vary with respect to at least two considerations:

1. The number of different entities to be described. In a trivial example of an information retrieval system that retrieves data concerning only two or three items (e.g., the number of chairs, tables, and lamps in a warehouse), the need to define will be trivial. In contrast, a chain of furniture shops or a large furniture museum will need detailed definitions to distinguish one type from another.
2. The definability of the entities concerned. It is clear that not all concepts are equally easily defined. Consider the following sequence of concepts:
   (a) Seat 34C on flight PA 6 from San Francisco airport on January 29, 1980.
   (b) An elephant
   (c) Heat
   (d) Lassitude

The airline seat is easily unambiguously defined. An elephant is quite difficult to describe but can be recognised from pictures. Once one knows what an elephant looks like, there is usually little doubt as to whether a particular object is an elephant or not. Heat can only be indirectly illustrated. It cannot be seen directly, though sometimes its causes or effects can be. It can be sensed, however, if one is close enough and it can be defined and measured in physical terms. Lassitude can be sensed and symptoms of lassitude can be observed. Not at all clear, however, is the relationship between lassitude and related concepts such as ennui, tiredness, weariness, exhaustion, boredom, etc. Unlike the aircraft seat, the elephant, and heat, there would appear to be no precise accepted definition of lassitude. If one were to search in an information retrieval system for material about "lassitude" one would probably have to try a variety of search terms, and the items retrieved as a result of the search would probably vary in the extent to which they were about lassitude.

Areas of study appear to vary in the extent to which the concepts they deal with are definable. Physical sciences tend to have "hard," i.e., relatively definable concepts such as temperature, molecular weight, size, velocity, etc. This is reasonable since the physical sciences deal with physical objects and the physical relationships between them. The "hardness" of these properties permits relatively easy measurement and calculation. One development can build upon another because the earlier achievements are clearly defined. The progress in achievement in the hard sciences is, in consequence, more palpable than in other areas of activity such as education, literature, political science, or social welfare.

The "softer" areas tend to be those which deal with human behaviour and social values. Each area of study appears to have a characteristic degree of intellectual hardness/softness. There seems to be variation within areas (e.g., welfare economics seems "softer" than econometrics) and subjects may change in hardness/softness over time. In other words, definability does not appear to be itself a linguistic problem. If it were, then coining new words might solve many difficulties. Rather, there appears to be something more basic that has effects which are difficult to handle linguistically. Bunge comments that "vagueness or blurredness has no positive aspect and is a conceptual rather than a linguistic disease, hence it is rather more difficult to cure.

The extent to which formal, logical notation and quantification are used is an indicator of hardness. It is an imperfect one since the use of such notation and quantification is not necessarily appropriate or well rooted in realistic definitions. The terminology of hardness and softness is potentially misleading. One of the meanings of the word "hard" signifies a firm consistency and its opposite is "soft." In that sense, the imagery of *intellectual* hardness and softness is appropriate. A different meaning of the word "hard" is "difficult." For that meaning, the proper opposite is "easy" rather than "soft."

It is in the second connotation of hardness as an indicator of difficulty that this imagery is misleading with respect to *intellectual* hardness and softness. The pages of formal notation and algebra which characterize writings in physics and chemistry look particularly unintelligible to the lay person. However, in an important sense it is even more difficult to make progress in fields where definitions are "soft" and unreliable, than when they are relatively "hard" and dependable. The foundations built by previous scholars cannot so easily be taken on trust but may need redefinition. New work may need to be built into rather than *onto* prior work. However one may view *difficulty,* let us simply accept that the definability of concepts—the intellectual "hardness" and " softness"—varies from one field of discourse to another.

To the extent to which terms are relatively low in definability, information retrieval is likely to be less satisfactory since retrieval, being a linguistic process, depends heavily on definitions.

In view of the importance of definition in communication, one would expect definability to emerge as fundamental in information studies in general and information retrieval in particular. Storer has referred to the distinction between hard and soft sciences as being possibly "the most powerful single variable in explaining disciplinary differences in the cultural realm." So far, however, research appears to have been limited. Studies of the information gathering habits of social scientists indicate a general similarity with the habits of physical scientists. Hindle has suggested that in patterns in use of books and journals, "softer" subject areas are characterised by much more diffuse reading than "harder subjects." In other words, the use of documents is more widely spread over different titles and over materials of a wider range of ages.

Signaling Through Time

Robert Fairthorne's delightful description of information retrieval as "marking" and "parking" catches nicely the expectation that what is marked and parked may be retrieved after some lapse of time. If that were not the case, then "discarding" or "dumping" would be more appropriate. The same emphasis on the elapse of time as a feature of information retrieval was made more explicitly by Calvin Mooers in a short paper that is said to contain the first use of the term "information retrieval." Mooers describes information retrieval as "communication through time."

The image of information retrieval as communication through time helps explain the lack of direct link between the originator of the message and the recipient. One can readily imagine messages (data, documents) as having hooks (tags, labels, or descriptors) attached to them and then being placed in some timeless void where they remain until an inquiry in the form of a set of one or more hooks reaches into the same void and pulls back any messages which have one or more hooks coinciding with those of the inquiry.

However, as one starts to work around the edges of this definition it becomes a little frayed. In one special case of information retrieval, there is an attempt to minimize the lapse of time. This occurs when every new batch of marked and parked information is automatically searched for material pertaining to specific inquiries. In professional jargon, a standing profile of reader's searches is routinely searched against a file in order to provide S.D.I. (selective dissemination of information). One might regard this as a sort of preemptive information retrieval, although the notion of a standing order would seem closer. Yet even here, some delay, even if minimised, is necessarily present because each of these processes of acquiring, marking, parking, and retrieving must take some time. Even in prompt on-line processing, the indirectness and sequential, discontinuous, two-stage nature of the process necessarily involves some time—even though it might be very little. A different sort of problem emerges from other examples of communication which take time and which do not easily fit accepted definitions of informal retrieval. A letter sent through the mail will take time to arrive. (Strictly, all communication processes must take *some* time even though they may be trivial.) A notice that is posted on a fence, such as "Trespassers will be prosecuted," or on a refrigerator, "Don't drink all the milk," will continue to inform people for as long as it remains posted. A documentary article in a newspaper may consciously be intended to inform readers in posterity.

The simplest conclusion from all this would seem to be that, although information retrieval can properly be regarded as communication through time, it is not the only form of communication in which time may be significant. Delay, one could conclude, is a necessary attribute of information retrieval but not exclusive to it. In information retrieval, the indirectness or discontinuity of communication permits and, indeed, *ensures* delay over and above the time required for communication itself. Both time and indirectness would seem to be significant in information retrieval and will be considered.

Indirectness

By the "indirectness" of information retrieval systems, we refer to the characteristic that the designers and operators do not know who will seek the indirect communication that the information retrieval system provides. Not only does one not know *who,* one also does not know *why* they will seek to use it or what perspectives and vocabulary they will have when they seek to use it. To some extent, this lack of prior knowledge is shared by other communication systems, notably in mass communication. One is, in general, unable to predict or later ascertain who heard a radio broadcast, read a newspaper, or heard a speech to a crowd—or how much of it they understood—or how beneficial the message was to them. In information retrieval situations, however, there is a further problem and that is that the user—with or without someone else acting as a mediator—needs to define what it is that needs to be retrieved. The vocabulary of the would-be user is necessarily somewhat different from that of the designer of the retrieval system, since no two persons' vocabularies are exactly alike, and may be substantially different especially if the designer (a category within which we include the indexer for present purposes) is distant in time, education, and culture from the would-be user. This problem of predicting rather than knowing what each future user of the system is likely to ask for and how he or she is likely to ask for it has long been recognised. Indexing and cataloging are, in part, predictive pastimes since the formal description of what data represent and what documents are about has to be modified by estimation of the probability that they will be sought and of the probable ways in which they will be sought. [19] For the most part, this seems to have been assumed more or less implicitly. In analysis, it has been described in terms of "thought experiments." The importance in practice of this indirectness varies according to the circumstances and, we suspect, with the degree of definability. Previously, we have noted three factors as affecting definability:

(a) The range of choices available: limited in most management information systems; unlimited in general libraries and archives.

(b) The definability of the things that might be retrieved: from specific aircraft seats to vague cultural concepts.

(c) The extent to which the individual seeking to use the system can describe what he or she needs to reduce distressing ignorance: from a telephone number to, say, background material on stoicism in modern Western culture.

Time and indirectness would both seem to reduce the closeness of match between the designer and the user in terms of approach to description and definition. Both, therefore, would seem to exacerbate the problems of matching characterised by these three dimensions. Strictly speaking, it is the fact of indirectness which *permits* the matching of definitions and it is the fact of time which inhibits adaptation of the system to the user. The user can, heuristicly, learn to understand the system better and the system, if computer-based, might be programmed to facilitate this heuristic learning.

With either manual or computerbased systems, other humans can, and often do, play a mediating role, as, for example, in doing a literature search on behalf of someone else who is too busy or less familiar with the retrieval systems available. Significantly, ascertaining what the user wants and translating it into a form suitable for the system(s) to be used are both regarded as important processes which not only take time but require special training. We conclude that:

- information retrieval involves communication through time, although not all communication through time is information retrieval;
- information retrieval is necessarily indirect communication;
- both the delay and the indirectness are liable to exacerbate existing difficulties caused by problems of definability.

Time

In some cases, library catalogs compiled more than a century ago are still in active use. The disadvantage of old catalogs is that older cataloging practice differs from contemporary cataloging in two ways. Descriptive cataloging (choice of form of entry for author, title, etc.) has evolved over the years. An extreme example-found in an ancient English library in a book-form catalog printed in 1790 and still in use-is the entry of books by the author, "Smith," under the letter F— because the genitive case of the Latin word for a smith (*faber*) begins with an F. Those whose work requires them to use old catalogs tend to learn how to allow for some of these vagaries. More serious is the shift in terminology for describing things over the years. In all aspects of human activity, new terms are coined and existing words change their meaning. Language evolves. Objects themselves may evolve. Consider, for example, the computer. Its appearance, power, and function have all changed radically in less than half a century. Finding antiquated terminology in library and other sorts of catalogs can be a source of amusement, of irritation, and of failure to retrieve. Inevitably, the use of words reflects the parlance and perspectives of the day. For example, Berman has drawn attention to the use of indexing terms which reflect sexist and racist attitudes which are now less acceptable in the United States than they used to be. From the point of view of information retrieval, the shifting of word usage over time and the evolving of new concepts, objects, and terms (which seem inevitable and behind which retrieval systems seem bound to lag) will mean that the retrieval system itself tends to become less accurate and less effective over time. The already imperfect description and definition, which are pivotal to effective retrieval, get worse.

Of course, the books should be recataloged continually according to contemporary cataloging practice, especially with respect to the subject headings used to describe what they are about. This requires, however, relatively expensive intellectual labor and the cost and benefits need to be weighed against the alternative uses of such money as is available. Most library users would be properly upset if their librarians ceased to buy new books of current interest in order to divert resources to the recataloging of old books which may be of limited interest.

Retrieval, Responsiveness & Relatedness

The design, use, and evaluation of retrieval systems depend heavily on various sorts of relatedness. There have been two problems in discussions of this area: (1) the elements and relationships have not always been analysed in enough detail; and (2) terminology has not always been clear and consistent. In particular, the *utilization of retrieved data* has not always been adequately distinguished from the *retrieval process* and the term "relevance" has been loosely used for more than one sort of relatedness. An attempt will be made to clarify the concepts and terminology involved.

The mechanism by which retrieval systems operate is the association (usually but not necessarily the matching) of arbitrarily chosen but predetermined attributes of the set of data that is to be susceptible to retrieval. The attributes that are used include authorship (as in a library catalog), date of publication (as, sometimes, in bibliographies), age (as in museum documentation), occurrence of words (as in the searching of texts), and so on. The list of possible attributes that could be used seems endless: location, size, chemical process, origin, etc. Nor need attributes be used alone: systems retrieving bibliographical data, for example, commonly operate on two or more attributes in combination, e.g., authorship, date of publication, language, and subject matter. The retrieval system responds to an inquiry by yielding such data as it finds that are highly associated with the attributes specified in the inquiry.

Retrieval Elements

We have defined the use of retrieval systems as including three distinguishable stages: the *formulation* of an inquiry; the *retrieval* of signals; the *utilization* of what has been retrieved. The effectiveness of each process can vary:

- The *formulation* of the inquiry may be more or less appropriate to the choice of attributes in the retrieval system. Much depends on the extent to which the person doing the formulation has an understanding of the data sought and of the characteristics of the retrieval system. The phrasing of the inquiry may be unskillful. [25]
- Aside from mechanical failures, the *retrieval* process may be ineffective in two ways: it may respond with data that has been incorrectly retrieved; or it may fail to yield data that should have been retrieved. In conventional terms, these would be referred to as failures in precision and in recall, respectively, For example, using authorship as the attribute for retrieval, "Mark Twain" might be used as the inquiry. The retrieval

system might correctly respond with data concerning works written by Mark Twain but fail to retrieve those written by Samuel Clemens—or, if it did, it might also wrongly include data concerning works by Severus Clemens or Susie Clemens.

- *Utilization* might be impaired if the inquirer did not have the necessary abilities (e.g., knowledge, cognitive skills) to become informed by the data retrieved.

From the analysis thus far there emerge several possibilities for things to be related to each other—or to have degrees of relatedness. These include but are not limited to:

1. the inquiry as formulated for the retrieval system;
2. any of a seemingly unlimited range of attributes;
3. data retrieved; and
4. benefit to the user.

Before considering sorts of relatedness, it is important to emphasize again the separateness of the retrieval process from the processes of formulation and of utilization. The difference between retrieval and utilization can be conveniently illustrated by what we might call the case of the disappearing user. Let us imagine that someone formulated and posed an inquiry concerning chocolate, cholesterol, and heart disease to a computer-based retrieval system. The retrieval system responds by yielding a set of data. The user becomes better informed as a result of perusing the data and benefits from a changed state of knowledge. Let us now imagine that, having posed the inquiry, the inquirer loses interest, is unable to await the response, or dies from a heart attack. In this latter scenario, there is no opportunity for utilization of the data, nor, therefore, for benefit to the user. Yet the retrieval system has performed in exactly the same way. The process of retrieval and the data retrieved are indistinguishable, in fact unchanged, from one scenario to another.

We can clarify the distinction between formulation and retrieval by extending this simple case. In some circumstances, the user may modify the formulation of the inquiry if it is thought that the data yielded would not be what is desired. In this case, what has happened is that a *different* search has been formulated, however slight the modification has been. Commonly, the user's knowledge has changed as a result of preliminary indications concerning the set of data that would be yielded. The response by the retrieval system to any given formulated search will not have been changed unless the retrieval system itself has also been altered in some way, e.g., new data added or the indexing modified.

Relatedness

In the evaluation of information retrieval systems, the term "relevance" has been loosely used to denote differing forms of relatedness. A practical approach is to define the most useful relationships and degrees of relatedness first and then give them distinctive names. We shall consider three different relationships for each of which the terms "relevant" or "relevance" has been used.

Responsiveness

Responsiveness refers to relatedness of the data retrieved to the inquiry as posed in terms of the attributes used as the basis for retrieval. To what extent *did* the system retrieve all and only the works that it contains by Mark Twain? The quality of the response to the inquiry by the retrieval system will be affected by several factors including the appropriateness and completeness of the data base, the suitability of the attribute(s) used as the basis for retrieval (in this case authorship), and the ability of the retrieval system to identify those data that fit the description offered by the inquiry—or fit it to the desired degree. If one wished to avoid talking of the "relevance" of the retrieved data to the inquiry, one might speak of the responsiveness of the system.

Utility

"Utility," is defined following usage in economics, as benefit accruing. If reading a document and being informed by it leads to an enhanced state of knowledge which enables one to achieve some goal, then we can describe that process as having been beneficial or useful—as having utility.

We need to note two other outcomes: having a harmful effect, sometimes referred to awkwardly as a "negative utility," "disutility," or "disbenefit;" and having no known effect that could be regarded as useful or harmful—no utility or benefit.

Utility is meaningful only in terms of some objective, explicit or implicit. Giving somebody money has the property of utility if becoming wealthy or purchasing things are goals for that person; if that person were trying to achieve spiritual growth through poverty, then the gift of money would be unhelpful—of negative utility. Utility, then, is in all cases dependent on an objective. People have objectives. Inanimate objects do not. Organizations have objectives only to the extent to which individuals and groups have objectives which they seek to achieve through the organization. Hence, utility is dependent not only on an objective but on the objective of one or more persons. Further, objectives imply values. There are values, implicit or explicit, which make one decide that it is desirable to pursue an objective, and a particular objective in preference over other objectives. Utility and objectives both derive from human values.

We are concerned here with information retrieval and the manner in which it might have utility. In principle, it would seem that being informed might assist in any of the objectives that one or more individuals might have: spiritual, physical, intellectual, professional, or social. These objectives might also be hindered. An obvious example of harmful information would be information that was, in fact, misinformation. The objective of getting from San Francisco to New York is likely to be hindered if one receives inaccurate information about the departure time of the airline flight and, as a result, misses the plane. Even so, although inaccurate information is likely to be the major cause of disutility associated with information retrieval, it is not necessary or proper to equate disutility with inaccuracy since it can happen that accurate information can also hinder the achievement of objectives. It is, after all, not absurd for someone to state honestly: "I would never have undertaken that task had I known more about what was involved, but I am glad that I did it!" Further, it is important to remember that if the utility derived from information retrieval can pertain to any human objective, then it is only to be expected that some of these objectives will appear obscure. They might seem irrational to other people. They might be kept a secret. They might lie deep in the subconscious and not be recognised even by the individuals concerned. They can be expected to reflect values of a very private nature as well as publicly proclaimed ones. There may be inconsistencies between professed objectives and those actually pursued. There will probably be conflicting objectives even for one individual.

Aboutness

Writings about retrieval and especially about the evaluation of information retrieval systems have been dominated by just one of the apparently unlimited range of attributes: subject matter, i.e., what documents are about. The term "aboutness" can be conveniently defined as referring to a coincidence of concepts, that is to say, if a book is "about" Australia, we infer that the book contains concepts that we associate with the subject "Australia." If it did not do so, we should deny that the book is "about" Australia. This is not entirely an objective matter since concepts have to be perceived and there may be some scope for disagreement in the perceptions by different people as to the concepts they perceive in a book and even in the concepts they associate with the subject "Australia" Hence, there is scope for honest difference of opinion as to what a book is about.

Consider, for example, an allegory. A person who fails to perceive the allegorical symbols will have a different opinion concerning what the text is "about" than someone who does perceive them. In an extreme case, most persons who saw a book on Buddhist mythology written in Tibetan would be able to perceive so little of the concepts that they would, if honest, have to say that they did not know what the book was about. This is a matter of conceptual perception as well as a linguistic problem. If the book on Buddhist mythology were translated into a language they could understand, then, if the concepts were unfamiliar, they would probably still understand little of what the book was about.

It is unwise to assume that a document has a single subject matter. It would seem more sensible to recognize that a document may, by general consensus, be concerned with a particular topic and yet have quite different meanings for particular individuals on particular occasions. In addition to the problems of the recognition of the concepts, there is also the problem of the definability of the concepts. Even with accurate perception, if there is not a rigorous, exclusive, unambiguous use of terms, the defining of the concepts perceived in the book may vary from one reader to another.

This might simply be a matter of using alternative and equivalent synonyms. However, to the extent that concepts are not susceptible to description in unambiguous terms—they are vague or "soft"—then it is to be expected that statements by different individuals as to what a book is about, i.e., which set of concepts they perceive to be represented, will vary. Different people will state different nonequivalent definitions as to what the book is about. The scope for honest disagreement concerning what something is about is important. However, in any given point in linguistic and cultural time and space, there is likely to be a great deal of agreement.

If there were not, then subject indexes would not work. On the assumption that indexes are expected to indicate what things are about, one can state that the effectiveness of indexes depends on and is determined, in part, by the degree of uniformity in perception of concepts, and common definition and labeling of those concepts. Retrieval using the attribute of what documents are about has been and can be expected to be of primary importance since subject access is difficult, useful, and technically interesting. It has dominated so much that it has, perhaps, hindered clarity of thought about the foundations of information retrieval theory. Retrieval by "aboutness" has to be seen as the use of one attribute among many. Our conceptual framework and definitions should be broad enough to include all attributes not just one.

Pertinence

In Relatedness I above, we were concerned with the general term: the relatedness of the retrieval system's response to the inquiry regardless of the attribute(s) being used as a basis for retrieval. We now consider one special case within the general class: when the attribute used as the basis for retrieval is topicality—the subject matter of the data. In ordinary speech one might well speak of one topic as being relevant to another topic. Such relationships (e.g., general to specific, overlap) can be difficult to understand or to define. For example, when retrieving by the attribute of topicality, data on "Freud" are related (relevant) but not identical to the topic of psychoanalysis. We might term this relatedness "pertinence " This sort of relatedness between properties of data within a given attribute could exist with other attributes than topicality.

Berieficiality

A relationship that is entirely different from either of the above is that between the retrieved data and the benefit of the user. It is in this sense, for example, that Wilson has sought to limit the use of the term "relevance" in *Two Kinds of Power* and it is implicit in all discussions of utility-theoretic indexing. Stated simply, it is assumed that retrieval systems are provided and used in order that their utilization will have beneficial effects. Social values are implied. This raises two questions: (1) Whose values? The users' or those of the providers of the service? and (2) Are we referring to actual benefits or expected benefits? These are critical questions. However, whatever answers are given, it is clear that the relationship is different in kind from both responsiveness and pertinence because factors external to the retrieval system affect the outcome: social values and the knowledge and cognitive skills of the users.

Implications for Information Retrieval

We have defined responsiveness as signifying the extent to which the retrieval system yields data associated with the attribute(s) specified in the formulated inquiry. We have defined beneficiality as the property of assisting in the achievement of objectives. We have noted that these objectives are necessarily the objectives of human beings and relate to human values even though they may sometimes be obscure and even seem irrational to other people. From this discussion the following conclusions would seem to follow.

An ideal information retrieval system would retrieve data and documents that would assist individuals in the pursuit of their objectives, i.e., values. This implies that the information retrieval system should be concerned with the utility of what is retrieved rather than what it is about, since utility, not aboutness, is the goal. In order to achieve utility, the ideal information retrieval system would need to know the objective(s) and value(s) of each user.

Since redundant information does not help achieve goals and may hinder their achievement, the information retrieval system would, ideally, also have to know the state of knowledge of the inquirer—both its extent and its limitations. Avoiding the retrieval of unneeded and unusable data is, after all, a major purpose of information retrieval systems. If a researcher sought material relevant to an inquiry concerning Freud, it is unlikely that it would be helpful to retrieve a document that had been written by that same researcher, even though it may be related to the subject of the inquiry.

It is not practical by any known technique to expect to know all of the objectives of people currently using an information retrieval system. It is still less reasonable to expect to be able to predict what future users' objectives and values might be. Even if one could, the most useful set of retrieved documents is likely to be unique for each inquiry. Further, since each person's mind is unique, even objectives that are ostensibly the same for different people may be different in practice. What is more, since redundant information is to be avoided, subsequent inquiries concerned with the same person's objective would call for different responses since the individual's state of knowledge will probably have changed in the meanwhile. Some things will have been learned, others forgotten. Therefore, an ideal information retrieval system based on utility would have a formidable set of design requirements. It would need to understand objectives that present inquirers might not be willing to admit to or might not consciously understand fully themselves; it would need to predict which persons might use the system in the future and what their objectives might be in that future; and it would in each case need to know not only what the individual's objective is but also that same individual's state of knowledge not at the point in time that the inquiry was made but at the point in time that the data are retrieved. This would have to be true for each and every individual who may come to use the system. What should be retrieved should vary even for different posings of the same question by the same person. All this is quite apart from the fact that the concepts and definitions used may be more or less ambiguous.

Although such an ideal system would seem to be what is needed, the compounding of inherently improbable achievements one upon another means that this ideal system is most likely to remain an inspiring but unrealised achievement. (Not that this might not be helpful. Witness the repeated homage to the inspirational role played by Vannevar Bush's seminal essay, "As We May Think," published in 1945.

The notion of imagining what future inquiries might be posed may very well be a useful device (*cf.* W. Cooper), but the combination of needing to know objectives, values, and future states of knowledge—including knowledge not yet known to anybody—casts grave doubt on the achievability of such an ideal system.

In the discussion of "aboutness" above, reasons were adduced as to why complete agreement is not to be expected concerning what documents are about. Nevertheless, within a given cultural and linguistic context, considerable consensus is likely. Indexing and retrieving books according to what they are currently perceived to be about is, therefore, a more practical matter than indexing them in relation to potential future inquiries.

If indexing and retrieval based on aboutness is more practical than indexing with respect to predictions of future inquiries and future knowledge, how does aboutness relate to utility? The answer would appear to be two-fold:

1. If we hold relentlessly to the importance of utility—of being beneficially informed—we can still regard aboutness as a sensible *predictor* of utility to the inquirer. If we seek to reduce our ignorance *about* Freud, a document about Freud is likely to make us more fully informed about Freud. Further, although this process does nothing to minimize the retrieval of knowledge that we already know, this redundancy is at worst inefficient rather than misleading since we can, presumably, ourselves filter out subsequently that which is already known to us.
2. in our discussion, we have tended to assume that the attribute used as a basis for retrieval would be its subject aboutness. Although a subject retrieval system could operate in isolation, this is a singularly unrealistic and unnecessary assumption, since constant use is in fact made of other attributes of identifying documents which might be useful. A few examples will demonstrate: Contextual attributes such as author, origin, date of creation, and extensions of these can be helpful. Indeed, in the case of archives, the principal means of arrangement and approach for documents is their administrative provenance. In libraries, a common mode of approach is to use the author's name as a means of identifying books on a subject on which it is thought that person might have written. Citations, by means of which an author refers in a document to another document, imply a relationship between the documents—a prima facie indicator that if one document is related to an inquiry, so might the other. The success of the various citation indexes is clear evidence of their value in supplementing subject indexes. Further,

a part of the formal information system is the information specialist who operates and may have designed it. Users of archives depend heavily on the archivist for guidance. Librarians have always included in their role the drawing on their experience with bibliography, with their collections and with their users in order to assist users (*cf.* the "reference interview"). In addition, it is foolish not to include as part of this picture the informal assistance played by friends and colleagues who can and do play a significant role in scholarship and in bureaucracies, to give but two examples.

Briefly, information retrieval based on what documents are deemed to be about (as opposed to prediction of what is unknown in relation to future enquiries) can be expected to work moderately well in practice because there is more or less consensus on what documents are about, because "aboutness" can plausibly be regarded as predictive of utility, and because, in practice, subject indexing is supplemented by other indicators of probable utility.

Information retrieval based on "aboutness" lends itself to automatic indexing since the occurrence and more especially the co-occurrence of terms in the text can indicate the apparent subject content of the document. This may be expensive and error-prone, but results likely to be of some use can be achieved.

The very same reasons which make the ideal information retrieval system unlikely also make implausible the concept of an "information counselor" in any sophisticated sense. Any person knowledgeable about sources of information can, in general, be helpful. However, the notion of an information counselor based on an analogy with a dietician, who can diagnose and prescribe information like a change of diet, would have to cope with the same problems as would the ideal information system: in addition to understanding objectives which the inquirer may imperfectly comprehend, the counselor would also need to understand the extent and nature of the inquirer's knowledge, and presumably be able to identify the point at which the inquirer has been beneficially informed to a sufficient extent. The analog of a dietician would be more apt if states of knowledge could be objectively assessed by blood count, encephalograms, and the like.

Summing Up

The foregoing discussion leads to the following conclusion:

1. The three sorts of relatedness—responsiveness, pertinence, and beneficiality—are different.

2. Since beneficiality (Relatedness III) is rooted in the utilization of retrieved data and in human values, the superficially startling conclusion follows that *relevance in the sense of utility cannot properly be used to evaluate information retrieval processes*. In this, we are using a strict, narrow definition: the ability of the system to yield a set of data responsive to the formulated inquiry. The proper basis for evaluation would be rooted in the responsiveness of the system in terms of the inquiry and the attributes used: "fitting the description" in Wilson's terms. Any use of beneficial effects cannot be an evaluation of retrieval processes only but must be either an evaluation of utilization or some combination of utilization and other processes (e.g., utilization and retrieval and, possibly, formulation, and even other logically prior activities such as identification of need) or concurrent activities (e.g., improvement of cognitive skills in order to improve utilization). Whoever uses benefit or utility in information retrieval evaluation should specify the boundaries of what is being evaluated.
3. It would be helpful if new, distinct terms were to be adopted to distinguish different sorts of relatedness ("relevance"). Confusion might be reduced. ideally, the terms should be applicable generally to sorts of relatedness and not restricted to specific examples of retrieval activities (e.g., subject-based retrieval as opposed to retrieval on the basis of other attributes) unless such narrower usage is justified and clearly stated.

We can speculate on the consequences of failure to find items. For this it is helpful to invoke a principle from cybernetics—the law of requisite variety—which states, in effect, that a system must have as many different responses as it encounters challenges. Otherwise, the system will fail for lack of being able to respond. In the context of retrieval systems, one might say that, if something appropriate is not retrieved for each and every inquiry, the system will fail. So it will if, for example:

- no signals are retrieved (no suitable books); or,
- if no term in the language of the retrieval system seems promising enough to be worth pursuing; or,
- if, for whatever reason, a promising term does not lead to the retrieval of appropriate signals.

It follows that requisite variety can be increased by attending to one or more of these causes. A more complete collection of retrievable objects (e.g., a bigger collection of appropriate books) will help. (We define completeness as being complete with respect to some range of inquiries.)

A wider range of index terms would also help, provided, of course, they lead to appropriate retrieval, as would more extensive and more reliable connections between index terms and retrievable objects. What are the consequences of failure? They would appear to be two-fold:

- The consequence of an *individual* failure is unlikely to be catastrophic since we are dealing with an open system. If the need is great enough, the inquirer can normally leave the library and try other sources: ask a friend, try another library, etc.
- The consequence of *repeated* failure is that, as the user perceives the *proportion* of failures to be increasing, there is likely to be a reassessment on the users' part of the perceived probable benefits of using the library. Usage is likely to be reduced and to be concentrated more narrowly on those sorts of inquiries which are perceived as being unlikely to result in failure. We consider this sort of reaction more fully.

Competence to Use Retrieval Systems

Those who would use retrieval systems are fully competent to do so. This is a most unwise assumption for the following reasons:

(a) There are many different retrieval systems. Consider the fact that Sheehy's *Guide to Reference Books* describes more than 10,000 different bibliographies and other works of reference.

(b) Typically, several retrieval systems are likely to contain material about a given topic, and many others may well contain at least a little material relating to that topic.

(c) Each system is more or less different from the others, even though the differences may sometimes be small and subtle. Further, retrieval systems commonly change. Published works may have new editions and computer-based retrieval systems are continuously being modified.

These are the reasons why a good reference librarian not only knows many reference sources, but also has the familiarity and understanding that come from frequent use, and keeps up-to-date. It is inconceivable that one could know too many sources, could be too familiar with them, or would be unnecessarily up-to-date. This is clearly a major challenge even for the dedicated professional information specialist. What, then, of the user who is not a professional reference librarian or information specialist? There are, of course, some exceptional individuals, but the general situation is entirely predictable:

(a) There is some vague (but generally incomplete) awareness that libraries have considerable potential for the retrieval of information.

(b) The number of retrieval systems known to any given user is likely to be small.

(c) The expertise that can come only from conscious attention to the complexities of the system is likely to be lacking in most cases.

It is difficult and unreasonable to imagine any circumstances in which this situation could be expected to be otherwise, since such expertise requires opportunity, time, and effort—and not just once but on a continuing basis. It is not at all clear that for everyone the benefits involved in being expert justify paying the price. The consequence is that the use of retrieval systems is bound to be far less in both frequency and effectiveness of use than is possible and beneficial. But to assert that this is "wrong" would be to forget the price involved (mostly nonmonetary) and to overlook the fact that the use of retrieval systems is a means, not an end. More use of libraries can sensibly be expected to follow—and only to follow—changes in the perceived benefits and perceived costs. What then could or should be done? Three sorts of practical activities would seem sensible:

(a) Greater awareness of the existence and of the potential usefulness of retrieval systems would permit *consideration* by the user of more use of them.

(b) A lower price—primarily, greater ease of use—can be expected to result in an increase of use.

(c) More effectiveness in retrieval systems should also help since that should increase the benefit. Yet, caution is in order since use will follow perceptions of cost-effectiveness as perceived by the user. (Because we are discussing use, we deliberately listed ease ahead of effectiveness.)

Some of the price (effort) can be reduced by using a competent intermediary (a reference librarian or information specialist). However, it is easily overlooked that using an intermediary may increase the price somewhat unless the user trusts and is accustomed to using the intermediary. Otherwise, for most people, a psychological effort and a change of habit—hence, a price—may be involved in asking for help. The style and demeanor of the reference librarian can increase or decrease the perceived price involved. In this rather intangible area, the interpersonal skills of librarians become important. So also is instruction (formal or otherwise) in library skills. Major problems include the providing of motivation and the development of good enough instruction. In a university context, a favourable attitude by faculty in the students' area of study and arrangements for credit for bibliographical instruction to count toward their degree both help. Pitching the instruction at the correct level and relating the learning experience to the user's personal interest both appear to be important. Unfortunately, skill as a librarian does not, in and of itself, guarantee skill as an instructor.

7

Understanding Common Library Practices on Collection and Protection

> Books constitute capital. A library book lasts as long as a house, for hundreds of years. It is not, then, an article of mere consumption but fairly of capital, and often in the case of professional men, setting out in life, it is their only capital.
>
> — *Thomas Jefferson*

Every year libraries around the world expend large sums of money on information resources for their users. Most of that money goes to acquiring materials the library owns, although each year the amount spent on leased electronic resources increases substantially. A small percentage of material has a short useful (shelf) life and everyone knows this at the time of purchase. However, the vast majority of the acquisitions have a substantial, if not indefinite, expected shelf life.

To realize a long-term shelf life, the staff must take steps to preserve the material. A major premise of this book is that collection development is the central function of collection management. However, collection management involves several other functions as well, including preservation and conservation of the collection. As there should be a concern for preservation and conservation throughout the collection development process, it is appropriate to place responsibility for preservation with the collection managers More and more libraries are placing preservation and binding under the direction of the chief collection development officer. There are several aspects to protecting the collection, including proper handling of materials, environmental control, security (to protect against theft and mutilation) and disaster preparedness planning, conservation (binding and preservation), and insurance. Most of these issues are broad concerns, and detailed discussion of them is beyond the scope of this book; however, this chapter briefly touches on each topic.

In a sense, all these factors work together to prolong the useful life of the materials in the collection. Even insurance fulfills this function, because claims payments help the library replace lost or damaged items. Problems of acidic paper have long been the major concern of those involved in conservation activities in the library. There is now a new challenge that may be more difficult to resolve than neutralizing the acid in paper. The challenge is electronic resources and their long-term preservation. We explore this issue later in the chapter. Two terms that we used in the preceding paragraphs are in common use, but have different meanings for different people. A 1998 article by Joseph Settanni addressed terminology definition issues. Settanni made the point that there is a hierarchy of activity in protection of collections: conservation to preservation to restoration. He defined *conservation* as "the overall or general attempt to prevent further damage and deterioration," and *preservation* as "the specific effort to not merely stop but reverse the various negative and unwanted effects of destructive chemical and other agents that can destroy." His definition of *restoration* is "the ideal goal of attempted reconstruction toward achieving the entire renovation of documents, artifacts, or physical structures to their original condition."

We take just a slightly broader view of the term *conservation*. If we were to modify Settanni's definition, it would be as follows: "attempt to prevent damage and deterioration, or further damage and deterioration." Essentially we see most "good housekeeping" practices as part of the conservation program. Our discussion starts with print materials and follows the conservation to preservation concept. (It is beyond the scope of this book to explore restoration in any detail.) In the last sections of this chapter we look at non-print and electronic resources.

Conservation

Proper Handling

Storage and handling are the two first steps in protecting a collection. Neither step requires extra expenditures on the part of the library. Libraries purchase storage units from time to time; the purchaser needs to give some thought to what is the most appropriate type of storage unit for the format. Too narrow and/or shallow a shelf will result in items being knocked off and damaged. Filling shelves and drawers too tightly is a poor practice. Equally harmful is allowing the material to fall over on the shelf (because proper supports are lacking) or slide around in a drawer, because either practice will lead to damage in time. Buying adjustable storage units provides the library a measure of flexibility. Anyone with extensive experience in shelving books (except a conservation specialist) probably has found a way to squeeze "just one more book" onto a shelf when good practice calls for shifting the material to provide proper space. This often happens when shelvers are under pressure to finish shelving a full book truck within a certain time period. Having sound performance standards is proper management; however, libraries must be certain that the shelving standard includes time for shifting materials.

Not factoring that in will result in cracked and damaged book spines, as well as torn headbands resulting from patrons' attempts to pull books out from a fully packed shelf. Books should be vertical or horizontal on the shelf, not leaning this way and that. Fore-edge shelving should be avoided because it places undue strain on the binding (which is designed for horizontal or vertical storage). Proper supports and bookends help to keep materials in good order. Poorly constructed or finished supports can be more damaging to materials than having none at all. Teaching people how to handle material properly is important. Training public service staff is an ongoing task; teaching proper handling techniques, if not already taught, will cost some time but will pay off in longer-lasting materials. One should make an effort to educate users in proper handling of materials as well.

Some librarians regard housekeeping issues as bad for the library's image. If the library effectively communicates the fact that monies spent on repair and replacement of materials damaged through improper handling ultimately means less money to buy new material, people will understand the importance of housekeeping. It does not take more than two or three items sent for rebinding to equal the cost of a new book. And, like everything else related to collection development, bindery fees are constantly increasing.

Environmental Control

Climate control in the library is essential to any successful conservation program. Few libraries are able to follow the example of the Newberry Library in Chicago, where a stack area 10 stories high is double-shelled, windowless, and monitored by a computerized environmental system. Something less complex, however, will still help extend the useful life of most materials. The major concerns for environmental control are humidity, temperature, and light. Architects and librarians should take these issues into account when planning a library building. This is often easier said than done, because the ideal environmental conditions for human comfort and for preserving materials don't match. For example, the design of the book stacks for the Newberry Library storage facility calls for a constant temperature of 60°F +/ 5°F.

Few people would be happy to engage in sedentary work all day in a room with a 60-degree temperature. Most library designs place human coin-fort ahead of material preservation. The only time designers can effectively meet both sets of requirements is in situations like the Newberry, where the stacks are closed to the public and even employees are in the stacks for only short periods. Still, this arrangement does not answer all concerns about the environment for preserving materials. There also are differences in the ideal conditions for preserving various types of materials. Thus, building design characteristics may present some problems for implementing a good conservation program.

Institutional emphasis on energy conservation can lead to cooler winter temperatures and warmer summer temperatures. Cooler winter temperatures are better for materials, but normally the temperature is still well above 65 degrees. The greatest damage occurs in summer, when reducing air conditioning costs becomes an institutional priority. (A related problem is that changes in air temperature affect relative humidity.) One way to reduce air conditioning costs is to turn off the system when the library is closed, but overnight shutdowns are damaging to materials. When the system is off for some time, such as the weekend, the temperature can rise dramatically. When the air conditioning is turned back on, the temperature falls fairly quickly. This “roller coaster” temperature swing is more damaging to materials than storing them at a steady, somewhat higher temperature. Temperature cycling is damaging (it ages paper prematurely), but so are high temperatures. For every rise of 10°C, book paper deteriorates twice as fast. With rapid fluctuations in temperature, the primary problem is the humidity level, which causes damage to the materials.

The Library of Congress Preservation Leaflet no. 2 recommends a temperature of 55°F in book storage areas and a maximum of 75°F (below 70°F, if possible) in reading areas, all with a 50 percent relative humidity. Paul Banks, a well-known preservation specialist who set the standards for the Newberry storage area, also recommended 50 percent relative humidity. For most libraries constructed after World War II, there is little chance of having temperature differentials in storage and reading areas, because the design concept called for integrating readers and materials. Also, in most libraries, the temperature and humidity range is much greater than +/– 5°F.

Why are conservationists concerned with humidity? Because changes in humidity can physically weaken materials, which, in turn, can create added costs for repair or replacement. Books (including bound periodicals) consist of a number of different materials-paper, cloth, cardboard, thread, man-made fabrics, adhesives, and sometimes metal (for example, staples). Often, a single book is made up of several different types of material from each category; for example, heavy endpapers, a moderate-weight paper for the text, and coated paper for illustrations. Each component absorbs and loses water vapor (humidity) at a different rate. Materials expand as they absorb moisture and shrink as the humidity falls. As the amount of water vapor in the air goes up or down, there is constant shrinking and swelling of the materials. With each expansion and contraction, the material weakens slightly. Overall, paper deterioration is the main problem with cycling. Humidity and heat combine to accelerate deterioration from paper acidity.

The differences in the rates of expansion and shrinkage for the different components in the book weaken the bonds between the components, making the book more likely to fall apart. (Humidity is also an issue with photographic materials.) Constant humidity stabilizes the materials. How much water vapor is normally present is important; paper fibers are subject to deterioration when humidity is somewhere below 40 percent. At 65 percent or higher, the chances of mildew and mold formation increase. The musty smell of the antiquarian bookshop may contain more than a hint of mildew or mold, something one does not want in the library.

Other materials (microfilms, videotapes, photographs, and so forth) have somewhat different ideal temperature and humidity storage requirements. The ideal range for microforms is 70°F +/– 50 with humidity at 40% +/– 5%. The same ranges apply to still photographs and safety motion picture film. In contrast, nitrate-based motion picture film must be stored below 55°F but can tolerate humidity up to 45 percent. Videotapes do best at 65°F +/– 5° and no more than 45 percent humidity. Audiodiscs (LPs, 45s, and so forth) can handle temperatures up to 75°F and 50 percent humidity. However, the upper limits for audiotapes are 70°F and 45 percent humidity.

The National Archives has set even higher standards for its new facility in College Park, Maryland. Text and map storage areas call for 70°F and 45 percent relative humidity. Black-and-white film, audiotapes, and sound recordings have a 65°F and 30 percent relative humidity limit. Glass negative, black-and-white photographs, slides, negatives, posters, and electronic materials will be in areas with 65°F temperature and 35 percent relative humidity. Storage areas for color photography film, slides, and photographs will be still cooler—38°F and 35 percent relative humidity. Coldest of all will be storage areas for color motion picture film and color serial film, at 25°F and 30 percent relative humidity.

Recalling basic chemistry, we know that increasing the temperature also increases chemical activity. Roughly, chemical reactions double with each 10°C increase in temperature. Freezing books would be the best way to preserve them; however, it is not likely that readers would be willing to sit about in earmuffs, overcoats, and mittens. One is fortunate to achieve a controlled temperature below 70°F in areas where people work for extended periods. One reason for wanting the lower temperatures is to slow down the chemical decomposition of wood pulp paper, which the majority of books and journals contain. However, lower temperatures only slow the process; they do not stop it. All formats are sensitive to temperature variations, and the ideal storage condition is an environment with minimal changes.

Lighting, both natural and artificial, influences conservation in two ways. First, it contributes to the heat buildup in a building. Naturally, designers take this into account when specifying the building's heating, ventilating, and air conditioning system. Fluorescent lighting is not a major heat contributor, but in older libraries where incandescent fixtures exist, the heat generated by the fixtures can be a problem. If the light fixtures are close to materials (i.e., in exhibit cases), there can be significant temperature differentials from the bottom to the top shelf in a storage unit. Windows and sunlight generate heat as well, and they create mini-climates. The Newberry Library's windowless storage unit eliminates the sunlight problem. Many libraries have designs featuring numerous windows to provide natural lighting (thus reducing electric costs) and to satisfy users' desire to see outside. The cost of these designs has been high in terms of money spent after a few years to reduce the sunlight problem and to repair damaged materials.

The second concern is ultraviolet radiation, a result of sunlight, fluorescent, and tungsten lights. Ultraviolet light is the most damaging form of light because it quickly causes materials to fade, turn yellow, and become brittle. Windows and fluorescent light fixtures should have ultraviolet screens or filters built in or installed. Tungsten lighting has the lowest levels of ultraviolet radiation, but even these lights should have filters. The longer one exposes materials to unfiltered light, the more quickly damage occurs. Nonprint materials are even more sensitive and they require greater protective measures than do print materials.

Air filters that reduce the gases in the air inside the library are useful, if expensive. Urban activities pump a variety of harmful gases into the air every day. Some enter the building as people come and go.

Few buildings have airlocks and ventilating systems that remove all harmful gases. Whenever it is economical, the ventilation system should remove the most harmful substances. Sulfur dioxide is a major air pollutant and a concern for library conservation programs, because it combines with water vapor to form sulfuric acid. Hydrogen sulfide, another common pollutant, also forms an acid that is harmful to both organic and inorganic materials. In addition to gases, air filters can also reduce the amount of solid particles contained in the building air. Dust and dirt include mold spores, which can cause problems if the air conditioning fails in warm, humid weather. Solid particles act as abrasives, contributing to the wearing out and wearing down of materials. Dusty, gritty shelves wear away the edges of bindings-and, all too often, dusting book shelves is not in anyone's job description.

Mold can be a serious problem for paper-based collections and people as well. For example, *Aspergillas furnigatus* can be toxic, in sufficient quantities, and many molds can cause serious (even debilitating) allergy problems for some people. A good source of information about controlling mold is the Northeast Document Conservation Center's "Technical Leaflet: Protecting Books and Paper Against Mold" (<http://www.nedcc.org/mold.htm>).

Finally, insects contribute to the destruction of books and other items in the collection. Silverfish enjoy nothing more than a feast of wood pulp paper, flour paste, and glue. Cockroaches seem to eat anything, but have a particular taste for book glue. Termites prefer wood, but wood pulp paper is a good second choice. Larder beetle larvae (book worms), though lacking intellectual curiosity, can devour *War and Peace* in a short time. Finally, book lice enjoy the starch and gelatin sizing on paper. Other, less destructive insects can infest collections in the temperate zones; in a tropical setting, the numbers and varieties increase dramatically. Control of insects presents a few challenges, because pesticides create pollution problems. Naturally, the best control is to keep the insects out. One way to control insects, especially cockroaches, is to keep food and drink out of the library. A second step is to keep the temperature and humidity as low as possible, because insects multiply faster and are more active at higher temperature and humidity levels. If the library faces a significant insect infestation, it is better to call on a commercial service rather than attempt to handle the problem with library staff.

What are the signs of insect infestation? Most of the insects that cause damage prefer the dark and to stay out of sight. When one sees them, it is a signal that the population may be so large that there is nowhere to hide. Obviously, if one finds "remains" of insects on shelves, windowsills, or the floor, it is a sign of potential trouble. Unusual dust, "sawdust," or colored powder on bookshelves is likely to be "frass" (insect droppings), and is a clear indication of a problem. A good source of information about pest management in libraries and archives is Chicora Foundation, Inc.'s *Managing: Pest in Your Collection* (<http://palimpsest.stanford.edu/byorg/chicora/chicpest.html>).

Gifts to the library require careful examination before being stored in any area where insects could get into the general collection. Shipments that arrive by sea mail also need careful study. As the concern for the environment increases, many in-library fumigation units have ceased to operate or been extensively (and expensively) modified. This may mean using commercial systems, with additional costs and delays in getting and keeping material on the shelf.

Security

We include physical security of the collection in our discussion of conservation because some of the issues are conservation issues-for example, mutilation and water/smoke damage.

A full library security program involves several elements. Broadly, the program's goals are to assure the well-being of people and to protect the collections and equipment from theft and misuse. This discussion emphasizes the collections, with only passing mention of the people and equipment issues; topics covered include theft, mutilation, and disaster preparedness. (For a fuller discussion of security programs, see chapter 14 in *Introduction to Library Public Services*, 5th edition.)

We tell people, only half in jest, that if a library wishes to identify its true core collection, all it has to do is prepare a list of all the lost and missing books and mutilated journal titles. Normally, these are the items that, for one reason or another, are (or were) under pressure from users, including high-use or, in the case of missing books, potentially high-use materials.

Every library loses books each year to individuals who, if caught by the security system, say they forgot to check the material out. Journals and other noncirculating material are subject to some degree of mutilation. Each incident of theft and mutilation means some small financial loss for the library, if nothing more than the cost of the material and the labor expended to make the item available. Other costs are the cost of staff time to search for the item, to decide how or whether to replace it, plus actual replacement and processing costs. Though a single incident seldom represents a significant cost, the total annual cost may be surprising, even if one calculates only the amount paid for replacement materials. The Loyola Marymount University library spends about $10,000 per year on replacement materials, and few of those replacements are for items that have become too worn to remain in circulation. This rate of loss occurs despite a high-quality electronic security exit system and targeting every book and every issue of every journal that goes into the collection. Needless to say, time and money expended to prevent theft or replace materials is time and money not spent on expanding the resources available to customers.

There are several givens to any security program. First, there will be some level of loss no matter what the library does. Second, the systems help basically honest people stay honest. A professional thief will circumvent almost any library security system, as Stephen Blumberg and David Siegelman demonstrated a few years ago. Therefore, the library must decide how important the problem is and how much loss it can tolerate. The goal is to balance the cost of the security program against the losses. The less loss the library will accept, the higher the security costs, so finding the proper balance is important.

Most libraries employ some mix of people-based elements and electronic systems for security. Door guards or monitors who check every item taken from the library are the most effective and most costly option. This method works well only when the person doing the checking is not a peer of the people being checked. That is, using students to check fellow students, much less their teachers, does not work well. Retired individuals are very effective. They interact well with users but also do the job without favouring anyone. The major drawback to exit monitors, after the cost, is, when there are peaks and valleys in the exit flow, there can be long queues during the peaks.

Electronic systems are common and may give a false sense of security. Every system has a weakness that the person who regularly "forgets to check out books" eventually discovers, and the professional thief knows. Also, some materials (for example, magnetic tape and videotape) cannot have the "target" deactivated without damaging the content, and some materials simply do not have a place for a target. Such systems are susceptible to electronic interference, such as frequencies generated by computers or even fluorescent light ballasts. Finally, the inventive thief can jam the operating frequency and no one on the staff will know the difference.

Mutilation is another ongoing problem, which, during a year, can generate a surprisingly large loss for the library. There are few cost-effective options for handling this problem. Having copy services available and at competitive prices will help. Monitors walking through the building will solve or reduce many other security problems, but will do little to stop mutilation. Studies suggest that even customers who see someone mutilating library materials will not report the activity to library staff. One option that customers do not like, but that does stop the mutilation of journals, is to supply only microform backfiles of journals that are subject to high mutilation. This option does not safeguard the current issues, and it requires providing microform reader-printers, which are more expensive than microform readers. There is also the occasional title that does not make its backfiles available in a microformat. Full-text CD-ROMs or Web-based services are a partial answer to some of the problems, because there is little user resistance to electronic material. However, if the person is seeking a color photograph or any color image there may still be a problem, especially if the library does not provide color printing or copier service.

Another option is to acquire multiple copies of high-use titles. Here again, one trades some collection breadth for a possible reduction in mutilation. Theft and mutilation are a part of doing business. How much they cost the library depends on the local situation. Those costs come at the expense of adding greater variety to the collections and, in the long run, they hurt the customer. Disaster preparedness planning is vital for the protection of people, collections, and equipment. Planners must think in terms of both natural and man-made disasters. Earthquakes, hurricanes, tornadoes, heavy rains, and floods are the most common natural disasters for which one should plan. The most common man-made disaster is water damage, which can be caused by a broken water pipe or sprinkler head, a faulty air conditioning system, or broken windows. In the case of a fire, water may cause more damage than the flames.

The following are the basic steps to take in preparing a disaster plan:

1. Study the library for potential problems. Often, the institution's risk management officer (insurance) is more than willing to help in that assessment.
2. Meet with local fire and safety officers for the same purpose.
3. Establish a planning team to develop a plan. This team may become the disaster handling team.
4. Establish procedures for handling each type of disaster and, if appropriate, form different teams to handle each situation.
5. Establish a telephone calling tree, or other fast notification system, for each disaster. A telephone tree is a plan for who calls whom in what order.

6. Develop a salvage priority list for the collections. If necessary, mark a set of floor plans and include them in the disaster planning and response manual. Most plans do not have more than three levels of priority: first priority is irreplaceable or costly materials, second priority is materials that are expensive or difficult to replace, and third priority is the rest of the collection. The LMU plan includes a category for hand-carrying one or two items from the immediate work area, if the disaster strikes during normal working hours. Establishing priorities can be a challenge for planners, because everyone has some vested interest in the subject areas with which they work.
7. Develop a list of recovery supplies the library will maintain on site (for example, plastic sheeting and butcher paper).
8. Include a list of resources-people and companies-who may assist in the recovery work.

Needless to say, after the planners finish the disaster plan, the library must put copies in the hands of each department and in the homes of the disaster team. It is also important to practice some of the procedures before disaster strikes. The LMU plan has been in place since 1991 and has been used three times, twice for water problems and once for an earthquake. With the water problems, the library was able to save all but eight books out of more than 15,000 that got wet. Had the staff not practiced its disaster response plan ahead of time, the loss rate would have been much higher. The library did not fare as well in the earthquake, because it is impossible to practice having book stacks collapse. Though LMU certainly fared better than libraries closer to the epicenter, it lost 1,237 books. Unfortunately, these losses could have been avoided if the shelving had been properly braced. The library staff knew where the problem stacks were and was waiting for funds to have the stacks retrofitted; however, the earthquake was quicker than the funding authorities.

Locating water, gas, and electrical system shut-offs is a good starting point for training the disaster team. Next, the team should check fire extinguisher locations to determine whether the units are operational and are inspected regularly. The team also should implement a program to train staff in use of the extinguishers. Usually, the local fire department will do this at no charge. There are three types of fire extinguishers: "A" for wood and paper fires, "B" for oil and electrical fires, and "C" for either type of fire. Match type to location and anticipated problems. Prepare floor plans, clearly identifying locations of shut-offs and extinguishers.

Salvage operations require careful planning and adequate personnel and materials. It is a good idea to develop a list of potential volunteers if the situation is too large for the staff to handle within a reasonable time. Keep in mind that the library can count on only about 72 hours of assistance from volunteers—that is, 72 hours from the time the first request for assistance goes out. Thus, there should be planning for what to do after 72 hours, if the disaster is major.

Water damage is a potentially destructive problem, as is the development of mold and mildew. Mold can develop in as little as 48 hours, depending on the temperature. What basic steps should one follow in a water emergency? The best way to handle large quantities of water-soaked paper is to freeze it and process the material as time and money allow. Planners should identify companies with large freezer facilities and discuss with them the possibility of using or renting their freezers in case of emergency. Often, such companies are willing to do this at no cost, because of the good publicity they gain from such generosity. Large grocery store chains and meat packing plants are possible participants. Refrigerated trucks can be most useful, if costly to rent. Getting wet materials to the freezing units is a problem: milk crates, open plastic boxes, or clothes baskets work well, because they allow water to drain. Cardboard boxes absorb water. Plastic interlocking milk crates are ideal, because they are about the right size for a person to handle when three-fourths full of wet material. Sometimes, local dairies are willing to assist by supplying free crates for the duration of the emergency. Freezer or butcher paper is best for separating the materials; never use newsprint, because it tends to stick and the ink comes off. Finally, find some drying facilities. There are three primary methods of drying wet books: (1) freezing freeze-drying, (2) vacuum drying, and (3) vacuum freeze-drying. Vacuum freeze-drying is the best way to handle wet items. Often, vacuum drying facilities are difficult to locate and can handle only a small volume of material at a time, so materials may be in the freezer for a long time while a small quantity is done whenever the source and funding permit. A variety of disaster-related online information, including Peter Waters's *Procedures for Salvage of Water-Damaged Library Materials*, is available from Conservation OnLine (CoOL, <http://palimpsest.stanford.edu>).

Two other steps are important when designing a disaster preparedness plan. One is to identify the nearest conservation specialist(s). Most are willing to serve as a telephone resource, and often they will come to the scene. A second important step is to arrange for special purchasing power. Although some groups, organizations, and companies may be willing to assist free of charge, many will not, and the library may need to commit quickly to a specific expense. Having to wait even a few hours for approval may cause irreversible damage.

Although most disasters are minor—a few hundred water-damaged items-a large disaster is always possible. One example was the April 1986 fire that struck the Los Angeles Public Library. For more than 10 years, there had been concern about the fire danger, but the hope that a new building would be constructed forestalled major modifications in the existing building. According to *Library Hotline*, it took 1,700 volunteers working around the clock to shrink-wrap and freeze the 400,000 water-soaked books (about 20 percent of the Central Library's collection). In addition, the city paid a salvage contractor $500,000 for his firm's services. One can only speculate what the costs and problems might have been with no disaster preparedness plan.

Preservation

By having the collection properly stored and handled in a controlled climate, and with sound security practices as well as a disaster preparedness plan in place, the library will lengthen the useful life of its materials and reduce preservation problems. However, if the library fails to employ good preservation methods, much of what it gains from those practices will be lost as items fade, decompose, or become unusable. Conservation should start with the purchase decision (which ought to include consideration of how well the material will stand up to the expected use) and should end with the question of what to do about worn, damaged materials and items identified in the weeding process.

One element in a library's conservation program is the basic binding and repair program. In-house repairs are fine as long as they employ good conservation methods and use materials that will not cause more harm. Repairers should do nothing that cannot be undone later, if necessary. For example, one should avoid using any adhesive tape other than a reversible adhesive, nonacidic tape to repair a torn page.

Most commercial binderies follow sound practices and employ materials that will not add to an already serious problem of decomposing books. An excellent overview of library binding practices, in a commercial setting, is Paul Parisi's "An Overview of Library Binding." Selecting a commercial binder should involve the chief collection officer, if the bindery operation is not under the supervision of that person. Most libraries spend thousands of dollars on bindery and repair work each year, and having a reliable and efficient binder, who uses the proper materials, benefits the library and its customers. Knowing something about bindery operations and the process the materials undergo can help the library staff responsible for selecting materials for binding to make better judgments about the type of- binding to order, given the probable use of the material. Most commercial binders are pleased to explain their operations and give customers and new library employees tours of their plant.

At present, the source of many conservation and preservation problems is acidic wood pulp paper. William J. Barrow is the person most often associated with identifying acid as the cause of the deterioration of wood pulp paper. The problem is not new, but people are now seeing the full implications of the findings of Barrow and other researchers. Estimates vary as to just how big the problem is. One project estimated that there were more than 600,000 brittle or moderately brittle books in a collection of 2 million books in the UCLA library system in 1979. *(A brittle book* is one in which a corner of a page breaks off when folded back and forth two or fewer times.) The estimate was based on a random sample of books in the collection. An estimated 1 million volumes in Widener Library (Harvard University) are in similar condition. In the early 1980s, the Library of Congress estimated that it had 6 million brittle volumes." According to Richard Dougherty, the Commission on Preservation and Access estimated that more than 25 percent of the world's greatest monographic collections are already embrittled beyond redemption." The problem grows with each passing day and nothing is done to stop the process. Unfortunately, few libraries have sufficient funding to do more than address a small percentage of the items needing attention.

Deanna Marcum published a short article in the *New York* Times in 1998 about the ever-growing problem of preservation. She outlined the stark facts and made a strong case that technology may be a greater problem than acidic paper. In the article, she noted that the U.S. National Archivist had advised government agencies that they "could delete certain computer files *if they kept paper copies*" (emphasis added). She also noted that the acidic paper issue was still a problem.

In the case of brittle books, short fibers and chemical residues from the paper manufacturing process are the culprits. The longer the fibers in the paper, the stronger it is. When ground wood pulp became the standard source for paper manufacturing, the long-term strength of paper dropped sharply. A weak paper combined with the acidic residue from sizing and bleaching, as well as lignin (a component of the wood used for paper), creates self-destructing material. At one end of the scale is newsprint, which is very acidic; at the other end is the nonacidic paper that more and more publishers are using in books. The Council on Library Resources' efforts to establish some guidelines for publishers, manufacturers, and librarians regarding the use of alkaline paper in book production are paying off. The CLR report stated that "alkaline paper *need not be more expensive* than acidic paper of the quality normally used in hardbound books."

The guidelines provide standards for both performance (acid content) and durability (folding and bending), as well as long-term book binding for the initial commercial binding. Though the guidelines will reduce future problems, they cannot help the present situation. Each year, the number of brittle items already in the collection increases. What can be done about materials that are self-destructing in the stacks? Maintaining environmental factors (temperature, humidity, and light) at the recommended levels slows the chemical processes; thus, this is a first step to take. For the already-brittle materials in the collection, the two concerns are permanence (shelf life) and durability (use). Permanence is the first issue, and there are several ways to stop the acidic activity. After the acidic action is under control, several options exist to enhance durability.

Several mass deacidification systems on the market are designed to process large numbers of books at one time. The only one with a reasonably long history of use is the Wei T'o process developed by Richard Smith. Probably the second best known system is the DEZ system. Developed with the support of the Library of Congress, the process received widespread press coverage after it encountered several problems, the most notable being an explosion at the test site. A good review of the history of deacidification systems is found in Michale V. Cloonan's "Mass Deacidification in the 1990s."

Options for Handling Brittle Materials

Given the magnitude of the acid paper problem, almost every library will be faced with a variety of decisions on what to do. Here, if nowhere else, collection development staff must enter the preservation picture. When an item in the collection deteriorates to the point that it cannot be rebound, what should one do? Ten options exist:

- Ignore the problem and return the item to storage.
- Withdraw the item from the collection and do not replace it.
- Seek a reprint edition on alkaline paper.
- Convert the material to microfilm and decide what to do with the original.
- Convert the material to an electronic format.
- Photocopy the material on alkaline paper and decide what to do with the original.
- Seek a replacement copy through the out-of-print trade.

- Place it in an alkaline protective enclosure made for the item and return it to the collection.
- Withdraw the item from the main collection and place in a controlled access storage facility.
- Deacidify and strengthen the item and return it to use.

Ignoring the problem is the most reasonable alternative for materials about which one is confident that long-term retention is unnecessary or undesirable and only a limited amount of use is probable. If there is little or no probability of use in the near future, withdrawing the item is probably the most effective option.

Seeking a reprint edition printed on alkaline paper is the least expensive option for materials that are worth long-term storage and probably will experience moderate to heavy use. Reprints are not available for all the items that are self-destructing; only the high-demand titles are reprinted. Several companies exist to serve the reprint market, for example, AMS, Scholarly Reprints, Kraus, Harvester Press Microform Publications, and Research Publications. *Guide to Reprints* (Guide to Reprints, Inc.), *Books on Demand* (University Microfilms), and *Guide to Microforms in Print* (Microform Review) are three sources of information about a broad range of titles. (*Note*: Just because an item is a reprint does not mean that it is printed on alkaline paper. Be certain to specify alkaline paper when ordering.)

Microformat and electronic storage of the brittle material are other options. Until the mid-1980s, microfilming was the most common way of storing the content of brittle materials in a secondary format. The cost of making the master negative is high, but once made, duplicate copies are relatively inexpensive to produce. Thus, if the primary collection development concern is with preserving the intellectual content of the brittle material and not with the item as an artifact, a microformat is a good solution. It may be possible to locate a master copy of an item, thereby reducing costs. Two places to check are the *National Register of Microforms Masters* (Library of Congress) and *Guide to Microforms in Print* (Meckler). The *Register* covers more than 3,000 library and publisher holdings worldwide and is produced by the Library of Congress. *Guide to Microforms in Print* is similar to *BIP*; it lists titles from commercial publishers around the world.

The Directory of Library Reprographic Services (Meckler) can be of assistance in identifying libraries with the capability of making a master. The Library of Congress has the most experience in working with analog videodisc technology as a preservation format. The advantages of the technology are high-density storage (54,000 graphic images stored on one disc) and random access to those images. In contrast, optical discs are used to store print material. A disc can hold about 3,000 pages of text or 200,000 catalog cards. Both technologies have potential for assisting in solving preservation problems. As one might expect, there is a relatively high cost associated with these systems, but as more organizations use optical or analog disc technology, it is reasonable to expect the cost to decline. However, it is now clear that digitization does not necessarily translate into long-term preservation.

Some publishers (and even the Copyright Office) have questions about the legality of converting copyrighted material to a disc format: How this differs in principle from microfilming, which no one seems to question, is unclear. Under U.S. copyright law (§ 108(e)), it is legal for a library to make a single complete copy of an out-of-print item after making a reasonable search for the item.

A photocopy of the original may be the best option when the library anticipates moderate use and cannot locate a reprint. There are commercial firms that will produce a bound photocopy on alkaline paper from an individual volume on demand. This is an especially good alternative when it is not necessary to preserve the original item. Photocopying and microfilming cause physical wear on bound materials, and a bound item may have to be taken apart to be duplicated properly. Generally, in the photocopy process, there is some loss in image quality; obviously, this may not be acceptable for items with high-quality photographs and illustrations. Several paper manufacturers (for example, Hollinger, Process Materials, and Xerox) offer buffered (alkaline) paper for use in photocopy machines. When binding the photocopies, it is necessary to specify that the binder use buffered materials. If alkaline paper or deacidified paper comes into contact with acidic material, the acid will migrate into the alkaline paper and start the process all over again.

The staff should think carefully before going to the out-of-print market for replacement copies. Although a replacement copy may be available at the lowest price of any of the options, will the replacement be in any better condition than the one it is to replace? Unless the replacement copy had better storage conditions than the library's copy, both will be in about the same state of deterioration. It is probable that the replacement copy will be less worn (as long as it is not an ex-library copy), but there will be little difference in the acidic state. Normally, the replacement copy's storage history is worse than the library's copy, and thus the replacement copy will be in greater need of preservation. Locating a replacement copy in the out-of-print market will take months or even years. During the search, the library must decide what to do with the item in hand. If it is brittle, should customers continue to use it while the library is waiting for a replacement copy that may or may not exist? Additional use may make it difficult, or perhaps impossible, to exercise other options, if the library fails to find a replacement. Although the out-of-print market is a frequent first choice, it is probably the least suitable for long-term preservation purposes.

Protective enclosures or containers provide a stopgap treatment. Enclosing the brittle item in an alkaline container (made of paper, plastic, or cardboard) protects it from unnecessary handling and light. This is a common method of storage for the original (hopefully deacidified) item when a surrogate copy is available for general use. The most common approach is to make custom-sized phase boxes for the item using alkaline cardboard. Bindery/archival supply firms and commercial binderies offer a wide range of prefabricated standard-sized phase boxes, as well as materials for constructing custom-sized boxes. Unfortunately, the materials, including alkaline mending tapes and adhesives, are expensive. To save a small amount of money, some libraries decide not to use the proper materials. Certainly, there is no need to use expensive mending materials on items that the library is likely to discard in time, but, all too often, librarians do not know which items will be kept and which will be discarded.

Secondary storage is a stopgap measure in most cases. It may become the most common first option when the quantity of brittle materials escalates beyond the library's ability to handle it. A controlled environment with limited handling would slow the destructive process and buy some time to determine which of the more permanent solutions to implement. The essential element is controlling the storage environment; merely placing the materials in a remote storage area with the same or worse climate control accomplishes little and may cause further deterioration. Another danger of remote storage is that the adage "out of sight, out of mind" frequently applies. Without a preservation officer or someone on the staff charged with supervising preservation activities, the storage area can become a dumping ground for materials that no one wants to think about. Even in a controlled environment, the disintegration continues day and night until something is done to stop it.

The following are some basic guidelines for preparing materials for storage :

1. Remove extraneous materials, such as paper clips, rubber bands, wrapping material, old folders, and any other material that is

not pertinent. If foreign matter, such as pressed flowers, must be saved as documentary evidence, place it in a separate enclosure.

2. Unfold and flatten papers wherever possible without causing damage to the folds. If the paper is brittle or inflexible, it may have to be humidified before unfolding. Remove surface soil with a soft brush.

3. Isolate newsprint because it is highly acidic and will stain adjacent paper. Newspaper clippings can be replaced with photocopies on alkaline paper or placed in a separate envelope. Fax copies are similarly unstable and should be reproduced or isolated, unless they are plain-paper faxes.

4. Note any badly damaged items; place them within individual folders and set them aside for professional conservation treatment. Do not undertake any first aid unless you have received training and are qualified to do so.

5. If it is necessary to place identifying information on the object itself, use a soft (no. 2) pencil and write on the verso or in the lower right margin. Repeat the identification on the storage folders and envelopes in pencil or typing. Never use ballpoint or felt-tip pens that might stain or bleed.

6. Identify boxes with labels that contain adequate information about the contents. This curtails unnecessary browsing and rifling through documents.

If materials should be humidified (see step 2), consult Mary Lynn Ritzen-thaler's *Preserving Archives and Manuscripts*.

Restoration is expensive, and libraries will never be able to restore all or even most of the brittle items they own. As noted earlier, the deacidification process is also expensive, and added to that are costs of restoring strength to the individual pages and binding. For a good description of the advantages and disadvantages of the various methods of preservation, see Robert Mareck's "Practicum on Preservation Selection."

To end this section on an upbeat note, in 1996 the Library of Congress (LC) began a major program to deacidify books in its collection. Prior to 1996 LC had a series of evaluation programs, one of which led to the destruction of its test facility in 1986. Between 1996 and 1998, more than 100,000 books had gone through the process, and Congress authorized a contract through October 2001 that will involve another 275,000 volumes. For additional information about the program, check <http://cweb.loc.gov/perserv/>.

Nonpaper Preservation Issues

Although this chapter emphasizes books and paper, other library materials also require conservation and preservation. In many cases, librarians, as well as technicians, do not fully understand how long a format may last without loss of information, or what problems may arise. However, various groups, such as the Council on Library Resources (CLR), the Mellon Foundation, and the National Endowment for the Humanities, are actively exploring the issue.

Like paper products, all photographic products (microfilm, photographs, motion picture films) are self-destructing on the shelves and in the cabinets of libraries and archives. There was some hope that electronic technologies would prove a more stable storage medium for older materials, but little testing has been done on their longevity. Already we know that there are serious concerns about the long-term value of digitization of print materials. The Library of Congress is using analog videodiscs to store images from old glass lantern slides, photographs, motion picture publicity stills, and architectural drawings.

Current estimates are that CD-ROMs will have a 30-year life. This may not be a major problem, because one can restore digital information. How ever, no one can predict what it will cost to periodically check the data and restore it as necessary. One major question is who will be responsible and have the necessary funding to carry out the work.

A 1998 article in *U.S. News & World Report* had a title that sums up current concerns about electronic data: "Whoops, There Goes Another CD-ROM." The author of the article described the frustration of NASA's Jet Propulsion Laboratory scientists when, in 1996, they tried to read magnetic data from the 1976 Viking Mars mission. What they found was that 10 to 20 percent of the data was missing-this in spite of the fact that the laboratory had tried to maintain the tapes according to "standard guidelines."

Anyone who has been a computer user for more than a few years knows something of the problem. Just try opening a word processing document that was created two or more versions before the current version, one that had not been opened in later versions. Even when one does open all the old documents in the newer version, one usually sees a warning message about the danger of possible loss of formatting and other information. Though the loss due to the migration from one version to the next may be small, the cumulative loss over 10 or more versions could be significant. Given the speed with which software and hardware companies "improve" their products, it does not require too many years to reach potentially troubling losses.

Gerd Meissner wrote an article for the *New York Times* about problems in preserving data in the German Federal Archives. In that piece he touched on many of the problems. "While shellac records or damaged microfilms can still be put to use today, one faulty data bit on a 10-year-old magnetic tape or a scratched optical disk often renders the rest of the stored information useless." Tracking down documentation, even from the company that produced the software or hardware, for old versions is difficult and sometimes impossible.

One of this book's authors had first-hand experience with the problem of digitized data and "long-term" preservation. LMU's campus has been growing in size over the last 20 years. The university acquired 20 acres of vacant land adjacent to the campus. Environmental impact reports are now part of any development plan. During part of the assessment, it was determined that there were at least two archeological sites within the boundaries of the projected campus expansion. Thus, in 1984 archeological field work was undertaken to assess the scope, character, and significance of the sites. More than five tons of material were carefully mapped, collected, and recorded. Each item had a unique (accession) number that would, in conjunction with the field notes, place the object vertically and horizontally in relation to all the other objects, as well as the surrounding matrix, the firm doing the work used an aging Tandy computer to generate the paper report (one copy) and "stored" the floppy disks.

Lacking an anthropology or archeology department, the paper copy of the report was handed over to various people in the university's facilities planning unit. In 1996, Dr. Evans was asked to develop a plan for handling the tons of material stored in the facilities and maintenance warehouse. Upon reading the narrative report, it became clear that there should be at least one more paper document-the list of accession numbers and the provenance data. Without that data, the five tons of cultural material were really just so much junk, from a research point of view. No one knew, or even remembered, a second volume being part of the file. A call to the archeological firm confirmed that there should be a very large second, or perhaps three or four, volume(s). The call also confirmed that the only other source was the old Tandy floppies, and they had no idea of where one could find a Tandy machine capable of reading the files. When Dr. Evans and some members of the local Native American community suggested, in light of the problem, that the material be reburied, the archeological firm began what turned out to be a 28-month effort to find a way to retrieve the data. We have no idea how much it cost the firm to recover the data, but in November 1998 they delivered four large volumes with the information. (Today, all the original volumes are in the LMU library's Archives and Special Collections department.)

The NASA Jet Propulsion Laboratory, the German Federal Archives, and LMU cases are just a sample of the problems that can arise with electronic data, and serve as cautionary examples of the dangers in committing to digitization as the preservation solution. We have doubts about the effectiveness of digitization-"long-term" in the preceding cases was less than 25 years. We agree with Roy Tennant's assessment: "Digital libraries are sitting on a time bomb. Yes, libraries are already familiar with deteriorating materials, but digital libraries face an even graver threat."

Librarians do have some recommended guidelines for checking some of these special formats. Staff should inspect and rewind motion picture film once every three years, inspect and rewind videotapes and audiotapes every two years, and inspect still photographs every three years. Peter Graham's paper dealing with electronic preservation is an excellent source if information about the issues related to preserving intellectual content in an electronic environment. The Commission on Preservation and Access published a mission and goals statement for digital consortia that should help resolve some of the unanswered questions about digitized data and long-term retention. The goals are :

1. Verify and monitor the usefulness of digital imagery for preservation and access.
   a. Establish the convertibility of preservation media.
   b. Foster projects to capture special types of documents.
   c. Insure the longevity of digitized images.
   d. Cultivate research on the application of intelligent character recognition.
2. Define and promote shared methods and standards.
   a. Sponsor forums to define production quality standards.
   b. Promote the development and use of the document structure file.
   c. Create appropriate bibliographic control standards.
   d. Address copyright issues.
   e. Organize a document interchange project.
3. Enlarge the base of materials.
   a. Encourage the involvement of service bureaus.

   b. Focus on the conversion of thematically related materials.

   c. Mount a large inter-institutional collaborative project.

4. Develop and maintain reliable and affordable mechanisms to gain access to digital image documents.

   a. Involve a broad base of constituents in technology development.

   b. Forge effective support structures for end users.

   c. Determine the efficacy of access to digital materials in the context of traditional library collections.

These goals are very similar to those for the paper preservation efforts that started almost 10 years ago. If these goals are as successful as the earlier ones, there is reason to think that the profession will resolve the digital preservation problems in time to save at least many valuable materials.

Cooperation

Because of the magnitude of the problems confronting libraries and scholars, it seems clear that cooperative preservation is essential. In the mid-1980s, under the leadership of CRL, the profession created the Commission on Preservation and Access. Two groups, ARL and RLG, have been collecting statistics on research library preservation activities and developing guidelines. The National Endowment for the Humanities has provided funding for microfilming projects. A program for educating preservation librarians was started at the Columbia University Library School; after that school closed, the preservation program was transferred to the University of Texas Library School. Many large libraries are hiring full-time preservation specialists. Two newsletters that allow one to keep up to date on conservation matters are *The Abbey Newsletter* (7105 Geneva Drive, Austin TX 78723) and *CAN: Conservation Administration News* (Graduate School of Library and Information Science, University of Texas, Austin, TX 78712). The American Institute for Conservation of Historic and Artistic Works (AIC) provides a forum for concerned individuals to discuss preservation and conservation issues. Naturally, ALA and many of its divisions have an active interest in this area, as do most other library associations around the world. One online source of information is Conservation OnLine (CoOL). We list some additional Websites at the end of this chapter.

In addition to national efforts, several regional preservation cooperatives exist. One such group project is the University Center of Georgia. This group started by educating staff members and raising awareness of preservation issues and concerns and what to do to help reduce the problems. The group's operating premises reflect the message this chapter attempts to convey :

> There are some areas in preservation that do not require a team of experts. Self-reliance should be developed in these areas. One area in which this could be done is basic housekeeping.
>
> Prevention is more cost-effective than treatment. Prevention will be stressed as a priority. (For example, preservation thinking will be built into the collection building process.)
>
> Preservation is an ongoing activity that is part of normal work flow. Awareness of this, and a sense of individual responsibility, will be fostered. (Again, this emphasizes the basic activities each staff [member] can perform that will help protect the collections.)
>
> Library and archival collections represent an investment that preservation can protect. (Preservation is an essential function, like cataloging or acquisitions, and should be funded as such.)
>
> Low-cost preservation activities are possible and desirable, but no-cost preservation is unrealistic.

Another example of a regional cooperative is MAPS (MicrogrAphic Preservation Service), a service established by Columbia, Cornell, and Princeton, the New York Public Library, and the New York State Library.

MAPS' focus is to assist libraries, archives, museums, and historical societies prepare their preservation microfilm for the digital present and future.... To simply reformat endangered materials into a form resistant to scanning or one that complicates scanning is a serious disservice to scholars and researchers of the future.

Efforts like these will help solve future preservation problems. All library professionals should do their part to avoid adding to these problems.

Insurance

Careful planning, proper handling, and the other elements discussed in this chapter will help prolong the useful life of collections. A good disaster preparedness plan will help reduce the scope of loss when disaster strikes. Because the odds are rather high that a disaster will strike eventually, where will the library get the funds to replace the materials damaged beyond salvaging? In fact, where will the library get the funds to salvage what it can? The obvious answer is some type of insurance. The section on developing a disaster preparedness plan suggests that one early contact for the planning team should be the institution's risk manager. This is the person who monitors safety conditions in the workplace and oversees the insurance programs that cover various loss situations, from fires to slippery floors to actions of the institutional officers. The risk manager for LMU visits the library once a year to discuss any new or outstanding problems, as well as to review the values assigned to the collections, equipment, and building.

The LMU risk manager and library staff have discussed and clarified the fact that there will be insurance coverage for salvage operations, after the institution's deductible limit is surpassed. Discussions regarding the collection valuation have been interesting, especially when it comes to what to do about coverage for special collections and archives materials. If a Shakespeare folio is stolen or destroyed by fire, it is highly unlikely that the library could ever replace it, even if the library insured each folio for several million dollars. The risk manager sees no point in paying an extra premium for something that cannot be replaced. That moved the discussion to facsimile works and the appropriateness of replacing an original with a top-of-the-line facsimile. To date, this is a topic of ongoing debate. Anyone who has dealt with homeowners' or renters' insurance representatives and policies can understand the complexities involved. Does the collection valuation increase or decrease over time? What does *replacement* mean? Will there be funds to process the material, or merely to acquire it? What damage is covered? In 1989, 12 ranges of shelving containing 20,000 volumes collapsed at the Colombia University library annex. Many, if not most, of the volumes were brittle, so the fall was very damaging. However, the embrittlement was a preexisting condition. After some long negotiations, the insurer agreed to pay for volumes with damage to the cover or text block attachments, but not for volumes with broken pages. There were questions about serial runs as well; this was finally resolved with the insurer paying for the entire run of backflles, if more than one-third of the run was damaged.

A relatively recent and major disaster took place in late July 1997 at Colorado State University. After an unusually heavy rainstorm, major flooding occurred on the campus, with much of the water damming up against the wall of the lower level of the library. The wall collapsed as result of the water pressure and a huge wave of water poured into the building. All of the materials on the lower level became water-soaked; more than 500,000 items, with an estimated value of more than $100 million. Recovery was still under way in 1999. Although insurance helped cover some of the costs, the final recovery was being assisted by donations of materials from libraries and publishers.

Working out reasonable arrangements in advance, such as who pays for salvage work, will reduce the pressure on everyone during a disaster. One cannot anticipate everything, but some issues are bound to arise, and, to the extent one can deal with those concerns ahead of time, there will be fewer distractions during recovery operations. Another element that bears predisaster discussion is how to value the collection. One common way is to use averages, such as one finds in *The Bowker Annual*, and multiply that figure by the number of units held. The problem with that approach, as was noted in an unsigned Lomment on the collection development listserv, is that local circumstances also determine the value of an item; "a single volume of *JAMA* from 1952 is probably worth $2.00, but as part of a set that is missing from 1952, it's worth $500!"

For a good discussion about replacement, actual cash value, average replacement cost, valuable papers, and records coverage, as well as other basic insurance topics and libraries, see Judith Fortson's "Disaster Planning: Managing the Financial Risk." Having insurance is a sound practice, because almost every library at some time will have a disaster of some type and size. Having insurance is one more step in protecting the library's and institution's investment.

Conclusion

This chapter highlights the many aspects of protecting the collections on which libraries and information centers expend large sums of money. Many of the issues raised are ones that virtually any library staff member can implement without major changes in duties or in training. Preparing for trouble always makes it easier to handle the trouble when, or if, it happens. Knowing what type of financial help one can expect to assist in recovering from a disaster can provide some peace of mind, if nothing else. Long-term preservation, though the primary responsibility of the large libraries, is also a concern, or should be, of all libraries and information centers. Working together, we will solve preservation problems, even if it takes a long time and great effort.

8

Analyzing the Role of Select Library Professionals in Library Organization

> Organization doesn't really accomplish anything. Plans don't accomplish anything, either. Theories of management don't much matter. Endeavors succeed or fail because of the people involved. Only by attracting the best people will you accomplish great deeds.
>
> —*Colin Powell*

ROLE OF THE LIBRARIAN

A librarian is the key functionary of any library. He is the chief of library organization. A librarian is various known as chief librarian, Director of library are. A librarian is an information professional trained in library and information science, which is the organization and management of information services or materials for those with information needs. Typically, librarians work in a public or college library, an elementary or secondary school media center, a library within a business or company, or another information-provision agency. Some librarians are independent entrepreneurs working as information specialists, catalogers, indexers and other professional, specialized capacities. Librarians may be categorized as a public, school, correctional, special, independent or academic librarian.

Traditionally, librarians have been associated with collections of books, as demonstrated by the etymology of the word "librarian" (Latin *liber*, 'book'). However, modern librarians deal with information in many formats, including books, magazines, newspapers, audio recordings (both musical and spoken-word), video recordings, maps, manuscripts, photographs and other graphic material, bibliographic databases, web searching, and digital resources. Librarians often provide other information services, including computer provision and training, coordination of public programmes, basic literacy education, assistive equipment for people with disabilities, and help with finding and using community resources.

Librarian Roles and Duties

Specific duties vary depending on the size and type of library. Olivia Crosby described librarians as "Information experts in the information age". Most librarians spend their time working in one of the following areas of a library:

1. *Public service librarians* work with the public, frequently at the reference desk of lending libraries. Some specialize in serving adults or children. Children's librarians provide appropriate material for children at all age levels, include pre-readers, conduct specialized programmes and work with the children (and often their parents) to help foster interest and competence in the young reader. (In larger libraries, some specialize in teen services, periodicals, or other special collections.)
2. *Technical service librarians* work "behind the scenes" ordering library materials and database subscriptions, computers and other equipment, and supervise the Cataloguing and physical processing of new materials.
3. *Reference or research librarians* help people doing research to find the information they need, through a structured conversation called a reference interview. The help may take the form of research on a specific question, providing direction on the use of databases and other electronic information resources; obtaining specialized materials from other sources; or providing access to and care of delicate or expensive materials. These services are sometimes provided by other library staff that have been given a certain amount of special training; some have criticized this trend.
4. *Collections development librarians* monitor the selection of books and electronic resources. Large libraries often use approval plans, which involve the librarian for a specific subject creating a profile that allows publishers to send relevant books to the library without any additional vetting. Librarians can then see those books when they arrive and decide if they will become part of the collection or not. All collections librarians also have a certain amount of funding to allow them to purchase books and materials that don't arrive via approval.
5. Archivists can be specialized librarians who deal with archival

materials, such as manuscripts, documents and records, though this varies from country to country, and there are other routes to the archival profession.

6. *Systems Librarians* develop, troubleshoot and maintain library systems, including the library catalogue and related systems.
7. *Electronic Resources Librarians* manage the databases that libraries license from third-party vendors.
8. *School Librarians* work in school libraries and perform duties as teachers, information technology specialists, and advocates for literacy.
9. *Outreach Librarians* are charged with providing library and information services for underrepresented groups, such as people with disabilities, low income neighborhoods, homebound adults and seniors, incarcerated and ex-offenders, and homeless and rural communities. In academic libraries, outreach librarians might focus on high school students, transfer students, first-generation college students, and minorities.
10. *Instruction Librarians* teach information literacy skills in face-to-face classes and/or through the creation of online learning objects. They instruct library users on how to find, evaluate and use information effectively. They are most common in academic libraries.

Experienced librarians may take administrative positions such as library or information center director. Similar to the management of any other organization, they are concerned with the long-term planning of the library, and its relationship with its parent organization (the city or county for a public library, the college/university for an academic library, or the organization served by a special library). In smaller or specialized libraries, librarians typically perform a wide range of the different duties. The following may be the representative examples of librarian responsibilities:

(a) Researching topics of interest for their constituencies.

(b) Referring patrons to other community organizations and government offices.

(c) Building collections to respond to changing community needs or demands

(d) Facilitating and promoting reading clubs.

(e) Suggesting appropriate books (“readers’ advisory”) for children of different reading levels, and recommending novels for recreational reading.

(f) Making and enforcing computer appointments on the public access Internet computers.

(g) Answering incoming reference questions via telephone, postal mail, email, fax, and chat

(h) Digitizing collections for online access

(i) Writing grants to gain funding for expanded programme or collections

(j) Developing programmes for library users of all ages and backgrounds.

(k) Managing access to electronic information resources.

Basic categories of workplace settings for librarians are routinely classified around the world as: public, academic, school, and special. Some librarians will start and operate their own business. They often call themselves information brokers, research specialists, knowledge management, competitive intelligence or independent information professionals.

Public Library

These institutions are created through legislation within the jurisdiction they serve. Accordingly, they are given certain benefits, such as taxpayer funding, but must adhere to service standards and meet a wide group of client needs. They are usually overseen by a board of directors or library commission from the community. Mission statements, service and collection policies are the fundamental administrative features of public libraries. Occasionally private lending libraries serve the public in the manner of public libraries. In the United States, public librarians and public libraries are represented by the Public Library Association.

Academic Library

Libraries that serve a post-secondary institution. Depending upon the institution, the library may serve a particular faculty or the entire institution. Many different types, sizes, and collections are found in academic libraries and some academic librarians are specialists in these collections and archives. A university librarian, or chief librarian, is responsible for the library within the college structure, and may also be called the Dean of Libraries. Some post-secondary institutions treat librarians as faculty, and they may be called professor or other academic ranks. Some universities make similar demands of academic librarians for research and professional service as are required of faculty. Academic librarians administer various levels of service and privilege to faculty, students, alumni and the public.

School Library Media Center

Libraries which exclusively serve the needs of a public or private school. The primary purpose is to support the students, teachers, and curriculum of the school or school district. In addition to library administration, certificated teacher-librarians instruct individual students, groups and classes, and faculty in effective research methods, often referred to as information literacy skills. Audio-visual equipment service and/or textbook circulation may also be included in a school librarian's responsibilities. Often, teacher-librarians are qualified teachers who take academic courses for school library certification and/or earn a Master's degree in Library Science.

Special Library

News, law, medical, government, nongovernmental organization, prison, corporate, museum or any other type of library owned and operated by an organization are considered as special library. They can be highly specialized, serving a discrete user group with a restricted collection area. In an increasingly global and virtual workplace, many special librarians may not even work in a library at all but instead manage and facilitate the use of electronic collections. Funding for special libraries varies widely. Librarians in some types of special libraries may be required to have additional training, such as a law degree for a librarian in an academic law library or appropriate subject degrees for subject specialties such as chemistry, engineering, etc. Many belong to the Special Libraries Association. There are also more specific associations such as the American Association of Law Libraries, Art Libraries Society of North America, the Medical Library Association, or the Visual Resources Association.

Training and Qualification

In the United States and Canada, a librarian might have a one or two-year master's degree in library and information science, library science or information science (called an MLS, MALIS, MSLS, MIS, MSIS, MS-LIS, MISt, MLIS, or MILS) from an accredited university. These degrees are accredited by the American Library Association and can have specializations within fields such as archiving, records management, information architecture, public librarianship, medical librarianship, law librarianship, special librarianship, academic librarianship, or school (K-12) librarianship. School librarians often are required to have a teaching credential, as well as a library science degree. Many, if not most, academic librarians also have a second, subject-based master's degree. This is especially true of four year colleges. In the UK and some other countries, a librarian can have a three- or four-year bachelor's degree in library and information studies or information science; separate master's degrees in librarianship, archive management, and records management are also available. In the United Kingdom, these degrees are accredited by the Chartered Institute of Library and Information Professionals and the Society of Archivists. In Germany and some other countries, the first step for an academic librarian is a PhD in a subject field, followed by additional training in librarianship.

In Australia, a professional librarian must meet the requirements set out by the Australian Library and Information Association (ALIA). There are three ways in which these requirements can be met: the individual must obtain an ALIA-recognized bachelor degree in library and information studies, complete a first degree in any discipline followed by an ALIA-recognized postgraduate diploma or masters course, or gain an ALIA-recognized library technician qualifications (undertaken at TAFE) followed by an ALIA-recognized bachelor degree in library and information studies. ALIA is responsible for accreditation of library specific qualifications for both librarians and library technicians. Professional Australian teacher-librarians require slightly different qualifications. In addition to having a degree that meets ALIA's accreditation process, teacher librarians must also hold recognized teaching qualifications. It is also possible to earn a doctorate in library and information science. Graduates with PhDs usually become teaching faculty in schools of library and information science, or sometimes occupy the directorship or deanship of university libraries.

Those undertaking research at the doctoral level can pursue a very wide range of interests including information technology, government information policy, social research into information use among particular segments of society, information in organizations and corporate settings, and the history of books and printing. It is common in academic and other research libraries to require the librarians to obtain Master's degrees in some academic subject, sometimes but not necessarily related to their professional responsibilities; in major research libraries, some of the librarians will hold Ph. D degrees in subject fields. Other advanced degrees often taken in conjunction with a degree in librarianship are law, management, health administration or public administration. Library associates, library technicians, and library assistants often have college diplomas but usually do not hold library-related degrees. Occasionally they also hold undergraduate or graduate degrees in other disciplines. These workers, sometimes referred to as para-professionals, perform duties such as database management, Cataloguing, ready reference, and serials and monograph processing.

The two largest library associations in the United States are the American Library Association (ALA) and the Special Libraries Association.

Many U.S. states have their own library association as well. Librarians may also join such organizations as the Association of College and Research Libraries and the Public Library Association and the Art Libraries Society. The Canadian Library Association serves Canada and there are provincial associations as well, such as the Ontario Library Association. In the United Kingdom, the professional body for Librarians is the Chartered Institute of Library and Information Professionals (formerly known as the Library Association). The International Federation of Library Associations and Institutions (IFLA) represents the interests of libraries and librarians internationally.

Recent issues of concern for U.S. libraries include implementation of the Patriot Act and the Children's Internet Protection Act. Many librarians around the world share American librarians' concern over ethical issues surrounding censorship and privacy. Some librarians join activist organizations like the UK-based Information for Social Change and the North American-based Progressive Librarians Guild. Within the American Library Association (ALA), some also join the Social Responsibilities Round Table. SRRT came into being amid the social ferment of the 1960s and is often critical of the American Library Association for not living up to its professed ideals. Another important activist organization is the Social Responsibilities Special Interest Section of the American Association of Law Libraries (AALL). These activist organizations are viewed as controversial by some librarians, while others view them as a natural extension and outgrowth of their own deeply-held library ethics. The increasing role of technology in libraries has a significant impact on the changing roles of librarians. New technologies are dramatically increasing the accessibility of information, and librarians are adapting to the evolving needs of users that emerge from the adoption of these new technologies.

The most significant example of how technology has changed the role of librarians in the last 50 years has been the move from traditional card catalogues to online public access catalogues (OPACs). Librarians had to develop software and the MARC standards for cataloguing records electronically. They had to purchase and run the computers necessary to use the software. They had to teach the public how to use the new technologies and move to more virtual working environments. The same could be said of other technology developments, from electronic databases (including the Internet), to logistical functions such as bar codes (or in the near future RFID). Many librarians provide virtual reference services (via web-based chat, instant messaging, text messaging, and e-mail), work in digitizing initiatives for works in the public domain, teach technology classes to their users, and work on the development of information architectures for improving access and search functionality. These examples illustrate some of the ways in which librarians are using technology to fulfill and expand upon their historical roles.

Librarians must continually adapt to new formats for information, such as electronic journals and e-books, which present both challenges and opportunities in providing access and promoting them to library patrons. Increasing technological advance has presented the possibility of automating some aspects of traditional libraries. In 2004 a group of researchers in Spain developed the UJI Online Robot. This robot is able to navigate the library, look for the specified book, and upon its discovery, carefully take it from the shelf and deliver it to the user. Because of the robot's extremely limited function, its introduction into libraries poses little risk of the employment of librarians, whose duties are not defined by menial tasks such as the retrieval of books.

Librarians in Popular Culture

Stereotypes of librarians in popular culture are frequently negative: librarians are portrayed as puritanical, punitive, unattractive, and introverted if female, or timid, unattractive, and effeminate if male. The negative stereotypes are a response to three aspects of the profession: librarianship is a predominantly female profession; the librarian is devoted to learning, literature, and information for their own sake; and the librarian occupies a position of authority. This authority is earned in two ways: the librarian possesses extensive, specialized knowledge that others depend upon; and the librarian occupies the pinnacle of a workplace hierarchy, however small it may be. The librarian is in charge of a library just as a principal is in charge of a school or a pastor is in charge of a church. In a culture that views women in positions of authority with deep ambivalence, negative librarian stereotypes function to reassure audiences that these women deserve neither legitimacy or respect. Men in the profession do not escape the sexist effects of negative librarian stereotypes. If stereotypical women librarians are generally portrayed as inadequately feminine, male librarians are generally portrayed as inadequately masculine.

Such inaccurate stereotypes are likely to have a negative impact on the attractiveness of librarianship as a profession to young people. This article provides a collection of descriptions of librarians in popular culture, i.e., literature, film, television, and games. Children's literature offers a generally positive portrayal of librarians as knowledgeable, helpful, and friendly, becoming more positive over the course of the 20th century. Adult literature, however, portrays the profession more negatively. Between these, portrayals of librarians in young adult fiction are neutral to negative. Here librarians are predominantly female, middle-aged, usually unattractive in some way, and mostly unmarried. Personality is mixed between positive traits such as intelligence, likeability, and kind-heartedness; and negative traits such as strictness, timidity, excess fastidiousness, and eccentricity.

While some provide assistance to the main characters, several are the villains of the story. Duties generally include reference, but may only show clerical tasks; however the amount of technology used by librarian characters has increased over time. A disproportionate number of the librarians represented in novels are in the detective fiction genre, frequently as an amateur detective and protagonist. Although the stereotype of the librarian as "passive bore" does not seem reconcilable with the intensity of a mystery, the stereotypical librarian does share many traits with the successful detective. Their mindset is focused, calm, unbiased in considering viewpoints, and focused on the world around them. By personality they are industrious perfectionists - and eccentric.

The drab and innocuous look of the stereotypical librarian is perfect for avoiding suspicion, while their research skills and ability to ask the right questions allow them to procure and evaluate the information necessary to solve the case. The knowledge they have gained from wide reading successfully competes with a private investigator's personal experience. For example, Jacqueline Kirby is drawn into the mystery in Elizabeth Peters' novel *The Seventh Sinner* (1972) due to her awareness of her surroundings. Wearing the stereotypical bun, glasses, and practical clothes, together with an eccentrically large purse, she is self-possessed and resourceful, knowledgeable in a variety of fields and skilled at research.

A sampling of librarians featured in works of literature include:

- Neal Stephenson's novel, *Snow Crash* features both the "Central Intelligence Corporation" (a commercialized melding of the Central Intelligence Agency and the Library of Congress) and a virtual librarian which assists the main character, Hiro Protagonist.
- In the *Discworld* book series by Terry Pratchett there is a librarian who has been magically turned into an orangutan. In these stories, librarians frequently have supernatural powers related to books and library work, including access to a form of hyperspace known as L-Space.
- In the comic book series *Batman*, Barbara Gordon is a computer-savvy librarian using the name Oracle. Before she was shot by the Joker, restricting the use of her legs, she was known as Batgirl.

- Lucien, from Neil Gaiman's comic book series The Sandman, tends to The Dreaming's library, where all the books that are dreamt of, but never written, are contained.
- Henry De Tamble (from the novel *The Time Traveler's Wife*) is a Chicago librarian with "Chrono Displacement" disorder; at random times, he suddenly disappears without warning and finds himself in the past or future, usually at a time or place of importance in his life.
- Jack and Annie in *The Magic Tree House* series of children's books become "Master Librarians".
- Irma Pince is the librarian in several of the Harry Potter novels. She is a minor character as a disciplinarian in the Hogwarts library.
- Malachi is the scholarly librarian in Umberto Eco's medieval murder mystery The Name of the Rose who unlocks the secrets of a labyrinthine library to the novel's protagonists.
- In Jo Dereske's Miss Zukas series, Helma Zukas is a prim librarian sleuth who swears in such terms as "Oh, Faulkner!"
- L.R. Wright's crime series features a librarian as partner of lead detective Karl Alberg.
- In "It" by Stephen King the central narrator is Mike Hanlon, a librarian in the small town of Derry, Maine. He is described as "the keeper of the lighthouse"
- In Kingsley Amis' comic novel *That Uncertain Feeling*, a Welsh librarian bored with his marriage casts his eye upon a new girl in town. In the film version, *Only Two Can Play*, the librarian was played by Peter Sellers.
- The manga series *Read or Die* (a.k.a. R.O.D.) features protagonist bibliophile Yomiko Readman, who works for the Library of England in search of rare and powerful books.
- Richard Peck's book, *Here Lies the Librarian*. "This book is dedicated to Living librarians everywhere And to my Dean Beth Mehalick Paskoff", who is Dean of Library and Information Sciences at Louisiana State University. On the cover is a cemetery with a gravestone that reads, "SHH!".
- Lilian Jackson Braun's popular mystery series *The Cat Who...* features Polly Duncan, head of the Pickax Library and companion of the main character, James Qwilleran. This series also features Qwilleran's two bibliocats, Kao K'o Kung (Koko) and Yum Yum.
- Charlaine Harris' "Southern Librarian" mysteries are solved by librarian Aurora "Roe" Teagarden.

- Scott Douglas' memoir "Quiet, Please: Dispatches from a Public Librarian."
- The eponymous character in Garth Nix's Lirael (2001) is an assistant librarian whose curiosity about the library she works in leads her into trouble and whose research skills save her. The head librarian is intimidating and the library itself a dangerous place.

According to Ann Seidl, director of the documentary The Hollywood Librarian, librarians in film are often portrayed as meek, timid, and unassertive in nature. After indexing hundreds of appearances of librarians in film, she found that "the shorter the reference to a librarian in a film, the worse the stereotype." By the 1950s, movies had established the stereotype of librarians as "spinsters" and "eggheads". Thus, female movie librarians are usually unmarried, prim, and introverted. They are usually young and may be attractive, but dress drably and are sexually repressed. The "fate-worse-than-death view of librarians" is particularly evident in movies such as It's a Wonderful Life and The Music Man. Male movie librarians - mild, intelligent, and timid - have fewer and less important roles.

Seidl's documentary discusses such stereotypes as:

- A wretched alternate fate is revealed for Mary Hatch Bailey (played by Donna Reed) in the movie *It's a Wonderful Life* (1946): "She's an old maid. She never married...She's just about to close up the library!"
- The staggeringly rude and unhelpful librarian (John Rothman) in Sophie's Choice (1982), who barks at Sophie Zawistowski (Meryl Streep) "Do you want me to draw you a map?!"

in contrast with such more well-rounded characters as:

- Librarian Bunny Watson (played by Katharine Hepburn) who teaches Richard Sumner (played by Spencer Tracy) a few things about modern research methods in the movie *Desk Set* (1957).
- The no-nonsense "Marian the Librarian" Shirley Jones in the movie *The Music Man*.

Librarians are usually ordinary people caught up in circumstances, rather than being heroes; likewise they are rarely villainous although they may have flaws, such as racism in Goodbye, Columbus.

Television

The portrayal of librarians on the small screen has usually followed the same stereotypes as those found in motion pictures. For example, in most animated cartoon series (such as Baby Looney Tunes or Rugrats) the librarian is often shown silencing the main/pivotal characters - especially younger children - when they're in a library area. Some even ban the characters from the libraries for making rude or strange noises. In creating the Australian miniseries *The Librarians*, however, co-producers and -writers Wayne Hope and Robyn Butler consulted with real librarians for research, and took their advice to avoid shooshing and cardigan-wearing librarian characters.

1. On the television series *All That*, there are several sketches that feature a silence-obsessed librarian (known as "The Loud Librarian" to some) that scolds someone for even making a coughing sound while she herself constantly makes loud noises while performing extremely inappropriate activities for a library (weeping openly at a soap opera she's watching, playing electric guitar, using power tools, etc.). She is eventually "fired" when Lori Beth Denberg leaves the cast in 1998.
2. In the television series *Buffy the Vampire Slayer*, Anthony Stewart Head played the role of Rupert Giles, school librarian in earlier episodes and Buffy's watcher.
3. In a *Star Trek* episode *All Our Yesterdays*, Ian Wolfe plays librarian Mr. Atoz: "The library serves no purpose unless someone is using it." Mr. Atoz's name apparently derives from the phrase "A to Z", a reference to his occupation as a librarian. Mr. Atoz's quiet competence speaks better for the profession than his obstinate belief that the Enterprise officers want to flee to the planet's past, as all the inhabitants have done. The episode was written by UCLA librarian Jean Lisette Aroeste.
4. In the 1967 episode of The Avengers (TV series), "Murdersville", a gun is used with a silencer after the librarian points to the SILENCE sign.
5. In an episode of *Seinfeld*, Cosmo Kramer (Michael Richards) dates a librarian from the New York Public Library, much to the chagrin of Lt. Bookman, the "library cop."
6. In one episode of Monty Python's Flying Circus wild animals are interviewed for the position of librarian.
7. In one episode of The Simpsons a librarian questions Reverend Lovejoy about a Bible he has checked out every weekend for the past 12 years, asking wouldn't it be easier just to buy one, to which the Reverend replies, "Perhaps...on a Librarian's salary..."

8. The television series Once Upon A Time centers around a librarian trapped in a witch's tower, who is forced to produce stories with a machine called 1Z2Z, and then read them.
9. In an Orwellian future, a librarian (played by Burgess Meredith) fills the title role of "The Obsolete Man" (1961) in an episode from *The Twilight Zone*.
10. On the May 24, 2007 episode of the Colbert Report, Colbert interviewed Wikipedia co-founder Jimmy Wales. During the interview, he showed on the screen the statement "Librarians are hiding something" and asked Wales how he would stop or prevent vandalism to Wikipedia based on that statement.
11. In a few episodes of That 70s Show, Shannon Elizabeth played Kelso's librarian girlfriend.
12. Al Bundy (Ed O'Neill) pulls off a typical claims returned trick on an old and bitter librarian in the Married... with Children episode "He Thought He Could" (1988).

Computer and Video Games

There have been several characters associated with the library field in the realm of interactive entertainment, often portrayed as guides and/ or purveyors of knowledge who help the user progress within the game:

- Miss Bluegarden, from the game *Secret of Evermore*.
- Myrna Bookbottom, the stereotypical meek English librarian, from the game *Freaky Flyers*.
- Brisketta, from the game *Brave Fencer Musashi*.
- The Daguerreo Librarian, the unnamed overseer of the Daguerreo Library in *Final Fantasy IX*.
- Darian, an anthropomorphic car from the children's educational game *Putt-Putt Travels Through Time*.
- Alan Dinsdale, Velma's former school librarian, from the game *Scooby Doo: Mystery Mayhem*.
- Eike, the librarian of Budehuc Castle, from the game *Suikoden III*.
- Geelo, from the game *Icewind Dale*.
- Aldus T. Giles, Assistant Correspondence Clerk of the Tarantian Library, from the game *Arcanum: Of Steamworks and Magick Obscura*.
- Grendor, a Rhynoc, from the game *Spyro: Season of Ice*.
- Mayumi Himuro, from the game *Divi-dead*.
- Jaard, from the game *Soulbringer*.

- Kairn, a librarian/vampire, from the game *Veil of Darkness.*
- Manaka Komaki, from the game *ToHeart2.*
- Kordava Librarian, the unnamed librarian of the city of Kordava, from the game *Conan: The Dark Axe.*
- Lady, from the game *Boktai 2: Solar Boy Django.*
- Lex, the bespectacled green worm caretaker of the Great Library, from the puzzle games *Bookworm* and *Bookworm Adventures.*
- Librari, the Elder of the Town Minish, from the game *The Legend of Zelda: The Minish Cap.*
- Marcus, from the game *Siege of Avalon.*
- Maria, from the game *Harvest Moon 64.*
- Mary, from the game *Harvest Moon: Friends of Mineral Town.*
- Master Librarian, the caretaker of Dracula's Long Library, from the game *Castlevania: Symphony of the Night.*
- Mop Top Island Librarian, an anthropomorphic onion, from the children's educational game *Pajama Sam 3: You Are What You Eat From Your Head To Your Feet.*
- Nightshade, the super-hero alter ego of librarian Mark Gray, from the game *Nightshade.*
- Natsume Oguro, a 15-year-old girl, from the game *.hack//INFECTION.*
- Onett Librarian, the unnamed caretaker of the Onett Library, from the game *EarthBound.*
- Phatt Island Librarian, the unnamed lady in charge of the library on Phatt Island, from the game *Monkey Island 2: LeChuck's Revenge.*
- Hester Primm, from the game *The Sims Bustin' Out.*
- Victorian Principles, from the game *Leisure Suit Larry 7: Love for Sail.*
- Mrs. Stapleton, from the game *Fallout.*
- Mr. Sullivan, from the game *Clock Tower.*
- Swofford, from the game *Geneforge 2.*
- Tar-Meena, an Argonian located within the Arcane University, from the game *Elder Scrolls IV.*
- Trish, from the game *Wild Arms Alter Code: F.*
- Sherman Trout, head of the Library of Congress, from the game *The Final Scene.*
- Cedrin Zil, from the game *Icewind Dale II.*
- *World of Warcraft* features several librarian characters: Mae Paledust, Brother Paxton, Donyal Tovald, and Milton Sheaf.

ROLE OF THE PERIODICALS LIBRARIAN

A periodicals or serials librarian is a librarian who works in the specialized area of serials librarianship. A periodicals librarian can have a variety of duties, but generally work specifically with the acquisition, collection development, organization, preservation, and sometimes Cataloguing of periodicals. Whereas many periodicals Librarians previously worked only with periodicals in print format, many now manage electronic periodicals also. While a periodicals librarians may work in any type of library, including academic, public, government, law, medical, or corporate libraries, a significant number work in larger public and academic libraries. In other libraries where there is no librarian assigned specifically to periodicals, one or more librarians may perform the duties of a periodicals librarian along with other duties.

Main Functions

The duties of a Periodicals Librarian are changing every day as technology and library patrons' demands change. The duties may include, but are not limited to, establishing and maintaining subscriptions to periodicals in print, microform, and electronic formats; providing personal assistance and guidance in identifying, locating, and using periodicals; designing and conducting instructional sessions on how to use electronic journals and databases; evaluating the existing Periodicals collection by performing collection analysis and usage studies; creating activities, programmes, or presentations to promote the Periodicals collection; establishing and maintaining contact with faculty, students, or other constituents to be sure the Periodicals collection is meeting their needs; assisting and instructing faculty of a college, university, or school on the integrating of Periodicals into the curriculum; supervising and developing student workers and support staff; managing budget allocations for materials, systems, and services; physical repair of Periodicals; supervising paraprofessional staff, other librarians, and student workers (Kane, 74-75). Advances in technology have significantly advanced the way that Periodicals departments in libraries function. For example, open url resolvers, systems which allow a libraries to give greater visibility and access to their electronic journal content (ODLIS). Many libraries have gone to electronic-only subscriptions on some periodicals, significantly expanding access for their patrons. Periodicals Librarians frequently set up access to electronic journals and other electronic resources, as well as to troubleshoot them when they do not work properly (Davis, 149).

Qualifications

In most western nations, a Periodicals Librarian must have a master's degree in library science to work in an academic or public library. Generally, the master's degree takes one to two years to complete. Many academic and public libraries in the United States require a master's degree from an ALA-accredited school of library science. Librarians working for the federal government are often required to have a master's degree in library or an equivalent in education and experience. Some may have additional degrees in a subject area (Kane, 75).

ROLE OF THE INDEXER

Basically, an index is a list of words or phrases ('headings') and associated pointers ('locators') to where useful material relating to that heading can be found in a document. In a traditional back-of-the-book index the headings will include names of people, places and events, and concepts selected by a person as being relevant and of interest to a possible reader of the book. The pointers are typically page numbers, paragraph numbers or section numbers. In a library catalogue the words are authors, titles, subject headings, etc., and the pointers are call numbers. Internet search engines, such as Google, and full text searching help provide access to information but are not as selective as an index, as they provide non-relevant links, and may miss relevant information if it is not phrased in exactly the way they expect. Indexes are designed to help the reader find information quickly and easily. A complete and truly useful index is not simply a list of the words and phrases used in a publication (which is properly called a concordance), but an organized map of its contents, including cross-references, grouping of like concepts, and other useful intellectual analysis.

Sample back-of-the-book index excerpt:

sage, 41-42. *See also* Herbs <□ directing the reader to related terms

Scarlet Sages. *See Salvia coccinea* <— redirecting the reader to term used in the text

shade plants <— grouping term (may not appear in the text; may be generated by indexer)

hosta, 93 <— subentries

myrtle, 46

Solomon's seal, 14

sunflower, 47 <— regular entry

In books, indexes are usually placed near the end (this is commonly known as "BoB" or back-of-book indexing). They complement the table of contents by enabling access to information by specific subject, whereas contents listings enable access through broad divisions of the text arranged in the order they occur. It has been remarked that, while "[a]t first glance the driest part of the book, on closer inspection the index may provide both interest and amusement from time to time." The indexer reads through the text, identifying indexable concepts (those for which the text provides useful information and which will be of relevance for the text's readership). The indexer creates index headings, to represent those concepts, which are phrased such that they can be found when in alphabetical order (so 'indexing process' rather than 'how to create an index'). These headings and their associated locators (indicators to position in the text) are entered into specialist indexing software which handles the formatting of the index and facilitates the editing phase. The index is then edited to impose consistency throughout the index. Indexers must analyze the text to enable presentation of concepts and ideas in the index that may not be named within the text. The index is intended to help the reader, researcher, or information professional, rather than the author, find information, so the professional indexer must act as a liaison between the text and the its ultimate user. Indexing is often done by freelancers hired by authors, publishers or book packagers. Some publishers and database companies employ indexers. There are several dedicated, indexing software programmes available to assist with the special sorting and copying needs involved in index preparation. The most widely known include Cindex, Macrex, and SkyIndex. Embedded indexing involves including the index headings in the midst of the text itself, but surrounded by codes so that they are not normally displayed. A usable index is then generated automatically from the embedded text using the position of the embedded headings to determine the locators.

Thus, when the pagination is changed the index can be regenerated with the new locators. LaTeX documents support embedded indexes primarily through the makeindex package. Several widely-used XML DTDs, including DocBook and TEI, have elements that allow index creation as part of the document too. StarWriter/OpenOffice.org Writer, Microsoft Word, WordPerfect, and most other Word processor have some facility for embedded indexing as well. An embedded index requires essentially the same amount of work to create as a conventional static index; however, this work differs slightly in character as the original source files are being edited, which may slow the process or prove distracting. An embedded index saves considerable work if the material will be updated even infrequently. Some principles of good indexing include:

(a) Ensure each of your topics/sections includes a variety of relevant index entries; use two or three entries per topic

(b) Understand your audience and understand what kind of index entries they're likely to look for

(c) Use the same form throughout (singular vs. plural, capitalization, etc.), using standard indexing conventions

Indexing pitfalls:

(1) Significant topics with no index entries at all
(2) Indexing 'mere mentions' — "But John Major was no Winston Churchill..." indexed under 'Churchill, Winston'
(3) Circular cross-references: 'Felidae. *See* Cats' — 'Cats. *See* Felidae'
(4) References to discussions of a single topic scattered among several main headings: 'Cats, 50-62' — 'Felidae, 175-183'
(5) Inconsistently indexing similar topics
(6) Confusing similar names: Henry V of England, Henri V of France
(7) Incorrect alphabetization: 'á-Linolenic acid' under 'A' instead of 'L'
(8) Inappropriate inversions: 'processors, word' for 'word processors'
(9) Inappropriate subheadings: 'processors: food, 213-6; word, 33-7'
(10) Computer indexing from section headings: e.g. 'Getting to know your printer' under 'G'

Indexer Roles

Some indexers specialize in specific formats, such as scholarly books, microforms, web indexing (the application of a back-of-book-style index to a website or intranet), search engine indexing, database indexing (the application of a pre-defined controlled vocabulary such as MeSH to articles for inclusion in a database), and periodical indexing (indexing of newspapers, journals, magazines). Some indexers with expertise in controlled vocabularies also work as taxonomists and ontologists. Some indexers specialize in particular subject areas, such as anthropology, business, computers, economics, education, government documents, history, law, mathematics, medicine, psychology, and technology. An indexer can be found for any subject.

References in Popular Culture

Kurt Vonnegut's novel *Cat's Cradle* includes a character who is a professional indexer and believes that "indexing [is] a thing that only the most amateurish author [undertakes] to do for his own book." She claims to be able to read an author's character through the index he created for his own history text, and warns the narrator, an author, "Never index your own book." Vladimir Nabokov's novel *Pale Fire* includes a parody of an index, reflecting the insanity of the narrator.

Standards

- ISO 999:1996 Guidelines for the Content, Organization, and Presentation of Indexes (this is also the national standard in the UK, Australia, and New Zealand)
- Indexing Society of Canada
- American Society for Indexing
- Australian and New Zealand Society of Indexers
- China Society of Indexers
- Society of Indexers
- Nederlands Indexers Netwerk (NIN)
- Booth, Pat 2001, *Indexing: the manual of good practice* (K.G. Saur), ISBN 3-598-11536-9
- Browne, Glenda and Jon Jermey 2007, *The Indexing Companion* (Cambridge University Press), ISBN 978-0-52168-988-5
- Mulvany, Nancy 2005, *Indexing Books*, Second Edition (University of Chicago Press) ISBN 0-226-55276-4
- Smith, Sherry and Kari Kells 2005, "Inside Indexing: the Decision-Making Process" (Northwest Indexing Press), ISBN 0-9771035-01
- Stauber, Do Mi 2004, "Facing the Text: Content and Structure in Book Indexing" (Cedar Row Press) ISBN 0-9748345-0-5
- Wellisch, Hans 1995, "Indexing from A to Z", Second Edition (HW Wilson) ISBN 0-8242-0807-2
- Harold Borko, Charles L. Bernier 1978, "Indexing concepts and methods ", ISBN 0-12-118660-1

ROLE OF THE LIBRARY TECHNICIAN

A library technician is a skilled paraprofessional trained to perform the day-to-day functions of a library, and assists librarians in the acquisition, preparation and organization of information. They also assist library patrons in finding information. The widespread use of computerized information storage and retrieval systems has resulted in library technicians assisting in the handling of technical services (such as cataloguing) that were once performed exclusively by librarians. Especially in small village libraries, a library technician may be the only person (or one of only a few) staffing the library. In larger libraries, they may help run certain departments and supervise library clerks, aides, and volunteers. Because libraries are increasingly using new technologies (such as automated databases, CD-ROM, the Internet and virtual libraries), the role of the library technician is expanding and evolving accordingly. Library technicians differ from librarians in terms of education and main duties. Library technicians typically require a library technician diploma from a community college, whereas librarians require a master's degree in library science from an accredited university. Library technicians will often carry out the practical tasks involved in daily library operation, whereas librarians generally perform the managerial, supervisory and administrative functions. For example, a librarian may be responsible for creating a library's collection development policies, which would include selection criteria for purchasing of items.

A library technician would then purchase items based on these criteria. Library technicians may also be graduates of a four-year college, or institute. They could also be holders of a certificate, associate degree, or bachelor's degree. Because the education of the library technician is practical, broad and skills-based, they are job-ready upon graduation; the only training they may require is that which is specific to their particular place of employment. Duties can vary with the type and size of the library but can include: cataloguing and classification of materials, data input to assist in acquiring print and nonprint materials, assisting in the provision of reference services, and circulation procedures. In a larger library in government or academia, senior library technicians with specialized and more extensive training (at the baccalaureate degree level) are often responsible for other technicians, clerical staff, student workers, and volunteers in a certain section or department.

In smaller libraries, where the foundations of organization and operation are already established, such paraprofessionals sometimes serve as the manager or even the sole staff member. A library technician who supervises or serves as library manager with the advanced training is more properly known as a library associate. The average salary for an experienced library technician (an associate degree with three to five years of experience) is around $31,000 per year in a good-paying district; those experienced technicians who serve as supervisors or managers and/or have a baccalaureate degree can earn slightly more. Using the latest information technologies, their goal is to bring together people, information and materials and meet the challenges of a constantly changing information environment. Library technicians work in environments as diverse as business corporations, professional firms, financial institutions, cultural organizations, public libraries and schools.

ROLE OF THE CURATOR

First we have to under what is curation in libraries. In fact curation may refer to:

(a) Digital curation, the preservation and maintenance of digital assets
(b) Sheer curation, a minimalist form of digital curation

Curation may also be:

(c) The work performed by a curator
(d) Archiving, historical record keeping
(e) Evidence management, indexing and cataloguing of evidence
(f) Cultural heritage management, conservation of cultural sites and resources
(g) Healing, medical curing of illness

Collection

A museum is distinguished by a collection of often unique objects that forms the core of its activities for exhibitions, education, research, etc. This differentiates it from an archive or library, where the contents may be more paper-based, replaceable and less exhibition oriented. A museum normally has a collecting policy for new acquisitions, so only objects in certain categories and of a certain quality are accepted into the collection. The process by which an object is formally included in the collection is called *accessioning* and each object is given a unique accession number. Museum collections, and archives in general, are normally catalogued in a collection catalogue, traditionally in a card index, but nowadays in a computerized database. Transferring collection catalogues onto computer-based media is a major undertaking for most museums. All new acquisitions are normally catalogued on a computer in modern museums, but there is typically a backlog of old catalogue entries to be computerized as time and funding allows.

Museum collections are widely varied. There are collections of art, of scientific specimens, of historic objects, of living zoological specimens, of cheese and much more. Because there are so many things to collect, most museums have a specific area of specialization. For example, a history museum may only collect objects relevant to a particular county or even a single person, or focus on a type of object such as automobiles or stamps. Art museums may focus on a period, such as modern art, or a region. Very large museums will often have many subcollections, each with its own criteria for collecting. A natural history museum, for example, will have mammals in a separate collection from insects. Because museums cannot collect everything, each potential new addition must be carefully considered as to its appropriateness for a given museum's defined area of interest.

Accessioning

Accessioning is the formal, legal process of accepting an object into a museum collection. Because accessioning an object carries an obligation to care for that object in perpetuity, it is a serious decision. While in the past many museums accepted objects with little deliberation, today most museums have accepted the need for formal accessioning procedures and practices. These are typically set out as part of a museum's Collections Management Policy or CMP. While each museum has its own procedures for accessioning, in most cases it begins with either an offer from a donor to give an object to a museum, or a recommendation from a curator to acquire an object through purchase or trade. Several issues must be considered in the decision to accept an object. Common issues include:

(a) Is the object relevant to the museum's mission and its scope of collecting, as defined by its governing body?
(b) Was the object lawfully acquired and if foreign in origin, imported in compliance with international law?
(c) Does the owner of an object have legal title to the object and therefore the right to transfer it?
(d) Are there any other parties with an interest in the object (e.g. heirs of a donor, descendant groups for cultural objects, etc.)?
(e) Is the object encumbered by any legal obligations or constraints (e.g., natural history objects that require special permits)?
(f) Would the object pose any threats or dangers to other objects or staff?
(g) Does the museum have the resources to properly care for the object (e.g., appropriate storage space, adequate funding)
(h) Is the object encumbered by any donor restrictions?

Answering these questions often required investigating an objects provenance, the history of an object from the time it was made. Many Libraries will not accession objects that have been acquired illegally or where other parties have an interest in the object. In art museums, special care is given to objects that changed hands in European countries during World War II and archaeological objects unearthed after the 1970 UNESCO Convention covering the transport of cultural property. Other disciplines have different concerns. For example, anthropology museums will pay special attention to Native American objects that may be subject to repatriation, and paleontology museums may look carefully at whether proper permitting procedures were followed when they are offered fossil collections. While in the past, museums often accepted objects with donor-based restrictions, many museums today ask that gifts be given unrestricted. Common donor restrictions include requiring that an object always be exhibited, or that a collection stays together. However, such restrictions can prevent museums from changing their exhibits as scholarship evolves and may introduce conservation issue for delicate objects not suited to continued display.

Final decision to accept an object generally lies with the museum's board of trustees. In large museums, a special committee may meet regularly to review potential acquisitions. Once the decision has been made to accept an object, it is formally accessioned through a Deed of Gift and entered into the museum's catalogue records. Each object is given a unique catalogue number to identify it. Objects are then packed for appropriate archival storage, or prepared for exhibition or other educational use. Once accessioned into the collection, museum objects must be appropriately cared for. New objects may be examined by a conservator and treated for any pre-existing damage. The object is then cataloged by a curator or other specialist with knowledge of the object's importance and history. The object will then be given an appropriate storage location. Museum storage conditions are meant to protect the object and to minimize any deterioration.

This often means keeping objects in a stable climate, preventing exposure to pests, minimizing any handling, and using only archival materials that will not deteriorate or harm the objects. Object safety also include providing appropriate security, and planning for disasters and other threats, and making sure that museum staff are trained in proper handling procedures. Different types of objects have different requirements, and many museums have specialized storage areas. For example, framed paintings may be stored in racks in one room while unframed paintings are kept in large drawers in another. Some objects have extremely specialized needs. For example, material from underwater archaeological sites may need to be kept wet, and some very rare and badly deteriorated objects require oxygen-free environments. At any given time, museums display only a portion of their collections. This is often because exhibition requires much more space than storage, and is impractical for the entire collection to be out. Museums may also contain many duplicate or similar objects and find that a few specimens are better suited to display than others.

In addition, certain objects, particularly works on paper and textiles, are damaged by light and must only be displayed for short periods of time. Museum collections are often made up of a variety of materials in a single collection including, but not limited to: canvas, oil and/or acrylic paints, wood, ivory, paper, bone, leather, and textiles. The biggest conservation issue for museum collections is the fluctuations in relative humidity and temperature. Relative Humidity (RH) is a measure of the percentage of saturation of the air. Temperature is not as important to the life of a work of art, but it is true that chemical reactions occur faster at higher temperatures. However, a museum must take into account the comfort of its staff and visitors and it has been widely accepted that 68°F-75°F does not cause a lot of problems for most artifacts and is comfortable for most humans. It has also been internationally agreed upon that the RH should be set at 50%–55%. This has become widely accepted because the lower limit was set at 45% since damage to organic materials begin to occur below this point. The upper limit is placed at 65% because mold flourishes at 70% RH. It is also cheaper for most institutions to maintain 50% RH rather than 45% or 60%. There is some exception when it comes to tropical climates since the indigenous artifacts are acclimated to RH levels higher than the "museum norm".

Changes can be made to a museum's RH to accommodate the changing seasons, but they must be made gradually. Humidity should change in 2% per month increments (an increase in 1°F will affect a decrease of about 2% RH).

Deaccessioning

Deaccessioning, the process of disposing, selling or trading objects from a museum collection, is not undertaken lightly in most museums. There are ethical issues to consider since many donors of objects typically expect the museum to care for them in perpetuity. Deaccessioning of an object in a collection may be appropriate if a museum has more than one example of that object and if the object is being transferred to another museum. It may also be appropriate if an object is badly deteriorated or threatening other objects. The decision to deaccession includes two parts. These are making the decision to deaccession and deciding the method of disposal. Generally, first choice is to transfer an object to another use or division in a museum, such as deaccessioning a duplicate object from a permanent collection into a teaching collection. Second choice is to transfer the object to another institution, generally with local institutions having priority. The American Association of Museums and other regional associations often operate lists or boards to help facilitate such transfers. Last choice is sale on the open market. Open market sales are generally expected to take place at auction rather than through private sale, and are typically most common in art museums due to the high monetary value of art collections.

A controversial example occurred when the last remaining complete Dodo mount in a museum collection at Oxford University was deaccessioned due to its deterioration in 1775. Another case was the sale of a J.M.W. Turner painting in the collection of Royal Holloway, University of London to the Getty Museum to fund the maintenance of the building, despite the fact that the original benefactor had expressly requested that the collection be kept intact. Many ethical guidelines for deaccessioning require that the funds generated by disposing of collection items be used only to increase or maintain the remaining collection. For example, the International Council of Museums (ICOM) Code of Ethics states that:

> "Money or compensation received from the deaccessioning and disposal of objects and specimens from a museum collection should be used solely for the benefit of the collection and usually for acquisitions to that same collection". In the United Kingdom, guidelines governing deaccessioning and other ethically difficult issues can be found in the Museums Association's *Code of Ethics*. In the United States, the guidelines on these matters are issued by the American Association of Museums. The American Association of Museums Code of Ethics takes the position that "in no event shall they [deaccessioning proceeds] be used for anything other than acquisition or direct care of collections".

Other museums may have additional restrictions on the use of funds from deaccessioning. For example, at some museums funds from deaccessioning a work of art can only be used to purchase a work of similar style or period (for example, funds from selling a 20th century American print could not be used to buy a 17th century Italian painting) and the name of the donor of the sold work remains associated with the purchased artwork. In common parlance, a curator or keeper of a cultural heritage institution (e.g., gallery, museum, or archive) is a content specialist responsible for an institution's collections. The object of a traditional curator's concern necessarily involves tangible objects of some sort, whether it be *inter alia* artwork, collectibles, historic items or scientific collections. More recently, new kinds of curators are emerging: curators of digital data objects, and biocurators.

Main Functions

In smaller organizations, a curator may have sole responsibility for the acquisition and care of objects. The curator will make decisions regarding what objects to collect, oversee their care and documentation, conduct research based on the collection, provide proper packaging of art for transport, and share that research with the public and scholarly community through exhibitions and publications. In very small volunteer-based museums, such as local historical societies, a curator may be the only paid staff member. In larger institutions, the curator's primary function is as a subject specialist, with the expectation that he or she will conduct original research on objects and guide the organization in its collecting. Such institutions can have multiple curators, each assigned to a specific collecting area (e.g. Curator of Ancient Art, Curator of Prints and Drawings, etc.) and often operating under the direction of a head curator. In such organizations, the physical care of the collection may be overseen by museum collections managers or museum conservators, and documentation and administrative matters (such as insurance and loans) are handled by a museum registrar.

In the United Kingdom, the term curator is also applied to government employees who monitor the quality of contract archaeological work under Planning Policy Guidance 16: Archaeology and Planning (PPG 16) and are considered to manage the cultural resource of a region. In the museum setting, a curator in the United Kingdom may also be called a "keeper". In the United States, the Board of Curators, which consists of nine members appointed by the state governor, is the governing body of the University of Missouri. More recently, advances in new technologies has led to a further widening of the role of curator. This has been focused in major art institutions internationally and has become an object of academic study and research.

In contemporary art, the title curator is given to a person who selects and often interprets works of art. In addition to selecting works, the curator often is responsible for writing labels, catalogue essays, and other supporting content for the exhibition. Such curators may be permanent staff members, be "guest curators" from an affiliated organization or university, or be "freelance curators" working on a consultant basis. The late twentieth century saw an explosion of artists organizing exhibitions. The artist-curator has a long tradition of influence. Notable among these was Sir Joshua Reynolds, founder of the Royal Academy, London. In some American organizations, the term curator is also used to designate the head of any given division of a cultural organization. This has led to the proliferation of titles such as "Curator of Education" and "Curator of Exhibitions". This trend has increasingly been mirrored in the United Kingdom in such institutions as Ikon, Birmingham, UK and Baltic, Gateshead, UK. In Australia and New Zealand, the person who prepares a sports ground for use (especially a cricket ground) is known as a curator. This job is equivalent to that of groundsman in some other cricketing nations. In France archive and museum curator posts are essentially reserved for French citizens (European citizenship does not apply) and recruitment is by special competition for state official service posts.

Education and Training

Traditionally, curators have held a higher academic degree in their subject. For larger organizations this is typically a Doctor of Philosophy. or a Master's degree - in subjects such as History, History of Art,

Archaeology, Anthropology, or Classics. Along with a higher degree, curators are usually expected to have contributed to their academic field, including, for example, delivering public talks, publishing articles or presenting at specialist academic conferences. In addition, curators need to have knowledge of the current collecting market for their area of expertise, and be aware of current ethical practices and laws that may impact their organization's collecting.

Recently, the increased complexity of many museums and cultural organizations has prompted the emergence of professional programmes in field such as public history, museum studies, arts management, and curating/curatorial practice. In the last decade or so, many curating courses have been established, including at the Royal College of Art, The MA course was established in 1992, co-funded by the Royal College of Art and the Arts Council of Great Britain. It was the first postgraduate programme in Britain to specialise in curatorial practice as it relates to contemporary art. The course is now funded by Arts Council England, and in 2001 the course title was amended to Curating Contemporary Art, more accurately to reflect the content and primary focus of the programme; Kingston University; Goldsmiths College, University of London; Birkbeck, University of London; Chelsea College of Art, University of the Arts London; California College of the Arts; Bard College; University of Rennes 2 – Upper Brittany; and Ontario College of Art and Design.

ROLE OF THE ARCHIVIST AND PRESERVATION

Basicall, in libraries, an archivist is a professional who assesses, collects, organizes, preserves, maintains control over, and provides access to information determined to have long-term value. The information maintained by an archivist can be any form of media (photographs, video or sound recordings, letters, documents, electronic records, etc.). As Richard Pearce-Moses wrote, *"Archivists keep records that have enduring value as reliable memories of the past, and they help people find and understand the information they need in those records."* Determining what records have enduring value can be challenging. Archivists must also select records valuable enough to justify the costs of storage and preservation, plus the labor intensive expenses of arrangement, description, and reference service. The theory and scholarly work underpinning archives practices is called archival science.

Main Functions

Practically Archivists' duties include acquiring and appraising new collections, arranging and describing records, providing reference service, and preserving materials. In arranging records, archivists apply two important principles: provenance and original order, sometimes referred to as *respect des fonds*. Provenance refers to the origin of records, essentially who created them. The idea of *respect des fonds* is applied by keeping records in their original order as established and maintained by the creator(s). This also means that records from one corporate body should not be mixed with records from another. Original order is not always the best way to maintain some collections though, and archivists must use their own experience and current best practices to determine the correct way to keep collections of mixed media or those lacking a clear original arrangement. American archivists are also guided in their work by a code of ethics.

Alongside their work behind the scenes arranging and caring for collections, archivists assist users in interpreting collections and answering inquiries. This reference work can be just part of an archivist's job in a smaller organization, or consist of most of their occupation in a larger archive where specific roles (such as processing archivist and reference archivist) may be delineated. Archivists work for a variety of organizations, including government agencies, local authorities, museums, hospitals, historical societies, businesses, charities, corporations, colleges and universities, and any institution whose records may potentially be valuable to researchers, exhibitors, genealogists, or others. Alternatively, they could also work on the collections of a large family or even of an individual. Applicants for archives jobs usually outnumber positions available.

Archivists are often educators as well; it is not unusual for an archivist employed at a university or college to lecture in a subject related to their collection. Archivists employed at cultural institutions or for local government frequently design educational or outreach programmes to further the ability of archive users to understand and access information in their collections. This might include such varied activities as exhibitions, promotional events or even media coverage. The advent of Encoded Archival Description, along with increasing demand for materials to be made available online, has required archivists to become more tech-savvy in the past decade. Many archivists are now acquiring basic XML skills in order to make their finding aids available to researchers online. Because of the varied nature of the job and organizations and work environment, archivists need to have a wide range of skills:

(a) Those who work in reference and access-oriented positions need to be good with people, so that they are able to help them with their research.

(b) An ability to apply some basic knowledge of conservation is needed to help extend the useful life of cultural artifacts.

Many different types of media (such as photographs, acidic papers, and unstable copy processes) can deteriorate if not stored and maintained properly.

(c) Although many archival collections consist solely of paper records, increasingly archivists must confront the new challenges posed by the preservation of electronic records, so they need to be forward-looking and technologically proficient.

(d) Because of the amount of sorting and listing, they need to be very logical and organized and be able to pay attention to detail.

(e) When Cataloguing records, or when assisting users, archivists need to have some research skills.

(f) Archivists are occasionally called upon to comment or provide some context for the records in their collection and so should know as much about their collection as possible.

Preservation

Preservation and maintenance of collections is an equally important process in the library. The books and other materials should be cleaned as frequently as necessary to keep away from dust, fungi and mildew. Napthalene bars should be kept in the shelves in perforated wooden boxes. DDT/Baygon or any other insecticide should be sprayed twice a week on the floors, walls, corners, ceilings and furniture. Care may be taken that books and other reading materials are not sprayed to avoid damage to them. Heat and humidity should be controlled by temperature control. If there is no such system the books should be kept away from direct sunlight and moisture.

Why the Books get Damaged

The books are damaged by (i) dust/dirt, (ii) insects, (iii) heat, and (iv) dampness. The books may be cleaned with neat and clean soft dusters or cloth piece. Use of vacuum cleaners may be made in removing dust from the books. Vacuum cleaners should be used to suck the dust from the books.

Insects Which Infest Books

There are several kinds of insects which infest the books due to poor house keeping. Such common insects are Silverfish. Firebrat, Booklice. Termite and White Ant. Booklice appear to live on mildew and fungi which can grow on damp books. Silverfish and firebrats are able to digest cellulose from paper and can eat glue, paste, leather etc. Books should be kept dry (relative humidity from 50 per cent to 65 per cent) so that moulds and fungi cannot grow and damage the paper or leather, thus providing ample food for booklice and silverfish. Books obtained and received from places where infestation is suspected should be dusted very carefully and kept apart from other books for about a year with frequent inspection to ensure that they are free from any infestation. If a large-scale infestation takes place, the books may be sent for thorough fumigation, to a firm specialising in fumigation or any Government agency like National Archives of India, New Delhi.

Care for Newly Purchased Books

When new books are purchased, they should be properly opened before they are borrowed and read by the readers. Keep each book on a table horizontally and open it in the middle and then turn a few pages at a time, rubbing at the inner margin until the beginning of the book is reached. Next turn over the book and repeat as before until the end side is reached. This process of opening a newly bound book tends to lessen the strain on the book where the sections are sewed and glued, and permits the leaves to be opened freely. If a book is valuable, every leaf should be turned over separately and pressed down gently beginning from the centre, first one way and then the other way. This will cause the back to bend evenly at all points and prevent premature breaking of the back.

It has been observed that books sewed by machine get weakend at the back after being used for sometime. In some cases, the glue becomes hard and cracks down the middle of the back. Such books when opened take the shape of V instead of the convexed curve which exists in properly bound books. This causes strain on the thread which ultimately breaks and the contents get separated. Such books should be rebound immediately so that the contents are not lost. The absence of roundness at the back of a book may be due to faulty backing, cheap glue and lightness of backing paper.

The books should be handled properly to prolong their life and save them from deterioration/damage. Books should not be jammed into the shelves or book cases with such compactness that it is literally impossible to pull them out without tearing their covers apart. Books should not be piled one over another and crushed out of shape. Books should be placed on the shelves in such a way that they do not rest on fore-edges of the cover, that is, they should be kept lying flat or resting on the tail edges.

Examination and Repair of Books

The stock of books should be examined occasionally and the books requiring minor repairs be repaired. Pages having torn print should be repaired with tissue paper, while any tear in the margin should be repaired with bond paper. Books bound with imitation leather or water-proof cloth should be cleaned with a damped cloth and little mild soap, while leather bound books should be treated with an oil dressing to keep the leather soft thus saving from cracks and decay. The oil treatment should be given after every two years. The oil in leather when dries, the fibres become dry and stiff, and thus deprived of its pliability the leather develops cracks. In leather dressing the Neat's-foot oil is used as the base. One simple formula consists of equal parts of pure Neat's-foot oil and castor oil. These are mixed together, heated, and allowed to cool before applying.

Books—Suggested for Reading

For detailed study on the care of books, following publications may bo consulted:

1. The Treatment of Leather Bookbinding—H.J. Plenderleith
2. The Conservation of Antiquities and Works of Art—H.J. Plenderleith.
3. Insects and Hygiene—J.R. Busvine
4. The Repairing of Books—S.M. Cocherell

Important Steps in Preservation and Maintenance of Collection

1. Books should be dusted thoroughly with soft cloth duster or piece of cloth and with vacuum cleaner frequently.
2. Books should be prevented form heat and dampness.
3. Books should be handled properly.
4. Napthalene bars in perforated boxes may be kept on the shelves.
5. DDT/Baygon or other insecticide should be sprayed in the library but not directly on the books.
6. Minor repairs and leather dressing of leather-bound books should be undertaken.

Training

The educational preparation for archivists varies from country to country. In Colombia, the Universidad de La Salle offers the degree of Professional in Information Systems, Library and Archival Sciences. It is a vocational training programme, within existing legal standards aimed at providing knowledge, skills and abilities required for the design and management of information systems and documentation of various sorts. Its projection for the future is based on the application of new information technologies and communications for the management of information services economically viable. The programme was created in 1971. Other institutions that offers a degree in Archival Science are:

1. Universidad del Quindío - Professional degree: Professional in Information and Documentation, Library and Archival Sciences.
2. Escuela Interamericana de Bibliotecología - Technological degree: Technologist in Archival Science.
3. Universidad Católica de Manizales - Technological degree: Technologist in Documentation and Archival Science.
4. Servicio Nacional de Aprendizaje - SENA - in chain training with the //plataforma.unipamplona.edu.co/tda Tecnológico de Antioquia - Technical degree: Professional Technical in Archives.

In France the oldest Archivist School is the *École des chartes*, founded in 1821. This prestigious *grande école* offers a diploma of "Archivist-Paleograph" after a three-year curriculum. A part of its alumni pursue to a State archivist career after a 18 month formation at the *Institut national du patrimoine*. Most positions are reserved for French citizens. Some universities offer Master's degree in Archival Science : Angers, Caen, Dijon, Lille III, Lyon III, Mulhouse, Versailles Saint-Quentin. In Ireland, the University College Dublin School of History and Archives offers a Masters of Arts degree in Archival Studies, recognised by the Society of Archivists. In the United Kingdom, there are currently five full- or part-time postgraduate courses in archives administration or management which are recognised by the Society of Archivists. Students are expected to have relevant paid or voluntary work experience before obtaining a place on the UK courses; many undertake a year's traineeship. Also, professional certification (after qualifying) can be pursued via the Registration Scheme offered by the Society of Archivists.

According to the most recent professional census of American Archivists published, most of those in the United States have earned a Masters degree. However, the exact type of degree can vary; the most common sorts of advanced degrees held by archivists are in archival science, history, library science, or library and information science. It is also possible for archivists to earn a doctorate in library, or library and information, science. Archivists with a Ph. D. often work as teaching faculty or deans and directors of archival programmes. In 2002, the Society of American Archivists published Guidelines for a Graduate Programme in Archival Studies. Also in the United States, Academy of Certified Archivists offers supplemental archival training by means of a certification programme. Critics of ACA certification object to its annual membership fees, the theoretical versus practical nature of its tests, and the need for members to re-certify every five years. Proponents note, however, that such requirements are comparable with certification programmes in other professions, and that certification strengthens professional standards and individual competencies. While many positions in government archives require certification from the ACA, it is not required by all employers in the United States.

Many archivists belong to a professional organization, such as the Society of American Archivists, the Association of Canadian Archivists, the Society of Archivists (UK/Ireland), the Colombian College of Archivists - CCA and the Australian Society of Archivists, as well as any number of local or regional associations. These organizations often provide ongoing educational opportunities to their members and other interested practitioners. In addition to formal degrees and or apprenticeships, many archivists take part in continuing education opportunities as available through professional associations and library school programmes. New discoveries in the fields of media preservation and emerging technologies require continuing education as part of an archivist's job in order to stay current in the profession. In 1898 three Dutch archivists, Samuel Muller, Johan Feith, and Robert Fruin, published the first Western text on archival theory entitled "Manual for the Arrangement and Description of Archives". Produced for the Dutch Association of Archivists, it set out one hundred rules for archivists to base their work around. Notably within these rules the principle of preserving provenance and original order was first argued for as an essential trait of archival arrangement and description.

The next major text was written in 1922 by Sir Hilary Jenkinson, the then Deputy Keeper of the British Public Records Office, entitled "Manual of Archive Administration". In this work Jenkinson states that archives are evidence and that the moral and physical defence of this evidential value is the central tenet of archival work. He further outlines his ideas of what an Archive should be and how it should operate. In 1956, T. R. Schellenberg, who is known as the "Father of American Archival Appraisal", published "Modern Archives". Schellenberg's work was intended to be an academic textbook defining archival methodology and giving archivists specific technical instruction on workflow and arrangement. Moving away from Jenkinson's organic and passive approach to archival acquisition, where the administrator decided what was kept and what was destroyed, Schellenberg argued for a more active approach by archivists to appraisal. His primary (administrative) and secondary (research) value model for the management and appraisal of records and archives allowed government archivists greater control over the influx of material that they faced after the Second World War.

As a result of the widespread adoption of Schellenberg's methods, especially in the United States of America, modern Records Management as a separate but related discipline was born. In 1972, Ernst Posner published "Archives in the Ancient World". Posner's work emphasized that archives were not new inventions, but had existed in many different societies throughout recorded history. In 1975, essays by Margaret Cross Norton were collected under the title of "Norton on Archives: The Writings of Margaret Cross Norton on Archival and Records Management". Norton was one of the founders of the Society of American Archivists, and wrote essays based on her decades of experience working in the Illinois State Archives. Archivists, like librarians, are taking advantage of Web 2.0 technologies such as blogs, wikis, and virtual environments as well as open access and open source philosophies.

Preservation in Libraries

Preservation is a branch of library and information science concerned with maintaining or restoring access to artifacts, documents and records through the study, diagnosis, treatment and prevention of decay and damage. It should be distinguished from conservation which refers to the treatment and repair of individual items to slow decay or restore them to a usable state. Conservation is occasionally used interchangeably with preservation, particularly outside the professional literature.

Although preservation as a formal profession in libraries and archives dates from the twentieth century, its philosophy and practice has roots in many earlier traditions. In library science, preservation is treated as an active and intentional process, as opposed to the passive sense of preservation that might be applied to paleontological or archaeological finds. The survival of these items is a matter of chance, from an information science perspective, while the preservation of them after their discovery is a matter of intentional activity. Human record-keeping arguably dates back to the cave painting boom of the upper paleolithic, some 32,000-40,000 years ago. More direct antecedents are the writing systems that developed in the 4th millennium B.C. Written record keeping and information sharing practices, along with oral tradition, sustain and transmit information from one group to another. This level of preservation has been supplemented over the last century with the professional practice of preservation and conservation in the cultural heritage community.

1. Oral tradition or oral culture, the transmission of information from one generation to the next without a writing system.
2. Antiquarian practices, including scribal practice, burial practice, the libraries at Pergamum, Alexandria and other ancient archives.
3. Medieval practices, including the scriptorium and relic collection

4. Renaissance and the changing conception of artists and works of art
5. Enlightenment and the Encyclopedists
6. Romantic movement's imperative to preserve

Slient Development

1. 1933: William Barrow introduces the field of conservation to paper deacidification when he publishes a paper on the acid paper problem. In later studies, Barrow tested paper from American books made between 1900 and 1949 and learned that after forty years the books had lost on average 96 percent of their original strength; after less than ten years, they had already lost 64 percent. Barrow determined that this rapid deterioration was not the direct result of using wood-pulp fibers, since rag papers of this period were also aging rapidly, but rather due to the residual sulfuric acid produced in both rag and wood pulp papers.

   Manufacturing methods used after 1870 employed sulfuric acid for sizing and bleaching the paper. Earlier papermaking methods left the final product only mildly alkaline or even neutral. Such paper has maintained its strength for 300 to 800 years, despite sulfur dioxide and other air pollutants. Barrow's 1933 article on the fragile state of wood pulp paper predicted the life expectancy, or "LE," of this paper was approximately 40–50 years. At that point the paper would begin to show signs of natural decay, and he concluded that research for a new media on which to write and print was needed.
2. 1966: The Flood of the River Arno in Florence, Italy damaged or destroyed millions of rare books and lead to the development of restoration laboratories and new methods in conservation. Instrumental in this process was conservationist Peter Waters, who lead a group of volunteers, called "mud angels", in restoring thousands of books and papers. This event awakened many historians, librarians, and other professionals to the importance of having a preservation plan. Many consider this flood to be one of the worst disasters since the burning of the Alexandria Library in ancient Rome. It spurred a resurgence in the profession of preservation and conservation worldwide.
3. 1987: Terry Saunders releases the film Slow Fires: On the Preservation of the Human Record which examines paper embrittlement resulting from acid decay
4. 1989: March 7 ["Commitment Day"] Major US print publishers

convene at NYPL to endorse a community-wide commitment to utilizing ISO 9706 certified permanent durable paper in order to combat the acid paper epidemic.

Notable Personalities

1. William Barrow (1904 – 1967) was an American chemist and paper conservator, and a pioneer of library and archives conservation. He introduced the field of conservation to paper deacidification through alkalization.
2. Paul N. Banks (1934 - 2000) was Conservator and Head of the Conservation Department at the Newberry Library from 1964 to 1981, and published regularly on bookbinding, book and paper conservation and problems related to conservation. He designed and implemented a curriculum for Columbia University's School of Library Science that dealt directly with preservation training.
3. Pamela Darling, author and historian, was Preservation Specialist for the Association of Research Libraries. Her works include materials to aid libraries in establishing their own comprehensive preservation programmes.
4. Carolyn Harris worked as head of Columbia University Libraries' Preservation Division from 1981 until 1987, where she worked closely with Paul Banks. She published extensive research throughout her career, especially dealing with mass deacidification of wood-pulp paper.
5. Peter Waters, former Conservation Officer at the Library of Congress in Washington, DC, worked in the areas of disaster recovery and preparedness, and the salvaging of water-damaged paper goods.
6. Nicholson Baker is a contemporary American novelist and author of *Double Fold*, a criticism of libraries' destruction of paper-based media.
7. Patricia Battin, as the first president of the Commission on Preservation and Access, worked to organize a national campaign both for the use of alkaline paper in publishing companies and for a national programme of preservation microfilming.
8. John F. Dean, Preservation and Conservation Librarian at Cornell University, has made contributions towards improving preservation efforts in developing countries. Specifically, Dean has created online tutorials for library conservation and preservation in Southeast Asia and Iraq and the Middle East.

It is remarkable to note that Paul Banks and Carolyn Harris Preservation Award for outstanding preservation specialists in library and archival science, is given annually by the Association for Library Collections & Technical Services, a subdivision of the American Library Association. It is awarded in recognition of professional preservation specialists who have made significant contributions to the field. Banks/ Harris award winners:

- Sally Buchanan 2001 - Buchanan received the award in recognition of years of service in the preservation field while an associate professor at the University of Pittsburgh School of Information Science
- Ellen McCrady 2002 - From 1975 to 2004, McCrady edited and published the "Abbey Newsletter", covering important information for preservation professionals. She also conducted research regarding papermaking and acid testing.
- John F. Dean 2003 - Since its inception in 1985, Dean has led the Department of Preservation and Conservation at Cornell University.
- Jan Merrill-Oldham 2004 - As the Malloy-Rabinowitz Preservation Librarian at Harvard University, Merrill-Oldham oversees the Weissman Preservation Center and the Preservation and Imaging Department.
- Paul Conway 2005 - Conway is an associate professor in the University of Michigan School of Information and has worked with Yale and Duke University after beginning his career at the Gerald R. Ford Presidential Library. His research and educational work focuses primarily on digital preservation and electronic media.
- Gary Frost 2006 - Currently the University Conservator at the University of Iowa Libraries, Frost has been an educator and practitioner in the field of library preservation for almost 40 years. Frost is actively involved in library preservation and maintains an online blog at Futureofthebook.com.
- Walter Henry 2007 - Henry, a conservator at the Stanford University Libraries and Academic Information Resources, is the creator of Conservation OnLine and the Conservation DistList
- Janet Gertz 2008 - Director for Preservation, Columbia University Libraries has been chair of ALCTS' Preservation and Reformatting Section (PARS). She has taught, spoken and published widely on topics ranging from traditional library

preservation, disaster preparedness, commercial binding, and preservation microfilming to digital preservation, audio preservation, preservation metadata and large-scale mass digitization. She is an adjunct faculty member in the Palmer School of Library and Information Science, Long Island University, and has been a guest lecturer at Rutgers' Preservation Institute and at Queen's College.

Environmental Controls

Environmental controls are necessary to facilitate the preservation of organic library materials and are especially important to monitor in rare and special collections. Key environmental factors to watch include temperature, relative humidity, pests, pollutants, and light exposure. In general, the lower the temperature is, the better it is for the collection. However, since books and other materials are often housed in areas with people, a compromise must be struck to accommodate human comfort. A reasonable temperature to accomplish both goals is 65-68ÚF however, if possible, film and photography collections should be keep in a segregated area at 55ÚF. Books and other materials take up and give off moisture making them sensitive to relative humidity. Very high humidity encourages mold growth and insect infestations. Low humidity causes materials to lose their flexibility. Fluctuations in relative humidity are more damaging than a constant humidity in the middle or low range. Generally, the relative humidity should be between 30-50% with as little variation as possible, however recommendations on specific levels to maintain vary depending on the type of material, i.e. paper-based, film, etc.

The Image Permanence Institute provides a downloadable calculator to assist in determining the ideal indoor temperature when taking into account the outdoor dew point. This calculator also provides information on the risk on condensation and how many days to mold based on the entered scenario. Pests, such as insects and vermin, eat and destroy paper and the adhesive that secures book bindings. Food and drink in libraries, archives, and museums can increase the attraction of pests. An Integrated Pest Management system is one way to control pests in libraries. Particulate and gaseous pollutants, such as soot, ozone, sulfur dioxide, oxides of nitrogen, can cause dust, soiling, and irreversible molecular damage to materials. Pollutants are exceedingly small and not easily detectable or removable. A special filtration system in the building's HVAC is a helpful defense. Exposure to light also has a significant effect on library materials. It is not only the light visible to humans that can cause damage, but also ultraviolet light and infrared radiation. Measured in lux or the amount of lumens/m^2, the generally accepted level of illumination with sensitive materials is limited to 50 lux per day. Materials receiving more lux than recommended can be placed in dark storage periodically to prolong the original appearance of the object.

More recent concerns about the impact of climate change on the management of cultural heritage objects as well as the historic environment has prompted research efforts to investigate alternative climate control methods and strategies that include the implementation of alternative climate control systems to replace or supplement traditional high-energy consuming HVAC systems as well as the introduction of passive preservation techniques. A new term "optimization" has come into use to represent the idea that rather than a flat line, consistent 24/7 condition for a collection's environment, fluctuation can occur within acceptable limits to create a preservation environment while also thinking of energy efficiency and taking advantage of the outside environment. Jean-Louis Bigourdan conducted a study on the effects of fluctuating environments on paper that changed the previous thought by showing that deterioration rates shown with cycling conditions showed no evidence that the change of one temperature to another or one RH to another caused a different mechanism of decay or accelarated decay. "Energy Savings and Collection Management" written by Peter Herzog, shows several options for saving energy.

Decision-Making and Criteria

Making a proper decision is an important factor before starting preservation practices. Decision making for preservation should be made considering significance and value of materials. Significance is considered to have two major components: importance and quality. "Importance" relates to the collection's role as a record, and "quality" covers comprehensiveness, depth, uniqueness, authenticity and reputation of the collection. Moreover, analyzing the significance of materials can be used to uncover more about their meaning. Assessment of significance can also aid in documenting the provenance and context to argue the case for grant funding for the object and collection. Forms of significance can be historically, culturally, socially, or spiritually significant. In the preservation context, libraries and archives make decisions in different ways. In libraries, decision-making likely targets existing holding materials, whereas in archives, decisions for preservation are often made when they acquire materials. Therefore, different criteria might be needed on different occasions. In general, for archive criteria, the points include:

1. the characteristics of a record (purpose, creator, etc.);
2. the quality of the information in the record;
3. the record in context (part of a series or not);

4. potential use and possible limitations; and
5. the cost against the benefits from its existence. For library criteria, the following are evidence of significance: 1) uniqueness, 2) irreplaceability, 3) high level of impact – over time or place, 4) high level of influence, 5) representation of a type, and 6) comparative value (rarity, completeness, integrity relative to others of its kind).

Selection

Since the 1970s, the Northeast Document Conservation Center has stated that the study of understanding the needs of the library is inherently important to the survival of archives and libraries. In order for the preservation of a collection to survive for a long time it is important that a systematic preservation plan is in place. The first step in planning a preservation programme is to assess the institution's existing preservation needs. This process entails identifying the general and specific needs of the collection, establishing priorities, and gathering the resources to execute the plan. Because budget and time limitations require priorities to be set, standards have been established by the profession to determine what should be preserved in a collection. Considerations include existing condition, rarity, and evidentiary and market values. With non-paper formats, the availability of equipment to access the information will be a factor (for example, playback equipment for audio-visual materials, or microform readers). An institution should determine how many, if any, other repositories hold the material, and consider coordinating efforts with those that do.

Institutions should establish an environment conducive to preservation changes, involve staff, and create an understanding among administration and staff. The first steps an institution should implement, according to the NEDCC, are to establish a policy that defines and charts the course of action and create a framework for carrying out goals and priorities. There are three methods for carrying out a preservation survey: general preservation assessment, collection condition surveys, and an item-by-item survey. General condition surveys can be part of a library inventory. Selection for treatment determines the survival of materials and should be done by a specialist, whether in relation to an established collection development policy or on an item by item basis. Once an object or collection has been chosen for preservation, the treatment must be determined that is most appropriate to the material and its repository. If the information is most important, reformatting or creation of a surrogate is a likely option. If the artifact itself is of value, it will receive conservation treatment, ideally of a reversible nature. With old media deteriorating or showing their vulnerabilities and new media becoming available, research remains active in the field of conservation and preservation. Everything from how to preserve paper media to creating and maintaining electronic resources is being explored by students and professionals in library and information science.

The two main issues that most libraries tend to face are the rapid disintegration of acidic paper and water damage (due to flooding, plumbing problems, etc). Therefore, these areas of preservation, as well as new digital technologies, receive much of the research attention. The American Library Association has many scholarly journals that publish articles on preservation topics, such as *College and Research Libraries, Information Technology and Libraries,* and *Library Resources and Technical Services*. Scholarly periodicals in this field from other publishers include *International Preservation News, Journal of the American Institute for Conservation*, and *Collection Management* among many others. Conservators should refer to the AIC Code of Ethics and Guidelines for Practice, which states that the conservation professional must "strive to attain the highest possible standards in all aspects of conservation." Ethics will play an important role in many aspects of the conservator's activities. When choosing which objects are in need of treatment, the conservator should do what is best for the object in question and not yield to pressure or opinion from outside sources.

One instance in which these decisions may get tricky is when the conservator is dealing with cultural objects. The AIC Code of Ethics and Guidelines for Practice has addressed such concerns, stating "All actions of the conservation professional must be governed by an informed respect for cultural property, its unique character and significance and the people or person who created it." This can be applied in both the care and longterm storage of objects in archives and institutions.

The AIC Code of Ethics and Guidelines for Practice also states: "While recognizing the right of society to make appropriate and respectful use of cultural property, the conservation professional shall serve as an advocate for the preservation of cultural property." This statement speaks to the conservator's need to balance his or her duty to conserve objects and maintain a collection with society's right to have access and use of objects for their own cultural/religious purposes. While it is obvious that a member of a religion should be able to have access to an object or text that has spiritual value to them, it would be against the conservator's ethics to then allow that object to incur damage from such use. The conservator should make sure that the care of the object is kept in mind when access to an object is granted. The object should remain in the best condition possible not only so it is preserved for prosperity, but also so that it can be studied by researchers and by members of the cultural or religious group that created it. It is important that preservation specialists to be respectful of cultural property and the societies that created it, it is also important for them to be aware of international and national laws pertaining to stolen items. The AIC Code of Ethics and Guidelines for Practice also states that:

> "The conservation professional should be cognizant of laws and regulations that may have a bearing on professional activity. Among these laws and regulations are those concerning the rights of artists and their estates, occupational health and safety, sacred and religious material, excavated objects, endangered species, human remains, and stolen property."

In recent years there has been a rise in nations seeking out artifacts that have been stolen and are now in museums. In many cases museums are working with the nations to find a compromise to balance the need for reliable supervision as well as access for both the public and researchers. Conservators are not just bound by ethics to treat cultural and religious objects with respect, but also in some cases by law. For example, in the United States, conservators must comply with the Native American Graves Protection and Repatriation Act (NAGPRA). The First Archivists Circle, a group of Native American archivists, has also created Protocols for Native American Archival Materials.

The non-binding guidelines are suggestions for libraries and archives with Native American archival materials. With all these issues of respect and cultural sensitivity to consider, conservation and preservation issues are sure to arise. The care of cultural and sacred objects often affects the physical storage or the object. For example, sacred objects of the native peoples of the Western United States are supposed to be stored with sage to ensure their spiritual well being. The idea of storing an object with plant material is inherently problematic to an archival collection because of the possibility of insect infestation. When conservators have faced this problem, they have addressed it by using freeze-dried sage, thereby meeting both conservation and cultural needs.

Some individuals in the library science community have explored the possible moral responsibility to preserve all cultural phenomena, in regards to the concept of monumental preservation. Other advocates argue that such an undertaking is something that the indigenous or native communities that produce such cultural objects are better suited to perform. Currently, however, many indigenous communities are not financially able to support their own archives and museums. Still, indigenous archives are on the rise in the United States.

It is noteworthy that in her book "Sacred Stacks: The Higher Purpose of Libraries and Librarianship," Nancy Kalikow Maxwell discusses how libraries are capable of performing some of the same functions as religion. Many librarians feel that their work is done for some higher purpose. The same can be said for preservation librarians. One instance of the library's role as sacred is to provide a sense of immortality: with the ever changing world outside, the library will remain stable and dependable. Preservation is a great help in this regard.

Through digitization and reformatting, preservation librarians are able to retain material while at the same time adapting to new methods. In this way, libraries can adapt to the changes in user needs without changing the quality of the material itself. Through preservation efforts, patrons can rest assured that although materials are constantly deteriorating over time, the library itself will remain a stable, reliable environment for their information needs. Another sacred ability of the library is to provide information and a connection to the past. By working to slow down the processes of deterioration and decay of library materials, preservation practices help keep this link to the past alive.

Regional Centers

1. The Northeast Document Conservation Center in Andover, MA. Since its inception in 1973, the Center has instructed institutions and organizations, as well as librarians, conservators, preservationists and museum professionals in preservation care and procedures. From 1995 to 2007, NEDCC presented its School for Scanning conference eleven times in cities across the United States. The school takes a leading role for digital preservation.
2. The Conservation Center for Art and Historic Artifacts in Philadelphia, PA. CCAHA is a non-profit conservation laboratory specializing in the treatment of art and historic artifacts on paper. The Center also trains museum and library professionals in disaster planning, records and archives management.
3. The Southeastern Library Network is a not-for-profit membership cooperative of libraries and other information organizations in the southeastern United States. Established in 1973, as the largest regional library network in the U.S., SOLINET provides a variety of preservation education programmes and workshops.

Vendor Services

Many private entities have provide preservation and conservation services and supplies. Listed here are many of these businesses.

Standard Functions of Preservation Programmes

(a) Collections Care refers to the general maintenance and preventive care of a collection as a whole. This can include activities such as security, environmental monitoring, preservation surveys and more specialized activities such as mass deacidification.

(b) Conservation refers to the treatment and repair of individual items to slow decay or restore them to a usable state. Conservation is occasionally used interchangeably with preservation, particularly outside the professional literature.

(c) Digital preservation refers to the maintenance of digitally stored information. This should not be confused with digitization, which is a process of creating digital information which must, in turn, be digitally preserved. Means of digital preservation include refreshing, migration, replication and emulation.

(d) Disaster Preparedness (RT: Disaster Plan / Business Continuation / Disaster Recovery / Disaster Mitigation Plan) refers to the practice of arranging for the necessary resources and planning the best course of action to prevent or minimize damage to a collection in the event of a disaster of any level of magnitude, whether natural or man-made.

(e) Reformatting refers to the practice of creating copies of an object in another type of data storage device. Reformatting processes include microfilming and digitization.

Media Specific Issues and Treatments

- Books
  - Sizing
  - Leather Binding
- Ephemera and Realia
- Paper
  - Acid-free paper
  - Japanese tissue
  - Mummy paper
  - Paper Splitting
- Parchment
  - Parchment repair
  - Preservation of Illuminated Manuscripts
- Moving image

    - Film preservation
    - Video recording
- Sound recording
    - Preservation of magnetic audiotape
- Oral history preservation
- Language Preservation
- Visual material
    - Still Photography
    - Architectural reprography, a variety of technologies and media used to make multiple copies of original drawings or records created by architects, engineers, mapmakers and related professionals.
- Optical media preservation
- Ink

Training

One of the biggest challenges in the field of preservation today is educating a library's community, especially librarians and other staff, in the best ways to handle materials as well as the conditions in which particular materials will decay the least. This challenge is exacerbated by the fact that preservation is a peripheral element of most library science curricula; indeed, there are few places where one can receive a specialized education in preservation. One of the primary degree granting institutions for library and archival preservation is the University of Texas at Austin's School of Information Science. The conservation and preservation programme is offered in partnership with the Kilgarlin Center for Preservation of the Cultural Record and trains both conservators and preservation administrators. There are a number of other preservation administration programmes in the United States including the University of Michigan School of Information which specializes in digital preservation management. Recently the Institute for Museum and Library Services (IMLS) has funded a number of digital curation education programmes around the United States, including at the University of North Carolina at Chapel Hill. Digital curation includes the activity of digital preservation management. Other conservation programmes in the United States focus on Art Conservation and are considered to be more museum focused than library focused. These programmes are all part of the Association of North American Graduate Programmes in the Conservation of Cultural Property (ANAGPIC).

The Rutgers Preservation Management Institute provides post-graduate training in preservation administration for working librarians who have already completed a Master's degree. UT Austin also offers certificates of advanced study in conservation and preservation to librarians who already hold their MLS. Another educational resource available to preservationists is the Northeast Document Conservation Center or NEDCC. This institution was founded in 1973 as a reaction to the growing problem of paper deterioration occurring in repositories in the New England area. The Center provides institutions and organizations, as well as librarians, conservators, preservationists, and museum professionals, with help in learning proper care and procedures to better preserve the integrity of their collections. The institution provides a variety of services such as imaging, surveys and consultations, and digitation. They also assist with disaster planning. The educational opportunities it provides include provision of workshops, conferences, and specialized trainings. Additional online courses are also available. For instance, some of the workshops offered by the NEDCC include: Basic Preservation, Collections Care, Emergency Preparedness, Integrated Pest Management (IPM), Identification and Care of Photographs, Basic and Intermediate Book Repair, Basic Paper Repair, Preservation of Scrapbooks, Preservation Technologies, Holdings Maintenance, Creating and Maintaining Digital Collections, Scanning Training, and Grant Writing. Additionally, the NEDCC is responsible for the creation of a Preservation Education Curriculum, which has been made available online to serve as an instructional aid for introductory preservation courses taught at Library and Information Science schools. Additional preservation education is available to librarians through various professional organizations, such as:

- American Institute for Conservation of Historic and Artistic Works
- American Library Association
- Amigos Library Services Preservation Service
- Association for Information and Image Management (AIIM)
- Association for Recorded Sound Collections
- Buffalo State College. Art Conservation Department, Buffalo, NY
- Campbell Center for Historic Preservation Studies, Mount Carroll, IL.
- George Eastman House. School of Film & Video Preservation Rochester, NY
- The Kilgarlin Center for Preservation of the Cultural Record
- Library Binding Institute

- New York University. Conservation Center, Institute of Fine Arts, New York, NY
- North Bennet Street School. Boston, MA
- Northeast Document Conservation Center (NEDCC)
- The Conservation Center for Art and Historic Artifacts in Philadelphia, PA
- Queen's University. Master of Art Conservation Programme, Ont, Canada
- Rare Book School (RBS) at the University of Virginia
- Society of American Archivists
- Southeastern Library Network (SOLINET)
- University of Delaware. Winterthur Art Conservation Programme, Newark, DE
- The National Archives

Public libraries: Limited, tax-driven funding can often interfere with the ability for public libraries to engage in extensive preservation activities. Materials, particularly books, are often much easier to replace than to repair when damaged or worn. Public libraries usually try to tailor their services to meet the needs and desires of their local communities, which could cause an emphasis on acquiring new materials over preserving old ones. Librarians working in public facilities frequently have to make complicated decisions about how to best serve their patrons. Commonly, public library aacademic libraries through interlibrary loan programmes. By sharing resources, they are able to expand upon what might be available to their own patrons and share the burdens of preservation across a greater array of systems.

Archival repositories and special collections: Archival facilities focus specifically on rare and fragile materials. With staff trained in appropriate techniques, archives are often available to many public and private library facilities as an alternative to destroying older materials. Items that are unique, such as photographs, or items that are out of print, can be preserved in archival facilities more easily than in many library settings.

Museums: Because so many museum holdings are unique, including print materials, art, and other objects, preservationists are often most active in this setting. Reformatting, or in any other way copying an item's contents, raises obvious copyright issues. In many cases, a library is allowed to make a limited number of copies of an item for preservation purposes. In the United States, certain exceptions have been made for libraries and archives.

An Analysis

There is a longstanding tension between preservation of and access to library materials, particularly in the area of special collections. Handling materials promotes their progression to an unusable state, especially if they are handled carelessly. On the other hand, materials must be used in order to gain any benefit from them. In a collection with valuable materials, this conflict is often resolved by a number of measures which can include heightened security, requiring the use of gloves for photographs, restricting the materials researchers may bring with them into a reading room, and restricting use of materials to patrons who are not able to satisfy their research needs with less valuable copies of an item. These measures can seem intimidating to less experienced researchers who might feel that these preservation measures are in place solely to keep materials out of the hands of the public.

There is also controversy surrounding preservation methods. A major controversy at the end of the twentieth century centered on the practice of discarding items that had been microfilmed. This was the subject of novelist Nicholson Baker's book *Double Fold*, which chronicled his efforts to save many old runs of American newspapers (formerly owned by the British Library) from being sold to dealers or pulped. A similar concern persists over the retention of original documents reformatted by any means, analog or digital. Concerns include scholarly needs and legal requirements for authentic or original records as well as questions about the longevity, quality and completeness of reformatted materials. Retention of originals as a source or fail-safe copy is now a fairly common practice. Another controversy revolving around different preservation methods is that of digitization of original material to maintain the intellectual content of the material while ignoring the physical nature of the book.

Further, the Modern Language Association's Committee on the Future of the Print Record structured its "Statement on the Significance of Primary Records" on the inherent theoretical ideology that there is a need to preserve as many copies of a printed edition as is possible as texts and their textual settings are, quite simply, not separable, just as the artifactual characteristics of texts are as relevant and varied as the texts themselves (in the report mentioned herewith, G. Thomas Tanselle suggests that presently existing book stacks need not be abandoned with emerging technologies; rather they serve as vitally important original (primary) sources for future study). Many digitized items, such as back issues of periodicals, are provided by publishers and databases on a subscription basis. If these companies were to cease providing access to their digital information, facilities that elected to discard paper copies of these periodicals could face significant difficulties in providing access to these items. Discussion as to the best ways to utilize digital technologies is therefore ongoing, and the practice continues to evolve.

REFERENCES

Kane, Laura Townsend. (2003). Straight from the Stacks : a first hand guide to careers in library and information science. American Library Association.

Sutton, Sarah A. (2007). "Serials/Electronic Resources Librarian". A Day in the Life : Career Options in Library and Information Science. Libraries Unlimited. pp. 103–107.

Glossary

Abstract: A brief summary of the main points in a book, article or other work.

Almanac: A publication, usually issued annually, containing facts and statistics.

Annotation: An evaluation or description of an entry in a catalog, bibliography or other work.

Anthology: A compilation of writings or poems from one or more authors focusing on a particular subject or literary form.

Atlas: A collection of maps.

Bibiographic: Database is a computer based list of library resources. Typically each record contains the call number, author, title, publishing information, and other card catalogue information.

Boolean logic: The algebraic system, developed by George Boole that is applied to Boolean expressions that contain Boolean operators such as AND, OR, NOT AND, and XOR (exclusive OR). This binary algebraic system is used primarily in switching circuits and database searches. Boolean operators are not to be confused with proximity operators such as NEAR.

Bound Periodical: Issues of magazines or journals that have been fastened together. Bound periodicals are arranged by call number.

Call number: An identification marker used in libraries to categorize and locate books and other resources. Each resource is assigned a combination of letters and numbers which correspond with a location in the library. For example the call number for the Publication Manual of the American Psychological Association is BF76.7 .P83 2001.

Catalogue: A complete and systematically organized enumeration of items, particularly the complete enumeration of a libraries' resources on a set of paper cards (card catalogue) or in an electronic database (bibliographic database).

Citation: The quoting or mentioning of a source. All works used in preparing a paper should be cited.

Citation search: A search, by name, of all references to an individual. Some databases have a specific citation search option, otherwise you use a full-text search. For an example of a database that has a specific citation search option go to the University of Michigan Library Database.

Descriptor: An index term used to identify a record in a database. It can consist of a word, phrase, or alphanumerical term. It can describe the content of the record or be an arbitrary code. When a descriptor is descriptive, it can be an effective search parameter.

Dissertation: A written treatise or thesis, usually lengthy, usually authored by a doctoral candidate, usually directed by a faculty advisor, and usually intended to advance the state of the art in a given discipline. There can be an oral component to the process, in which the dissertation must be defended in front of critical judges. Dissertation searches are valuable because of their currency.

Document delivery: The transfer of a database record, or other information resource, to the end user. It can involve direct internet or email transfers, CD delivery via mail, paper delivery via mail, or delivery via interlibrary loan.

Free-text search: 1. is a simple word or character search, usually with very few Boolean, proximity, or scope limiting options. It is simple and fast. 2. a search in which all the entries are freed from their original format of presentation. Text that originated in a journal article looks much the same as text that originated in a glossary or chat room. 3. the deliberate limiting of the scope of the search parameters to include only records that are available free of charge.

Full text database: A collection of records containing complete versions of the original source, rather than just bibliographies, abstracts, or abridgements. An example is JSTOR. A related concept is that of a full text search which searches only sources that are complete, and ignores those records that are mere abstracts or descriptors.

Interlibrary loan (EUA) or interlibrary lending (UK): When patrons of a library arrange for resources from other libraries to be sent to their library. This resource sharing system is being promoted by the International Federation of Library Associations and Institutions (IFLA).

Journal: A periodical publication that presents articles in a specific subject area. They are usually scholarly. An example is *The Journal of Marketing Research*.

Keyword searching: The searching of a database using a significant word from the title, abstract, or descriptor of a record as a point of reference to the article's overall content. This type of search is usually the best type to start with.

Literature search: A systematic and thorough search of all material, print or electronic, published on a given topic. This can include books, journals, newspapers, catalogues, encyclopedias, dictionaries, atlases, bibliographies, handbooks, manuals, indexes, yearbooks, gazetteers, directories, chronologies, almanacs, and guides.

Online catalog: A record of the holdings of an institution (usually a library), or group of institutions, that can be found on the internet. An example is UCSD's "Roger".

Periodical index: An alphabetized listing of works that are published at regular intervals of more than one day.

Plagiarism: The passing off as your own, the work of others'. Original sources are not given credit.

Primary source: The originator of a primary record. A primary record is a resource created by the same people that initially experienced or used it. They create the records for their own purposes, records that often remain unpublished. Sometimes they witness an event, sometimes they are involved in an event, and sometimes the record is directly created by the event.

Scholarly article: An article, usually in a scholarly journal, that deals with academic subject matter at an advanced level.

Search strategy: A generalized set of technique used in the process of determining what information you currently have, determining what information you need, and determining how to get it. Some possible strategies include; controlled vocabulary searches, specific entry searches, browsing, general scanning, broad to narrow searches, adjacent item browsing, subject tracings searches, keyword searches, citation searches, literature searches, cross reference searches, and chat room questions and other direct people contact searches.

Truncation: The shortening of a search word, field, or record. In the case of truncating a search word, this is a strategy used to search among multiple variants or spellings.

Bibliography

Banned Books Week (2010). Celebrating the Freedom to Read. Retrieved October 5, 2010, from American Library Association: http://www.ala.org/ala/issuesadvocacy/banned/bannedbooksweek/index.cfm

Chan, Lois Mai, McGraw-Hill, (1994). *Cataloguing and Classification: An Introduction*, second ed. New York.

CLA Copyright Grassroots Advocacy Kit. (2010). Canadian Library Association. Retrieved November 3, 2010.

Dainton, Fred (2001). *Doubts and Certainties*. Sheffield Academic Press.

Davis R, Shrobe H E, Representing Structure and Behavour of Digital Hardware, IEEE Computer, Special Issue on Knowledge Representation, 16(10):75-82.

Day, Alan Edwin (1998). *Inside the British Library*. Library Association Publishing (UK).

Dorrell, Ed. "Students 'inundate' LSE with complaints over Foster library". Architects Journal.

Hayes P, Naive (1978). physics I: Ontology for liquids. University of Essex report, Essex, UK.

Hayes P, The Logic of Frames, reprinted in Readings in Knowledge Representation, pp. 288-295.

Hjorland, Birger (2008). What is Knowledge Organization (KO)?. Knowledge Organization. International Journal devoted to Concept Theory, Classification, Indexing and Knowledge Representation 35(2/3):pp. 86-101.

Hoetzlein R., (2007). The Organization of Human Knowledge: Systems for Interdisciplinary Research. Available at: http://www.rchoetzlein.com/quanta

Kane, Laura Townsend. (2003). Straight from the Stacks : a first hand guide to careers in library and information science. American Library Association.

Kenny, Sir Anthony (1994). *The British Library and the St Pancras Building*. British Library.

Pople H, Heuristic methods for imposing structure on ill-structured problems, in AI in Medicine, Szolovits (ed.), AAAS Symposium 51, Boulder: Westview Press.

Reitz, Joan M. (2004). *Dictionary for Library and Information Science*, Libraries Unlimited, p. 103.

Richard J. Goodram (1990). *The Virtual Library: collections on demand* (Memex Research Institute White Paper #2). Chico: California State University, p. 1.

Scherer, Jeffrey (2005). "Lights and Libraries." *Library Hi Tech* 17:4: 358-371.

Smith, Dorothy (December 1992). "The NREN—The next library revolution?". *Alki* 8 (3): 5–8.

Sutton, Sarah A. (2007). "Serials/Electronic Resources Librarian". A Day in the Life : Career Options in Library and Information Science. Libraries Unlimited. pp. 103–107.

Thomison, Dennis (1978). *A History of the American Library Association: 1876-1972*. Chicago: American Library Association.

Tudhope, D. & Lykke Nielsen, M. (2006). Introduction to special issue: Knowledge Organization Systems and Services. New Review of Hypermedia and Multimedia, 12(1), 3-9.

Walkowitz, Daniel J.; Knauer, Lisa Maya (2009). *Contested Histories in Public Space: Memory, Race, and Nation*, Duke University Press, p. 103.

Wiegand, S.A. (1996). "Reality Bites: The Collision of Rhetoric, Rights, and Reality in the Library Bill of Rights." *Library Trends 45, (1)*, 76-86.

Woolwine, David E. (2007). "Libraries and the Balance of Liberty and Security." *Library Philosophy and Practice (E-Journal)*, Libraries at University of Nebraska-Lincoln.

Wrightson, Denelle and John M. Wrightson (2005). "Acoustical Considerations in Planning and Design of Library Facilities." *Library Hi Tech* 17:4: 358-371.

Index

■■■